KU-207-445

Your Rights

The Liberty Guide

Edited by John Wadham

Fifth Edition

Liberty

National Council for Civil Liberties

with

Pluto Press

LONDON • BOULDER, COLORADO

Fifth edition published 1994 by
Pluto Press
345 Archway Road, London N6 5AA
and
5500 Central Avenue, Boulder, Colorado 80301, USA

Previous editions published 1972, 1973, 1978, 1989 by Penguin

British Library Cataloguing in Publication Data
A catalogue record for this book is available from the British Library

Library of Congress Cataloging in Publication Data
Your rights : the Liberty guide / edited by John Wadham. – 5th
    ed.
        p.   cm.
    Rev. ed. of: Civil liberty. 3rd ed. 1978.
    Includes bibliographical references and index.
    ISBN 0-7453-0778-7 (cloth)
    1. Civil rights–Great Britain. I. Wadham, John, 1952–   .
II. Liberty (Great Britain) III. Civil liberty.
KD4080.C55   1994
342.41'085–dc20
[344.10285]   94-1041
                                                               CIP

ISBN 0 7453 0778 7 Hardback
ISBN 0 7453 0779 5 Paperback

Designed and produced for Pluto Press by
Chase Production Services, Chipping Norton, OX7 5QR
Typeset from author's disks by
Stanford Desktop Publishing Services, Milton Keynes
Printed in Finland by WSOY

Contents

List of contributors   ix
Preface to the fifth edition   xi
Introduction   xiv
Table of statutes   xvi

1 The right of peaceful protest   1
  1.1 The historic right of peaceful protest   1
  1.2 The regime for regulating public protest   3
  1.3 In practice – organising a protest action   14
  1.4 Public order offences   23
  1.5 Stop press   30
  1.6 Further information   30

2 The right of free expression   32
  2.1 The right to speak freely?   32
  2.2 Defamation – libel and slander   34
  2.3 Obscenity and libel   39
  2.4 Blasphemy   41
  2.5 Racial hatred   42
  2.6 Contempt of court   42
  2.7 Secrets and confidentiality   47
  2.8 Copyright   49
  2.9 Controls on broadcasting, films, videos and cable   51
  2.10 Whose freedom?   54
  2.11 Further information   55

3 The right of privacy   56
  3.1 Confidential information   56
  3.2 Telephone tapping and the interception of mail   57
  3.3 Bugging and surveillance   58
  3.4 Intrusion or harassment by neighbours and others   59
  3.5 Unwanted letters and telephone calls   59
  3.6 Power of officials to enter your home   60
  3.7 Privacy and the media   70
  3.8 Further information   72

4 *The right to know*   73
   4.1   Computer records   73
   4.2   Credit reference agency records   78
   4.3   Non-computerised records: some common features   79
   4.4   Health records   80
   4.5   Housing records   83
   4.6   Social work records   84
   4.7   School records   85
   4.8   Other records   85
   4.9   Stop press   86
   4.10   Other rights of access   86
   4.11   Further information   87

5 *The right to complain*   89
   5.1   Government departments   89
   5.2   Local government   90
   5.3   Health services and care services   91
   5.4   The police   94
   5.5   Courts and legal services   101
   5.6   Financial professions   104
   5.7   The media   105
   5.8   Public utilities   107
   5.9   Transport and travel agencies   109
   5.10   Miscellaneous complaints   110
   5.11   Compensation for the victims of crime   110
   5.12   Complaints and European law   111
   5.13   Other international treaties   126
   5.14   The Citizen's Charter   126
   5.15   Further information   127

6 *The rights of suspects*   128
   6.1   Police powers to stop and search persons
          and vehicles (without arrest)   129
   6.2   Police powers to search premises   133
   6.3   Police powers of arrest   138
   6.4   Police detention   142
   6.5   The rights of suspects in the police station   146
   6.6   The right to make notes   153
   6.7   Special powers under the Prevention of Terrorism Act 154
   6.8   Stop press   160
   6.9   Further information   160

7 *The rights of defendants*   161
   7.1   Principles and procedures   161
   7.2   Representation and legal aid   162

7.3 Trial by jury or trial by magistrates 164
7.4 Committal proceedings 165
7.5 The right of appeal 167
7.6 The right to bail 168
7.7 Spent convictions and the rehabilitation of offenders 170
7.8 Stop press 174
7.9 Further information 179

8 *The rights of prisoners* 180
8.1 Reception 181
8.2 Complaints and requests 181
8.3 The courts 182
8.4 Access to lawyers 182
8.5 Visits and letters 183
8.6 Telephones 185
8.7 Marriage and founding a family 185
8.8 Women prisoners 185
8.9 Categorisation and allocation 186
8.10 Discipline, adjudication and punishment 187
8.11 Segregation and transfer 188
8.12 Medical treatment 190
8.13 Work, exercise and education 190
8.14 Parole 192
8.15 Further information 194

9 *The right not to be discriminated against* 196
9.1 Race discrimination 196
9.2 Sex discrimination 208
9.3 Sexual orientation 215
9.4 Disability discrimination 225
9.5 Further information 226

10 *The rights of immigrants* 231
10.1 Immigration control 231
10.2 Coming to settle 233
10.3 Coming to work 236
10.4 Coming for temporary purposes 237
10.5 Enforcement of immigration controls 238
10.6 Refugees 241
10.7 Rights to British nationality 243
10.8 Further information 244

11 *The rights of mental patients* 247
11.1 Applications for compulsory detention 248
11.2 Detention of offenders 252

11.3 Mental health review tribunals	253
11.4 Rights in mental hospitals	254
11.5 Further information	256
12 The rights of children and young people	**257**
12.1 Parental responsibility	258
12.2 Decision making	259
12.3 Money and financial support	261
12.4 Citizenship and nationality	261
12.5 Education and schooling	262
12.6 Children, young people and the courts	264
12.7 Further information	267
13 The rights of workers	**268**
13.1 Unions	269
13.2 Contracts of employment	273
13.3 Drug taking, drinking and workers' rights	280
13.4 Women	281
13.5 Health, safety, sickness and disability	284
13.6 Dismissal	287
13.7 Redundancy	289
13.8 Industrial action	291
13.9 Claims	292
13.10 Further information	294
14 The rights of travellers	**296**
14.1 The right to travel	296
14.2 The right to stop	296
14.3 The right to a site	299
14.4 The right to housing	300
14.5 The right to education	302
14.6 The right to healthcare	303
14.7 The right to welfare benefits	304
14.8 The right not to be discriminated against	305
14.9 Stop press	306
14.10 Further information	306
Index	308

List of contributors

Ruth Bundy is a solicitor practising in Leeds specialising in criminal and immigration work, and is also involved in the conduct of inquests.

Jo Cooper is a solicitor advocate who specialises in public order law, particularly cases concerning demonstrations. He is a former convenor of the Crime Committee of the Haldane Society of Socialist Lawyers and remains a member of its Executive Committee. He writes a regular column, *Public Order Review*, for Legal Action.

Fiona Fairweather is a solicitor and senior lecturer in law at the University of East London. She has written and lectured widely on police powers and is co-author (with Howard Levenson) of the Legal Action Group's *Police Powers: a practitioner's guide*.

Bill Forrester has been Gypsy Liaison Manager for Kent County Council since 1989, and held a similar position within Essex County Council from 1980. He has been involved with traveller issues from 1973, first with NCCL (now Liberty) and later for the Minority Rights Group. He is chair of the Advisory Council for the Education of Romany and other Travellers and author of *The Travellers' Handbook*, published in 1985.

Maurice Frankel is the director of the Campaign for Freedom of Information.

Tess Gill is a barrister specialising in employment and environmental law. She was formerly executive member and chair of NCCL (now Liberty). She is a member of the European Commission's network of experts on the implementation of equality directives.

Malcolm Hurwitt is a solicitor and a president of mental health review tribunals. He was a member of the executive committee of NCCL (now Liberty) for thirty years and has twice been chair of NCCL. He was formerly a part-time adjudicator under the Immigration Act, and is now a Trustee of the Civil Liberties Trust.

Isobel Manley is a solicitor who works for Bradford Law Centre where she has been since 1985. She deals mainly with employment and discrimination. She is chair of the Law Centres' Federation and a member of the Legal Action Group management committee.

Daniel Milnes is a second-year law student at Durham University who works as a volunteer at Bradford Law Centre during vacations.

Andrew Nicol is a barrister practising in London. He previously taught law at the London School of Economics. He is the co-author of *Media Law: the Rights of Journalists and Broadcasters*.

Ijeoma Omambala is a barrister in private practice specialising in discrimination law.

Jay Sharma has worked in London law centres since 1987. His current areas of work and interest are refugees, the harmonisation of migration policies in Europe, racism and xenophobia. He is active in the Law Centres' Federation and convenes its Working Party on Europe.

Victoria Teggin is a London barrister. Previously she was the legal assistant for the National Council for Civil Liberties.

John Wadham is a solicitor and is the Legal Director of Liberty. He has been working for Liberty since 1990. He is the author of a number of articles on civil liberties and human rights and the civil liberties section of the *Penguin Guide to the Law*.

Nicola Wyld is a solicitor and has worked as an advice and policy worker with the Children's Legal Centre for the past 5 years. Prior to that she worked in a legal aid firm specialising in children's law. The Children's Legal Centre promotes the principle that children and young people should be able to participate as fully as possible in all decisions affecting their lives according to their level of understanding.

Preface to the fifth edition

The last edition of the *Guide* was published in 1989, five years ago and there have been some very substantial changes in the law since then. Also over that period there seems to have been an increasing interest in legal rights. We hope that one effect of this will be that people will be more conscious of the fact that they may have rights. The increased complexity of the law and the gradual erosion of rights over the last fifteen years makes it all the more important that we all know what rights we have. Since 1989 we have also changed publishers and Pluto has taken over this publication. We look forward to a long and happy association with them.

No book of this length can possibly do justice to the vast subject matter that we have attempted to cover. It cannot possibly pretend even to be a detailed guide to any one area of the law. It is not designed for lawyers although we hope that, like previous editions, they will have it on their shelves for easy reference.

Our primary aim is to provide easy access to a whole range of the most fundamental civil and political rights that are available. This publication is aimed at individuals who themselves have had their human rights violated and we hope that it provides a commonsense approach to those rights. We hope also that it can help to put those rights into practice. Unfortunately, in many cases the book serves only to highlight aspects of the law in which rights are inadequate and remedies non-existent. In many other cases we can only indicate the right direction and suggest that people get in touch with lawyers and other experts.

We have not included in this edition the sections on Scotland and Northern Ireland because the law is very different and our sister organisations, the Scottish Council for Civil Liberties and the Committee for the Administration of Justice (in Northern Ireland), have their own publications.

The law is stated as at 1 January 1994. The law is always changing and over the next two or three years it is likely that there will be substantial alterations in the following: the Royal Commission on Criminal Justice and now the government have made many recommendations which will change the criminal justice system and the rights of defendants, young people and suspects (in the Criminal Justice and

Public Order Bill), the police disciplinary system (in the Police and Magistrates Courts Bill), the complaints procedure for newspapers; the right of access to information may improve and it is likely that a right of privacy will be established. The rights of travellers will be further restricted and the government intends to impose criminal sanctions on some forms of trespass and protest (again, in the Criminal Justice and Public Order Bill). Unfortunately all these changes are likely to reduce our rights.

Finally I would like to thank all the contributors for their hard work and generous cooperation. The services of the contributors have been provided free of charge so that the profits from this book can go to furthering the work of Liberty. Thanks also go to Ken Akanwo, Celia Hughes, Marianna Masters and Nettie Pollard and all the staff at Liberty and all of the editors and contributors to the previous editions of this guide. I would also like to thank Anne Beech and all at Pluto.

John Wadham
February 1994

Liberty is an independent organisation commited to defending and extending the rights explained in this book. To do this it depends on its members and donations. Please help to maintain your rights by photo-copying and completing this form.

Surname/s ....

Forenames ....

Title .... (Mr/Mrs/Miss/Other)

Address ....

....

Town ....

County .... Postcode..........................

(BLOCK CAPITALS PLEASE)

I wish to give a donation of £100 ☐ £50 ☐ £25 ☐ £10 ☐ Other ☐
and/or I wish to become a Member
(please tick membership required):

£20 Individual membership ☐   £25 Two people at same address ☐

£6 Student ☐   £10 Two students   "   "   "   ☐

£6 OAP ☐   £10 Two OAPs   "   "   "   ☐

£6 Unwaged ☐   £10 Two unwaged   "   "   "   ☐

£3 Prisoner ☐

PLEASE TICK THE METHOD OF PAYMENT:

Cheque/PO made payable to Liberty ☐

Visa/Access Card No. ☐☐☐☐☐☐☐☐☐☐☐☐☐☐☐☐☐☐

Signed ....

Date ....

Total amount enclosed £ ....

Introduction

Liberty (the National Council for Civil Liberties) was founded in 1934 to defend civil and political rights. The need to establish an independent watchdog had resulted from the observation of the police handling of the hunger marches in 1932. For sixty years Liberty, a non-party, non-denominational voluntary organisation, has fought for human rights. It has taken up test cases, led campaigns, briefed legislators and politicians, researched and reported, advised and defended and has often been at the centre of fierce controversy.

One of the key roles of Liberty has always been to encourage and spread a greater awareness of individual rights. It is to this aspect of Liberty's work that the *Guide* is especially directed. Rights cannot be enjoyed without knowledge of their existence. Justice cannot be obtained without awareness of the remedies available to correct injustice.

The need for a guide like this and for Liberty itself is now greater than ever. Human rights are increasingly vulnerable. Our society is scarred by racism and an increasing number of racist attacks. Miscarriages of justice are regularly uncovered and yet there are proposals to restrict the rights of suspects. Censorship is widespread and attacks on the media increase. The Prevention of Terrorism Act remains on the statute book. There is increasing intolerance against travellers and other minority groups. Our immigration laws and procedures violate accepted international norms. Discrimination against women remains deeply imbedded in our laws and institutions.

There are, however, positive signs. There is increasing support for a system of positive enforceable rights – increasing support for a fundamental Bill of Rights. In the absence of such a Bill, our system of statute and common law provides few positive rights. Parliament has never guaranteed rights of free speech or of assembly, for example. Such rights can only be resumed in the absence of restraint, in the silence of the law.

This approach has a number of consequences. Firstly, as positive rights are not enshrined in the law they cannot be invoked to protect individuals from abuses. The contraints exist but not the counterbalancing rights. Secondly, the boundaries of rights are uncertain and unknown:

because they are not written down they are more likely to be vague, open to interpretation and be vulnerable to the exercise of official discretion. Thirdly, such vague and unclear rules cannot represent something that we can respect and fight for, they cannot be taught in schools, or indeed be part of our culture.

It is not the task of this guide to argue the case for a Bill of Rights. This we have done elsewhere. The only fundamental rights that do exist are contained in the European Convention on Human Rights (which is discussed in Chapter 5) and despite the success of Liberty in bringing cases to the European Commission and Court of Human Rights the procedures for enforcing rights under this mechanism are slow and cumbersome. Furthermore, legal aid to bring cases is limited. The Convention is not enforceable in our courts and its value to an aggrieved individual is, therefore, limited.

We hope that this guide is of practical value to everyone in our society. Attacks upon our rights can come unexpectedly and from many quarters. It is dangerous to assume that we will need – ourselves – one day the knowledge provided by this guide. In any case human rights are universal entitlements, attacks upon the rights of one person inevitably undermine all of us. It is in this spirit that we produce this guide.

Andrew Puddephatt
General Secretary
Liberty

Table of Statutes

Access to Health Records Act (1990) 80, 81, 190
Access to Medical Reports Act (1988) 82
Access to Personal Files Act (1987) 83, 84
Agriculture Act (Safety, Health and Welfare Provisions) (1956) 286
Asylum and Immigration Appeals Act (1993) 231, 241–2, 243

Bail Act 241
British Nationality Act (1981) 243

Caravan Sites Act (1968) 300
Children Act (1989) 65, 250, 257, 259, 303
Child Support Act (1991) 258, 261
City of London Police Act (1839) 7
Companies Act (1985) 287
Conspiracy and Protection of Property Act (1875) 27
Consumer Credit Act (1974) 78
Copyright Act (1956) 278
Copyright Act (1988) 49, 51
Courts and Legal Services Act (1990) 199
Criminal Damage Act (1971) 26
Criminal Justice Act (1988) 26
Criminal Law Act (1977) 136
Customs and Excise Management Act (1979) 139

Data Protection Act (1984) 73, 74, 75, 77, 86, 173, 278
Disabled Persons (Employment) Acts (1944) (1958) 287

Employment Act (1980) 268
Employment Act (1988) 271, 273, 292
Employment Act (1990) 271
Employment Protection Act (1975) 290
Employment Protection (Consolidation) Act (EPCA) (1978) 268, 269, 274, 275, 278, 283–4, 287, 289, 290
Equal Pay Act (1970) 210, 214, 268, 281, 282

Factories Act 190–1
Firearms Act (1968) 136, 140

Fire Precautions Act (1971) 285
Fire Services Act (1947) 61
Football (Offences) Act (1991) 139

Gaming Act (1968) 136

Health and Safety at Work etc. Act (1974) 191, 271, 284–5
Highways Acts 298
Housing Act (1985) 62, 222, 234

Immigration Acts (1971) (1988) 136, 152, 157–8, 231
Indecency with Children Act (1960) 216
Industrial Relations Act (1971) 268
Insolvency Act (1986) 290
Interception of Communications Act (1985) 57

Justices of the Peace Act (1361) 29

Legal Aid Act 254
Local Government (Access to Information) Act (1984) 86
Local Government Act (1988) 224
Local Government Finance Act (1992) 63

Malicious Communications Act (1988) 60
Mental Health Act (1959) 248
Mental Health Act (1983) 241, 247, 255
Metropolitan Police Act (1839) 7
Mines and Quarries Act (1954) 285
Misuse of Drugs Act (1971) 133, 136, 280

National Assistance Act (1948) 65
Northern Ireland (Emergency Provisions) Act 159, 160

Obscene Publications Act (1959) 39, 52, 53, 136
Offences Against the Person Act (1861) 24
Official Secrets Act (1911) 47
Official Secrets Act (1920) 139
Official Secrets Act (1989) 34, 47, 87, 139

Patents Act (1977) 278
Police and Criminal Evidence Act (PACE) (1984) 2, 25, 97, 128–34,
    136–40, 141, 142–3, 144, 146, 156, 184, 239–40
Prevention of Crime Act (1953) 26
Prevention of Damage by Pests Act (1949) 65
Prevention of Terrorism (Temporary Provisions) Act (PTA) (1989)
    146, 149, 152, 154–60
Prison Act 180

Public Health Act (1936) 65
Public Health (Control of Diseases) Act (1984) 64
Public Meeting Act (1908) 12
Public Order Act (1936) 136
Public Order Act (1986) 2, 3, 5, 6, 10, 11, 12, 15, 23, 24, 25, 42, 133, 136, 207, 208, 219, 299, 306

Race Relations Act (1976) 182, 196, 198, 201, 203, 205, 268, 298, 305
Rehabilitation of Offenders Act (1974) 37, 170, 176, 279
Representation of the People Act (1983) 12
Rights of Entry (Gas and Electricity Boards) Act (1954) 62
Road Traffic Act (1988) 141

Sex Discrimination Act (1975) 209, 214, 215, 220, 221, 268, 281, 282, 283
Sex Discrimination Act (1986) 209, 213, 281, 282, 283
Sexual Offences Act (1956) 139, 217
Sexual Offences Act (1967) 218
Single European Act (1987) 232
Social Security Act (1986) 63, 269, 284
Sporting Events (Control of Alcohol etc.) Act (1985) 129

Taxes Management Act (1970) 63
Telecommunications Act (1984) 59
Theft Act (1968) 133, 139
Town and Country Planning Act (1990) 63
Town Police Clauses Act (1847) 7
Trade Disputes Act (1906) 268
Trade Union Act (1871) 268
Trade Union Act (1913) 272
Trade Union Act (1984) 268, 272, 273
Trade Union and Labour Relations Act (1974) 268, 291
Trade Union and Labour Relations Act (1992) 9–10
Trade Union and Labour Relations (Consolidation) Act (1992) 272
Trade Union and Labour Relations (Consolidation) Act (1993) 268
Trade Union Reform and Employment Rights Act (1993) 268–9, 275, 280, 284
Transport and Works Act (1992) 281

Unsolicited Goods and Services Act (1971) 60

Wages Act (1986) 269, 276
Wireless Telegraphy Act (1949) 59

1

The right of peaceful protest

This chapter deals with:

* The historic right of peaceful protest.
* The regime for regulating public protest.
* In practice – organising a protest action.
* Public order offences.
* Further information.

There have been many times in the past – even in the recent past – when the public demonstration of support for a cause, or opposition to a policy or government, have changed the course of history. Despite legislation designed to limit its effectiveness, 'people power' remains a very potent political force, whether at a national or local level; whether to do with political causes or single issues; whether in support of striking workers or bereaved families or in opposition to unpopular legislation. Even when people have nothing else to fight with, it is often their solidarity with each other – to stand together and be counted – which proves their most powerful weapon.

1.1 The historic right of peaceful protest

The historic right to demonstrate is as deeply rooted in our political culture as the right to govern. It is one of the basic building blocks of our constitution. And like most of our 'constitutional rights' it is difficult to trace to a single source because our constitution has never been written down in a single place, unlike the American constitution, for example. So there is no specific law which confers a legal right to demonstrate. But senior judges have often referred to the right of peaceful protest. One of the most famous judges of the last forty years, Lord Denning, said:

> The right to demonstrate and the right to protest on matters of public concern ... are rights which it is in the public interest that individuals should possess; and indeed, that they should exercise without impediment so long as no wrongful act is done.

1

In 1985 the government explicitly recognised that: 'The right to assemble, demonstrate and protest peacefully within the law is fundamental to our democratic way of life.'

These very important rights are not 'given' to us by Parliament, but are ones which, as individuals, we already have. They are rights which, in principle, we can exercise how we want and when we want, subject only to the restrictions that our elected governments or the courts impose.

For as long as there have been governments there have been rules to restrict demonstrations which might threaten their future, or the success of their policies. At the heart of public order law is the natural tension between the amount of freedom we demand as demonstrators and the amount of latitude we as electors want our Parliament to legislate for. Over the centuries the law in this area has developed piecemeal, adapting to the prevailing attitudes and concerns of the governments and courts of the day. Nowadays the law does three things:

- It grants police certain powers (for example, to impose conditions on a march, to search people, or to make arrests).
- It imposes obligations on people who organise demonstrations (for example, to give the police advance notice).
- It restricts the exercise of our right to demonstrate (for example, by saying that in some circumstances we can only do so at a particular time or in a particular way).

Where to find the law

The most important statutory provision is the Public Order Act 1986. This sets out a procedure for regulating public protest under which the police can sometimes impose conditions on a march, or exceptionally seek to ban it altogether. The Act also contains the main criminal offences which relate to public order, ranging from riot to disorderly conduct (see 1. 2, below). Another significant statute is the Police and Criminal Evidence Act 1984 which gives the police very wide general powers to arrest and detain people suspected of committing criminal offences.

Even after these major pieces of legislation, public order law is far from unified. This is because, as well as their powers under these statutes, the police retain some of the powers first given to them in ancient legislation, which have never been repealed. There are also numerous bye-laws, which are passed by local authorities and are specific to a particular area. These often restrict our rights or impose obligations on us. Other legislation sometimes refers to rights to demonstrate. Picketing during industrial disputes, for example, is regulated by employment laws.

An important source for today's law is guidance in the form of case-law showing how the courts have approached particular situations in the past. All laws have to be interpreted – what exactly counts as a 'public place', for example – and the precedents from previous court decisions are a useful indication of how they might react if the same situation were to occur again.

1.2 The regime for regulating public protest

The Public Order Act 1986 sets out the powers of the police to impose conditions on marches, and on static demonstrations such as rallies, pickets and vigils. Police powers arise not only to prevent 'disorder' but also to prevent disruption to the normal life of the community – leaving it to the police to balance freedom of expression against traffic flow, the rights of traders, shoppers, etc. Following mass support for pickets in recent industrial disputes, the Act also allows the police to intervene if they believe a demonstration is intended to be intimidating. The Act refers to marches as 'processions' and to all other static demonstrations as 'assemblies'.

As well as the Public Order Act 1986 there are limits on the use of the highway for demonstrating and for other activities in the street, such as collecting money or selling newspapers, which are often associated with demonstrations.

Marches
In the terminology of the Public Order Act, a 'procession' is simply defined as people moving together along a route; the law does not provide a minimum number to constitute a procession. Most processions are lawful. The participants are exercising their right to pass along the highway (see p. 13). A procession may become an obstruction of the highway (see p. 27) if the use of the highway is unreasonable. The Public Order Act 1986 gives police extensive controls over processions. Organisers of most processions must give advance notice to the police. The police may impose conditions on processions and, in limited circumstances, have them banned. Failure to comply with these provisions is a criminal offence.

Who is the organiser?
There is no legal definition. For a big procession an official organiser will probably have been selected well in advance of the date. For a spontaneous event the organiser could be anyone who takes the lead.

Advance notice
The rules are designed to ensure that the police are told, in advance, about the vast majority of political marches. Specifically, they say that notice should be given of any procession if it is intended to:

- Demonstrate support for or opposition to the views or actions of any group.
- Publicise a cause or campaign.
- Mark or commemorate an event.

Notice need not be given if it is not *reasonably practicable to do so* in advance. This is intended to allow for a completely spontaneous procession, for example when a meeting turns itself into a march or, as Christian CND put it, when it is necessary 'to call acts of witness or protest at short notice'. If a prosecution is brought it will be for the magistrates' court to decide whether notice of any kind could have been given. A last minute telephone call to the police – a record should be kept of the call – is advisable to show you are prepared to follow the spirit of the law.

Notice is also not required if it is a funeral procession or a procession commonly or customarily held. This will include the Lord Mayor's Show in the City of London, the Notting Hill Carnival, and other annual local parades including those organised by religious groups. If a protest march occurs regularly (weekly, annually) at the same time along the same route then no notice should be required.

Where notice is required it must be in writing and must include:

- The date of the procession.
- The time it will start.
- The proposed route.
- The name and the address of the organiser.

The written notice must be delivered to a police station in the area where the procession is planned to start (or the first police area in England on the route if it starts in Scotland) either *by hand* or by *recorded delivery six clear days* in advance. 'Six clear days' means, effectively, a full week in advance, for example on Saturday for a procession the following Saturday.

If a procession is planned at short notice (less than one week) then the organiser is required to deliver written notice *by hand* as soon as reasonably practicable.

Offences connected with notice
The organiser commits an offence (maximum penalty fine at level 3[*]) if either:

- Notice was not given as required.
- The date, starting time or route differs from that given on the notice.

* Fine levels are outlined at the end of this chapter on p. 29.

There is no power of arrest, but the police could rely on their general power of arrest (see p. 129). In practice it has proved very difficult for the police, in the handful of prosecutions brought under this section of the Act since 1987, to prove that a particular person was the organiser of the march. Unless the police can do so, their powers to prosecute are greatly curtailed. Even if they can, it is a defence if you can prove either:

- You were not aware that notice had not been given or not given in time.
- The different date, starting time or route was due to circumstances beyond your control or was changed with the agreement of the police or by direction of the police.

Police conditions on processions

There is no guarantee that the police will allow your proposed procession to take place as you want it. In advance, the Chief Constable (or the Commissioner in London) can impose conditions relating to the route, number of marchers, types of banners, duration, or restrict entry to a public place. These conditions must be in writing. After the procession has begun the most senior officer on the spot can impose similar conditions which do not have to be in writing. The Public Order Act 1986 says that conditions can only be imposed if the senior officer reasonably believes that the procession may result in:

- Serious public disorder.
- Serious damage to property.
- Serious disruption to the life of the community.

The senior officer may also impose conditions if he or she reasonably believes that the purpose of the organisers is to intimidate others 'with a view to compelling them to do an act they have a right to do, or to do an act they have a right not to do'. The conditions must be ones which the officer believes are *necessary* to prevent the disorder, damage, disruption or intimidation. Failure to comply with a condition is a criminal offence (see below).

Banning processions

The Public Order Act 1986 leaves unchanged the power of the police to ban all or a 'class' of processions in a local area for up to three months. If a Chief Constable (or the Commissioner in London) is satisfied that the powers to impose conditions will not be sufficient to prevent serious public disorder if the procession takes place, then he must apply for a banning order.

Outside London, the Chief Constable applies to the district council for a banning order. The district council is not obliged to make the order, but it must have the Home Secretary's consent to any banning order it makes. In London, the Commissioner makes the order with the Home Secretary's consent.

A banning order can cover all or part of a district (or all or part of the Metropolitan Police area or the City of London) and can ban all processions or just those within a certain class (for example, processions marking the death of a political terrorist). A blanket ban of all processions is often imposed, even though it is designed to prevent one march only. The standard formula is to ban 'all public processions other than those of a traditional or ceremonial character'. Failure to comply with a banning order is a criminal offence (see below).

Static demonstrations, rallies and other assemblies

In addition to the powers that the police have used effectively for many years (breach of the peace, obstruction of the highway, local bye-laws, etc., see p. 28) to move or disperse a crowd which has assembled for a common purpose, the Public Order Act 1986 gives the police specific powers to control public assemblies. These are similar to the powers which the police have to impose conditions on processions (see above). It should be noted that there is no power to ban an assembly and no advance notice need be given to the police of an assembly.

A 'public assembly' is twenty or more people gathered together in a public place which is at least partly in the open air. A public place is any highway (including the pavement) and any other place to which the public or a section of the public can have access and therefore includes parks and gardens, shopping precincts, shops and offices, restaurants and pubs, cinemas, football stadia, rights of way, etc. A public assembly could be twenty people spaced across a wide entrance, but probably not four sets of five pickets at different factory gates.

Police conditions on assemblies

Conditions may be imposed on a public assembly which restrict:

- The place – for example by forcing pickets to move from the factory gates.
- The duration – for example by reducing a twenty-four hour vigil to four hours.
- The numbers – for example by reducing a mass picket from thousands to twenty.

Similar to the powers concerning processions, the Chief Constable (Commissioner in London) can impose conditions in advance (in writing) or the most senior officer on the spot can impose conditions as soon as twenty people have assembled. The grounds for doing so – such as the fear of serious public disorder – are also the same as for processions.

Whilst Parliament's intention was clearly to give the police greater control over picketing in particular, the courts have said that it was not intimidation when the conduct complained of was 'abuse, swearing and shouting' as workers crossed a picket line, and that causing 'discomfort' to guests entering South Africa House did not amount to intimidation.

It is an offence to defy a condition or a banning order
If you *know* that a condition has been imposed on either a procession or a public assembly it is an offence if you do not comply with the condition, either as an organiser or as an ordinary participant. It is also an offence to incite others not to comply with it. If you *know* that a procession has been banned it is an offence for you to organise, to take part or to incite others to take part in it.

In principle the police can arrest organisers or demonstrators, which in a large gathering gives them extremely wide discretionary powers as to whom they choose to remove from the scene. The maximum penalty for organisers or inciters is three months' imprisonment or a fine at level 4 (currently £1000) and for participants a fine at level 3 (currently £400). It is a defence to prove that any failure to comply with a condition was beyond your control.

Demonstrations near the Houses of Parliament
At the beginning of each Parliamentary session, the Metropolitan Police Commissioner is instructed by Parliament to give directions under the Metropolitan Police Act 1839 to police officers 'to disperse all assemblies or processions of persons causing or likely to cause an obstruction, disorder or annoyance' within a specified area around Westminster whenever Parliament is sitting (see map overleaf).

The police must rely on their general powers of arrest or powers to prevent a breach of the peace (see p. 28). You commit an offence (maximum sentence, a fine at level 2) if you fail to disperse after you are made aware of the Commissioner's directions, which normally means that the police must read them to you before they can arrest you. It is a defence to show that the free passage of MPs would not have been obstructed by you. The directions do not affect processions or meetings on a day when Parliament is not sitting.

Additional powers in London and other towns
There are several nineteenth-century statutes (Metropolitan Police Act 1839, City of London Police Act 1839, Town Police Clauses Act 1847) which enable the Commissioner of Police in London and the City or local councils outside London to make regulations and give directions

to prevent obstruction and to keep order. Directions are given to constables and are not required to be made public. There are no conditions that must be satisfied before directions can be given, and, therefore, little scope to challenge them as excessive or unjustified. When lawful directions have been given, if you do not comply with police instructions (for example, not to continue down a particular street) you commit an offence or you could be charged with obstructing the police (see p. 27).

Police directions are often used to restrict protest events. For example, when a 'Stop the City' demonstration was planned, the City of London Commissioner issued directions under which the police arrested people who distributed leaflets or gathered in groups of three or more. During the News International dispute at Wapping the Metropolitan Commissioner's directions, which were renewed monthly during the dispute, gave the police authority to close streets and stop any person walking or driving in any street in Tower Hamlets. In Salisbury the district council made an order banning 'hippies' from the town centre for two days and restricted them to a designated route.

In the City of London, anti-terrorist roadblocks were originally set up under police powers to stop and search suspected offenders (see p. 129). But after protests the police conceded in practice that they had no special grounds to think that the people caught up in the roadblocks were terrorist suspects. The roadblocks continued, but were subsequently justified by reference to directions issued by the City of London Police Commissioner. Their legality remains to be tested by the courts.

The wide power to issue directions can very easily be abused by the police, who sometimes compensate for what they perceive to be gaps in the law by relying on their discretionary powers. Many people feel that fundamental decisions about our civil rights should be taken by Parliament and not left to the discretion of Chief Officers.

Picketing

For more than a century, trade unions and organised groups of workers have used picketing as a powerful means of protecting their employment rights and improving the conditions in which they are expected to work. In recent years, picketing has been used by campaigning and protest groups as an effective way of bringing their views to public attention. The law gives special status to picketing when it is related to an industrial dispute – and this is reaffirmed in recent legislation – but no special exemption under the criminal law. However, most picketing is lawful unless it causes an obstruction of the highway (see p. 27).

You are protected under the civil law if you picket in connection with an *industrial dispute* at or near your workplace for the purpose of peacefully obtaining or communicating information or peacefully persuading any person to work or abstain from working (Trade Union and Labour Relations Act 1992). Employers have increasingly used the civil courts to get injunctions in order to limit severely the effectiveness of picketing. Injunctions have been granted on the basis that it was not the workplace of some or all of the pickets or that the picketing was not peaceful. Unions who continue to picket in breach of an injunction are in contempt of court and liable to pay very heavy fines. By injunction the court can limit the location and number of pickets and impose conditions on their conduct.

In a *non-industrial situation*, the court granted an injunction to a firm of estate agents whose premises were being picketed by local people protesting against the firm's alleged involvement in the eviction of tenants. The court was satisfied that the pickets, although peaceful, were interfering with the firm's trade.

No legal case has been decided which specifies that a particular number of pickets at a location will always be lawful. But a government Code of Practice, which the courts can refer to, suggests that the number of pickets at any entrance to a workplace should not generally exceed six. In applications for injunctions, the civil courts have tended to set the upper limit of the number of pickets that must be allowed at six. Other cases have given the police very wide discretion to limit the number of pickets if they believed this was necessary to prevent a breach of the peace or an obstruction of the highway.

Secondary picketing – picketing at a workplace or premises where you do not work – is not a criminal offence and it is not the job of the police to enforce the civil law on picketing, even if an injunction is in force.

Police powers and picketing

Giving the police greater power to control and restrict picketing was a primary purpose of the Public Order Act 1986. Any picket of twenty or more people is a 'public assembly' and therefore subject to police conditions under the Act (see above). The police are likely to be present at a picket of whatever size. In addition to the power to impose conditions, the police possess a wide range of public order powers to restrict and control picketing and to arrest pickets for various offences, including:

- Obstruction of the highway (see p. 27) – on the basis of too many pickets, even if they are moving; or a single picket trying to compel a driver to stop and listen.
- Obstruction of the police (see p. 27) – for example, refusing to comply with lawful directions when the police are acting to prevent a breach of the peace.
- Using threatening, abusive or insulting words or behaviour (section 4 Public Order Act 1986, see p. 24).

- Disorderly conduct likely to cause harassment, alarm or distress (section 5 Public Order Act 1986, see p. 25).

The police often rely on their powers of arrest (including the use of reasonable force) to remove people who are taking part in a mass picket and then either offer cautions (see p. 138), or when cases come to court, consent to bind-overs being offered and the charges dismissed (see p. 28).

If you decide to defend a charge which relates to picketing, you should be aware that the police or Crown Prosecution Service may try to persuade the court that it should be a condition of your bail that you stay away from the picket until your trial, which could be several months away.

Meetings

Private meetings
A meeting is private if the public are not free to attend, in payment or otherwise (for example, the meeting of a trade union branch or a political party). A private meeting remains private even though it is held in a public building like a town hall. Organisers can refuse entry or require someone to leave. Private meetings are governed by the rules of the organization involved, or by conditions specified by the organisers together with any requirements, for example, as to maximum numbers which apply to the premises where the meeting takes place. Unless the police are invited by the organisers they have no right to enter a private meeting and can be invited to leave unless they are present to prevent crime or an imminent breach of the peace.

Public meetings
A public meeting is a meeting which is open to the public to attend, with or without payment, and is held in a public place (a place to which the public have access on payment or otherwise). Many private premises, including town halls and council buildings, church halls, football stadia, pubs, etc., become 'public places' when public meetings are held there. A meeting could be any number of people and there is no duty to advertise it or to offer tickets widely. Local council meetings are public (except for confidential parts of the agenda).

If you are the organiser of a public meeting on private premises you must ensure that you comply with the terms and conditions for the use of the hall, etc., including all fire and safety regulations, and that the meeting is conducted in an orderly manner. Stewards should be easily identifiable but they should not wear a uniform to promote a political objective or signify membership of a political organisation. They must not try to take over the functions of the police or use force to promote a political objective (these acts would be illegal). They can assist in the admission and seating of members of the public and in the control of disorder or to remove members of the public who go too far in their heckling.

It is an *offence* under the Public Meeting Act 1908 to try to break up a lawful public meeting by acting in a disorderly manner or to incite others to do so. The maximum penalty is six months' imprisonment and/or a fine on level 5. If a police officer is present and reasonably suspects you of trying to disrupt the meeting then, at the chairperson's request, he or she can ask you for your name and address and it is an offence if you fail to give these details or give a false name or address (maximum penalty a fine on level 1). These offences do not carry a power of arrest, although the police could rely on their general powers of arrest (see p. 138).

If there is serious disruption or aggressiveness, and if the police believe that you are involved, then, relying on their common law powers to prevent a breach of the peace, the police could ask you to leave the meeting, threatening you with arrest if you refused, or they could arrest you for an offence under section 4 or section 5 of the Public Order Act 1986 (see p. 24).

Any meeting of twenty or more people which is wholly or partly in the open air is a 'public assembly' and subject to conditions being imposed by the police under the Public Order Act 1986 (see p. 6). Organisers should be aware that plain-clothes police officers may attend political meetings without authority for the purpose of collecting information.

Election meetings
The Representation of the People Act 1983 makes special provision for public meetings held at the time of local or national elections. All candidates are entitled to use rooms in local schools and other publicly owned meeting halls, free of charge, for election meetings *provided that* the meetings are open to the public and are intended to further the candidate's prospects by discussion of election issues.

Some local authorities have refused permission to the National Front to use their premises for election meetings on the grounds that they did not intend their meetings to be genuinely open to the public or because damage was likely to be caused to the premises. In 1986, the Court of Appeal upheld the right of a British National Party candidate to be allowed to use a schoolroom for an election meeting and ruled that a candidate who was refused such access could sue the local authority to enforce his rights under the election law.

The Representation of the People Act makes it an offence, punishable with a fine at level 3 (see p. 29), to disrupt, or to incite others to disrupt, an election meeting. If a police officer reasonably suspects you of trying to disrupt the meeting, then, at the chairperson's request, he or she can ask you for your name and address and it is an offence if you fail to give these details or falsify them. Police powers for public meetings also apply to election meetings.

Using the highway

The law provides a specific right to use a public highway. It is the right to pass and repass along the highway (including the pavement), and the right to make ordinary and reasonable use of the highway, which includes processions. Lord Denning said in one case that the right to meet together, to go in a procession, to demonstrate and to protest on matters of public concern was undoubted in English law.

But the use of the highway must be reasonable; any unreasonable obstruction of the highway is a criminal offence (see p. 27). There may also be bye-laws – laws relating to a particular area – that restrict activities which are incidental to the right to use the highway (see the following two sections).

Street collections, leafleting, petitions, posters and newspapers

Generally speaking the law allows a wider latitude for collecting money for charitable operations than for commercial or political ones, both of which are more closely regulated by licensing. 'Charitable purposes' means any charitable, benevolent or philanthropic purpose. It includes the relief of poverty and the advancement of religion or education at home or abroad, but it does not include collections to raise funds for a political party or for a political campaign, like CND or animal liberation. However, the law relating to these subjects is confused and inconsistently applied by the police. If in doubt, check with the local authority and the police beforehand.

There is no need to obtain a licence or certificate for handing out leaflets or collecting signatures for a petition. A leaflet must have on it the name and address of the printer. Some bye-laws contain restrictions on the places where leafleting may take place; check the bye-laws at the town hall. The police may also move leafleters if they appear to be causing an obstruction. It may be an offence to hand out leaflets which are threatening, abusive or insulting or which are intended to stir up racial hatred.

A petition to Parliament is governed by special rules and must conform to special wording. Copies of the rules can be obtained from:

House of Commons
Westminster
London SW1A OAA
Tel: 071 219 3000

Sticking up posters in public places is quite legal, so long as:

*   You have the consent of the owner of the hoarding, fence or wall in question, and the poster is no more than six feet square.
*   It advertises a non-commercial event, including political, educational, or social meetings there is no bye-law to prevent it.

Persons over eighteen may sell newspapers in the street or from door to door, as long as the sale is for campaigning purposes. If the sale is for profit it becomes street trading or peddling (if door to door), both of which are illegal without a licence. Sometimes difficulty is caused because the police believe that the newspaper or magazine is less of a campaigning document and more a device merely to raise money for a political organisation. Also, the sale of newspapers may obstruct the highway, which is a criminal offence (see p. 27).

Bye-laws

Many activities on the highway and in other public places such as parks and gardens and on common land are restricted by local bye-laws. Bye-laws for parks may, for example, prohibit public meetings, bill-posting, the erection of notices, stalls and booths, and the sale or distribution of pamphlets and leaflets. They will usually give the police and local authority officials the power to remove anybody who breaches the bye-laws.

Ministry of Defence bye-laws are used, for example, to keep trespassers out of United States Air Force bases. The RAF Greenham Common bye-laws list twelve prohibited activities, beginning with entering the protected area except by way of an authorised entrance, and including affixing posters to perimeter fences.

A copy of the bye-laws should be on sale at the local town hall and also available for inspection. It is an offence to breach a bye-law. The penalty is set out in the particular bye-law or, if not, is a fine up to £100. Recent cases show that when a charge is brought, bye-laws can be challenged on the basis that they are *ultra vires*, that is, beyond the scope of the Act of Parliament which creates them, or that they are obviously unreasonable or inconsistent with or repugnant to the general law.

For the right to use the highway for industrial and consumer picketing (see p. 27).

1.3 In practice – organising a protest action

It is easy to be intimidated by all the laws that exist to regulate the expression of public protest. But the most successful protest groups see the restrictive legal framework as one of the necessary challenges that their own good organisation can overcome, or at least accommodate. Although the police have been given very wide powers under the Public Order Act 1986, the actual *exercise* of these powers has been remarkably rare since the Act came into force. Conditions are not routinely imposed on demonstrations, and banning orders have not been used as extensively as opponents of the legislation first feared. In fact, only a handful of the hundreds of thousands of prosecutions brought under the Act since 1987 have been for offences connected with organising marches or assemblies, defying banning orders or even breaching conditions imposed by police. The vast majority have been for the public order offences ranging from riot to disorderly conduct (see p. 23) each of which involved specific offensive conduct by the defendant, usually at the demonstration itself.

The following sections show how complying with the law and nego-tiating with the police can be fitted into the arrangements that organisers will be making, in any event, in preparation for a protest of significant size. Obviously, organisers will choose which of the following are appropriate or desirable for the particular sort of protest they are planning.

A checklist for organisers

Stewards and legal observers

An efficient stewarding operation avoids many of the interactions between protesters and police that have the potential for conflict. Protesters are usually quite happy to follow sensible instructions so long as they know that they are part of the organisers' plan rather than some arbitrary decision made on the spot by an officious police officer. Stewarding therefore gives confidence to your protesters, whilst also enabling information about particular difficulties to reach the organ-isation room, or chief stewards at the protest, very quickly.

Stewards should be briefed prior to the protest on what exactly they should be doing, and who they should report to in the event of difficulty. They are part of the organisation of the event and should be identifiable as such both to police and protesters by bibs, arm bands, special T shirts or badges (but obviously not a quasi-military uniform, see p. 11). At the event itself they should have a map of the proposed route, and the telephone number of the organisation room (see below).

Some organisations have ad hoc groups of legal observers who are prepared to attend demonstrations and make an independent note of numbers and movements of police and protesters. In the event of arrests, they will make immediate notes of witnesses' names and addresses. Observers can be a great help if events turn sour, but in any case their presence at a demonstration can be reassuring to protesters and police alike. It is important that they perceive themselves to be independent of the protest itself and its organisation. They may therefore wish to be identified in a way that distinguishes them from other people on the march, including stewards, for example by special badges, arm bands or bibs. Often law students or lecturers from local colleges are prepared to provide this service if given enough notice. Inexperienced legal observers should be briefed by a solicitor, perhaps the standby solicitor (see legal cover section on p. 17), preferably in good time before the protest. An organisation based in London that can sometimes provide support of this kind is the Legal Observers' Group (address in Further information – see p. 30).

Stewards and legal observers should know where to meet immediately after the event for a debriefing where any feedback or information they have (notes from legal observers) can be retrieved. They should also be available to come to a defendants' meeting, which should be pencilled in for two or three days after the event, in case anyone at the demonstration is arrested. Arranging such a meeting provides a safety net which will enable you to begin to draw all your resources together should there ever be a defendants' group that needs to rely on them.

Advance publicity and press liaison
Prior to the event itself, advance publicity should include a clear statement of the venue for assembly, the time of departure (for a march) and the time and place of the eventual rally. Any venues you advertise ought – as a matter of good practice – to have been agreed with the owners/local authority/police in advance (see below). Otherwise, if you are forced to change any of these arrangements your supporters may never get to the protest.

Demonstrations are designed to be widely seen and their intended message understood. You might prepare a brief press statement to be sent out to the media in advance setting out the message you want them to grasp – and, hopefully, to broadcast on your behalf – about why the event is taking place. Ideally, this should include contact telephone numbers of one or two people who are prepared to be quoted speaking on your behalf and a reference point at the protest itself so that journalists know where to go if they want to get an official statement or reaction to something that has happened. Journalists might be given the telephone number of the organisation room, but telephone interviews during the protest itself should be kept short.

The advantage of preparing a press release in advance is that local journalists will put the event in their news diary which may ensure fuller coverage. Also, they may be more interested in difficulties you have with the police in the run-up to the event, especially if you decide to tell the press that you are preparing to challenge proposed conditions.

Organisation room
On the day of the event itself there ought to be a reference point away from the demonstration – a union office, for example – with at least two separate phone lines. One of these numbers should be circulated widely so that arrested people will be likely to have a leaflet with them in the police station with it written on. This will also be the number used by stewards or legal observers if they want to contact the organisation room where necessary during the event itself. The other phone line can be used for outgoing calls – to the police station, to the standby lawyer (see below), or perhaps to the press.

Legal cover
Ideally you will have arranged a standby lawyer well in advance of the action who is prepared to be contacted during the demonstration itself and to follow through with representation for arrested demonstrators if they require it. The standby lawyer should be a criminal solicitor with particular experience of dealing with demonstrations. If you do not know of such a lawyer, organisations like those listed below will help you find one in your area. If you experience difficulties negotiating with the police in advance, the standby lawyer may be prepared to help you.

It may be worthwhile making contact with lawyers' groups who are committed to civil liberties in good time before a proposed action. Again, full addresses are included in Further information (see p. 30):

- Haldane Society of Socialist Lawyers.
- Lawyers Against Apartheid.
- Legal Aid Practitioners' Group.
- Society of Black Lawyers.
- Society of Labour Lawyers

Debriefing
Taking time to listen to feedback from those who have helped you organise the event is more than just good practice – where there have been arrests such an exercise is essential. It is also an opportunity to recognise the job done by stewards and legal observers, to thank them and to make sure you have their contact numbers for the next time you need them.

Defendants' meeting
At the briefing for stewards and legal observers you will probably have arranged a defendants' meeting at a given venue and time two or

three days after the event. Although you hope it will not be needed, such a meeting may make a very significant difference to those who may attend (see p. 30).

Dealing with police

Whenever it is anticipated there may be police interest in a proposed action it will be worth weighing the benefits and costs of speaking to the police well in advance as part of your preparations. Sometimes it will be a legal obligation to do so (see p. 3).

The benefits of establishing contact with the police are likely to include, if not necessarily good will, at least some cooperation. With some or all of the above measures in place you will be in a strong position to satisfy the police that you will be able to regulate your own event without needing outside help. Confident organisers who impress with their thoroughness and practicality are more likely to be able to convince sceptical police that a proposed event should proceed exactly as planned. Where they are able to do so, the worry that the event might be hi-jacked by police interference will be eased, and organisers will then be able to concentrate on getting their political message across to the public.

The costs might include the fact that the police may use your information to trigger the use of their powers to restrict a protest or, exceptionally, to ban it altogether. It is worth remembering that communications to police – especially those in writing – could be used in court if the police wanted to show that a particular person was an organiser of an illegal demonstration.

If you decide to speak to the police in advance of the event you should be fully prepared with details of arrangements for stewarding and crowd control, first aid and access by emergency vehicles, maps and plans, a detailed time schedule and an estimate of numbers. Relying on your own knowledge of the community and any other events likely to take place on the same date, try to anticipate police objections. Keep a full note of any objections they raise. Where you have already arranged legal cover, your standby lawyer may be prepared to help you sort out difficulties with the police.

Despite their substantial human resources and weaponry, the police are very often intimidated by the idea of large numbers of people taking to the streets to make their protest heard. Where police react in a hostile way, it is often through fear of the unknown. In practice, most police forces respond positively to constructive engagement – they like to know that someone who is organising a demonstration has anticipated the likely numbers and thought about the route, stewarding and safety. They also like to know that there will be someone at the protest to whom they can talk sensibly in an emergency.

Challenging police decisions

Even when the police threaten to impose conditions, organisers have a great deal of discretion about whether and when to challenge the police decision. Sometimes organisers are quite happy to agree to police alterations to their original proposals – a minor alteration to the proposed route, perhaps – knowing that this means in practice that the police are unlikely to interfere further with a route they have themselves adopted. Organisers may even prefer to adapt their protest to what they consider to be unreasonable police requests simply to ensure the event goes ahead without its political message being blunted by unnecessary conflict with the police. If organisers wish to challenge unacceptable police conditions they might do so in a number of ways.

Mobilising political support

Although the police regard their own decisions as 'operational', in practice they involve setting priorities between the interests of different groups in society. Ultimately, where the right balance lies is really a political matter and the police are sensitive to criticism from MPs and councillors, local interest groups or trades councils. Members of the police committee may be concerned by 'operational' policing decisions they consider to be oppressive.

Mounting a legal challenge

With the help of legal advisers, organisers could test the legality of police conditions through a court case in advance of the action itself. In order to seek a judicial review of a police decision you would need to argue that either:

- The decision was improperly reached (for example, because the proper procedure was not followed or improper considerations were taken into account).
- The decision was so unreasonable or arbitrary that no reasonable chief officer could have reached that conclusion.

It would be relevant to show that negotiations were still open. Cases brought to challenge banning orders show that courts are very unwilling to interfere with police decisions, especially if to do so would involve substituting their own assessment of the facts, and the possible prospects of disorder, damage, disruption or intimidation, for the assessment made by senior police officers.

Applications for judicial review must be made to the Divisional Court of the High Court in London. Urgent applications can be heard quickly. In many instances, however, you will be informed of conditions to restrict processions or assemblies too late to apply to the court. There is no one with immediate power to overrule the senior officer on the spot if he decides to impose conditions.

Where protesters themselves defy police conditions it will be for the police to decide whether to make arrests and seek prosecutions. If in a subsequent trial it turns out that the conditions were indeed invalid, the prosecutions would fail and arrested persons may be entitled to damages.

Help from Liberty
Liberty has been able to advise many of its supporters, including unions and political groups, about the best way to challenge police operations which threaten to defeat civil liberties. In the past our organisation has supported lawyers and lay people who have challenged such decisions and has itself been prepared to take test cases where important issues of principle have been at stake. In the first instance, you or your solicitor may want to write or talk to Liberty's Legal Officer at the address below. Liberty will either be able to help you or will refer you to a specialist solicitor or campaigning group who have dealt with similar problems in the past.

Liberty
21 Tabard Street
London SE1 4LA
Tel: 071 403 3888

Supporting defendants
Where people have been arrested at a protest event and charged with offences, they become defendants in the criminal process, facing the possibility of a criminal record and sometimes a substantial fine or even prison. It is often very frightening for protesters to be torn from the cosy solidarity of a demonstration to find themselves facing the music all on their own. An important part of what organisers can do for defendants, as their cases progress over the months that may elapse before a trial, is to retain and build on that original sense of solidarity. Defendants may be helped by support and reassurance in many different ways – it will often be a question of adapting your resources to the calls that are made on them – but one of the most straightforward and practical measures is to ensure that there is always someone from your organisation at court with them for each appearance.

In the immediate aftermath of the event, however, there are some standard procedures to be performed, starting with the defendants' meeting. This will have been pencilled in for two or three days after the event just in case it may be needed. Too soon, and defendants may still be in custody. Too late, and a lot of your resources, especially witnesses, will have dispersed, perhaps for good.

Defendants' meeting

A defendants' meeting puts people who have been charged with offences in touch with the people who organised the event, perhaps for the first time. Defendants may need immediate help with lawyers or legal aid, for example, or even just floors to sleep on if they have to remain away from home for a court hearing. The meeting is an opportunity to give defendants reassurance if they need it, and to tell them what support they can expect from your organisation. There may be questions about bail conditions, legal aid or bind-overs, for example, or how their cases are likely to develop. The standby lawyer may be prepared to attend such a meeting, but will not give specific legal advice to defendants about their individual cases.

The defendants' meeting is a very important practical opportunity to match defendants to the witnesses who saw them being arrested. It is useful to do this quickly while memories are fresh. Often witnesses will not have met the defendants before and will not know them by name. Unless they come to a meeting and see the defendant, the only method of matching them to the right arrest is by their description of the arrested person, or by the time and location of the arrest. Where there have been many arrests, particularly at a mobile protest like a march, there is often great confusion about location, order and times of arrests. Often the only way to sort out which witnesses saw which arrests is to have everyone in the same room at the same time.

Defendants might want to provide passport photos of themselves – or, if you have a camera at the meeting, might want you to take photos of them – to help with identification. This is often an enormous help for you, for witnesses and for lawyers where there are more than a handful of arrests. Make sure defendants are happy for you to circulate their photos and other information about themselves they want to give you.

Supporting the legal team

Once a lawyer is instructed by a person arrested for a criminal offence, the relationship is a personal one between the client and the lawyer and is therefore subject to professional confidentiality. Although the lawyer will not be prepared to speak about the details of the client's case to anyone else, most sympathetic lawyers will wish to retain a close contact with any organisation that has their clients' best interests at heart. Moreover they may wish to rely on you to get things done that they do not have the knowledge or resources to do themselves.

Sometimes several different solicitors will be acting for different defendants. Unless you are able to help them with an overview of what happened when and where during the course of the whole event, individual solicitors may never get the full picture. It is very important, for example, for them to know which arrests may be linked with each other. Accurate information about the time and location of arrests will be very helpful when defence lawyers seek film or photographs of the event from journalists who covered it. It is best to get this overview completed when events are fresh in everyone's mind and you have willing supporters to help.

Preparing material for defendants and their solicitors

At the earliest opportunity – within a few days of the defendants' meeting – organisers should marshal all the material they have at their disposal and make it available to defendants and their lawyers. This will include brief accounts of the following matters. Where more is needed later, defendants will know exactly who to ask:

- Facts about the event itself – who you are, how you prepared for the event. Negotiations with the police before and at the event. Who spoke for the organisation, who represented the police. What conditions were imposed/agreed. What steps were taken by police/organisers to publicise conditions. Whether any conditions were broken. Include a map of the route showing, if possible, location and time of arrests. Also reports – in the form of brief statements – where stewards and legal observers have observations about the event that might be relevant. Include telephone numbers to enable lawyers to contact individuals direct if their evidence may be helpful.
- Full list of defendants' names, addresses and telephone numbers, including, if possible, time and location of arrest, police station taken to, offence they are charged with, date and venue of first court appearance. If defendants are happy to supply passport-sized photos of themselves (or wanted you to take photographs at the defendants' meeting) you can include a photocopied sheet with them all on.
- Full list of witnesses' names, addresses and telephone numbers, marked (if known) with the names of the defendants whose arrest they saw.
- List of media representatives – especially photographers and television news teams – who you think were at the event. A useful source are the by-lines on media coverage – this can be followed up in the local library without having to buy all the newspapers. Wherever a news story might be helpful it should be circulated. You might also include the list of organisations you sent your press release to. Lawyers may then be able to follow up whether they had anyone at the event.
- List of defence solicitors, so you know who to circulate information to. It will also help solicitors to communicate with each other if they know who else is being represented by whom.

Dealing with the press

In the run-up to the trials of defendants who plead not guilty – sometimes a delay of many months – you may want to look closely at the media coverage of the event and respond constructively by telephone to journalists, by 'letters to the editor' or by press release to anything that is said that you know is not true.

The police are adept at public relations and will normally have their own publicists, who are experienced journalists, handling press enquiries about the event and its aftermath. It is a sad fact that the media often takes this version as gospel, presuming the guilt of anyone unfortunate enough to have been arrested. Whilst there are no doubt other factors at play this may *sometimes* be due to their perception that there is no other reliable source to challenge what the police say.

As well as information from your organisation you may be able to put the media in touch with ordinary protesters who had a very different impression of the way the event took place. If you know that celebrities at the event, such as local politicians, are likely to be supportive, you can ask them if they, too, are prepared to be interviewed.

It will give confidence to defendants to see that you are active about putting media coverage right. It also advertises the work that you are doing just in case defendants or potential witnesses did not know how to get in touch.

1.4 Public order offences

The right of protest may only be exercised peacefully. Otherwise, a wide variety of offences may be committed. The Public Order Act 1986 introduced new offences like disorderly conduct, as well as updating some old offences like riot. But there are many offences elsewhere in the law which may be used against activities in public, such as assault, criminal damage and having an offensive weapon. Some specific offences connected with marches, assemblies and meetings were set out earlier in this chapter. The most widely exercised non-statutory powers arise in relation to perceived breaches of the peace.

Serious offences of violence

The three main offences in the Public Order Act 1986 for group violence are riot, violent disorder and affray.

Riot

It is an offence of riot if you use violence where at least twelve people are together using or threatening violence for a common purpose and in such a way that 'a person of reasonable firmness' witnessing the events would fear for his or her safety.

This is the most serious of public order offences. Prosecutions are becoming less common because of the difficulty of proving a 'common purpose'. The offence can only be tried in the Crown Court and the Director of Public Prosecutions must consent to the case being brought. The maximum penalty is ten years' imprisonment.

Violent disorder
You are guilty of violent disorder if you use or threaten violence where at least three people are together using or threatening violence and in such a way that a person 'of reasonable firmness' would fear for his or her personal safety.

This offence is used especially for group violence, such as disturbances commonly associated with football hooliganism, or where weapons are used. It can be tried in either the Crown Court or the magistrates' court. The maximum penalty is five years' imprisonment.

Affray
It is an affray if you use or threaten violence to somebody else in such a way that a person 'of reasonable firmness' would fear for his or her personal safety (*effrayer* is the French word meaning to frighten).

Street fighting, with or without weapons or missiles, is an affray. It can be tried in either the Crown Court or the magistrates' court. The maximum penalty is three years' imprisonment.

Grievous bodily harm and actual bodily harm
Serious assaults on individuals include the offences of inflicting grievous bodily harm and assault occasioning actual bodily harm. These offences are set out in the Offences Against the Person Act 1861.

If you cause or inflict grievous bodily harm on somebody or wound them (that is, cut the skin), the maximum penalty is life imprisonment. If the person dies, the charge may be murder or manslaughter. If the injury is less serious, such as bruising or grazes, the charge may be assault occasioning actual bodily harm, with a maximum penalty of five years' imprisonment.

Less serious offences

Threatening, abusive or insulting words or behaviour
It is an offence under section 4 Public Order Act 1986 if you use any, or a combination of, threatening, abusive or insulting words or actions towards somebody else, *and:*

- You intend the other person to believe that violence is going to be used; *or*
- The other person is likely to expect violence; *or*
- Violence may well be provoked.

This rather complicated offence is normally used where threats, abuse or insults are likely to cause a breach of the peace: rival football supporters hurling abuse, threats at the picket line, abusive language by rival demonstrators. The charge is often used against protesters who, in the view of the police, go beyond the bounds of ordinary protest, but in all cases the behaviour must be directed towards another person. It is an offence if the words are on a banner or placard or even a T shirt or badge.

This offence can only be tried in the magistrates' court; there is no right to trial by jury. The maximum penalty is six months' imprisonment and/or a fine of £2,000.

Disorderly conduct

It is an offence under section 5 of the Public Order Act 1986 if you use threatening, abusive or insulting words or behaviour or disorderly behaviour within the hearing or sight of a person likely to be caused harassment, alarm or distress. There must be a victim present at the scene of the crime. That person must be identified but need not be brought to court. Police officers are unlikely to be victims of this offence.

This is the lowest-level public order offence. It is intended to cover minor acts of hooliganism, especially behaviour directed at the elderly and other vulnerable groups. It was much criticised when it was introduced in the Public Order Act because it covered behaviour which was generally not considered to be criminal. In particular, it covers behaviour which falls short of violence or the threat or fear of violence.

The offence carries a unique two-stage power of arrest, allowing police to arrest only if the demonstrator has been warned to stop the disorderly conduct and has then gone on to repeat it. In practice, however, police will often be able to use their broader 'general arrest powers' under the Police and Criminal Evidence Act (see p. 138) or their breach of the peace powers (see p. 28) which both allow for arrest without a warning. The offence can only be tried in the magistrates' court. The maximum penalty is a fine on level 3; there is no power to send a person convicted of this offence to prison.

Assault

You are guilty of common assault (under the common law) if you engage in an act which intentionally or recklessly causes another person to expect immediate personal violence, anything from a punch or a kick to throwing something at somebody. If injury is caused, a more serious charge of assault may be brought (see above). Common assault can only be tried in the magistrates' court. The maximum penalty is six months' imprisonment.

You are guilty of a separate offence with a similar penalty if you assault a police officer in the execution of his or her duty (see p. 27). At a trial the prosecution would have to show that the police officer was acting lawfully. In practice, especially in a confused demonstration situation, proving beyond doubt that police action was lawful can be difficult.

Criminal damage

You are guilty under the Criminal Damage Act 1971 if you damage or destroy property or threaten to do so intentionally or recklessly and without lawful excuse. There is a full range of offences from arson with intent to endanger life (maximum penalty life imprisonment) to damage of property under £2,000 (to be increased to £5,000 in 1994) in value (magistrates' court only with a maximum penalty of three months' imprisonment and/or a fine up to £1000). The damage need not be permanent. Even graffiti designed to wash away with rain may be criminal damage.

Offensive weapons

You are guilty under the Prevention of Crime Act 1953 if you have an offensive weapon in a public place without lawful authority or reasonable excuse. There are three types of weapon: one designed for causing injury such as a knuckleduster, dagger or flick-knife; one adapted for causing injury like a broken bottle; and one intended for use to cause injury, such as an ordinary knife or a spanner. The offence can be tried in the Crown Court (maximum penalty two years' imprisonment) or in the magistrates' court (maximum penalty three months' imprisonment and/or a fine up to £2000).

Under the Criminal Justice Act 1988 it is an offence to have a knife in a public place, but not a folding pocket knife with a blade of not more than three inches. Mere possession of a knife or other article with a blade is an offence (maximum penalty a fine of £400 in the magistrates' court) unless you can prove you had a good reason for carrying it, for example, for use at work, for a hobby, for religious reasons or as part of a national costume (for stop and search powers, see p. 129). The courts have said that the 'good reason' has to relate to the time the knife is found. A good reason for having it five days before was not good enough, and nor was just forgetting you had it with you.

Offences connected with processions, assemblies and meetings

It is an offence to breach a condition imposed by the police on a procession or an assembly or to breach an order banning processions in your locality (see p. 5). You may commit an offence if you wear a uniform in public signifying association with any political organisation or with the promotion of any political objective (trial in the magistrates' court, maximum penalty three months' imprisonment and/or a fine on level 2). You commit an offence if you organise or train members of a quasi-military organisation (maximum penalty in the Crown Court two years' imprisonment and in the magistrates' court six months' imprisonment and/or a fine on level 5).

Police obstruction

It is an offence if you wilfully obstruct a police officer in the execution of his or her duty. This is widely used by the police at demonstrations and in other public order contexts. Wilful obstruction of a police officer means simply doing any act which makes it more difficult for police to carry out their lawful duty (magistrates' court only, maximum penalty one months' imprisonment and/or a fine on level 3). It is used against those who refuse to move on or to keep back, or against those who interfere with police work, for example, by objecting to a lawful arrest or search. There is no specific power of arrest for this offence and so the police have to rely on their 'general arrest powers' where the circumstances permit. Where an arrest can be justified, no warning need be given in advance.

'Watching and besetting'

It is an offence under the Trade Union and Labour Relations (Consolidation) Act 1992 (maximum penalty six months' imprisonment and/or a fine on level 5 – see p. 29) to intimidate others, if, for example you:

- Use violence to intimidate someone or their family or damage property.
- Persistently follow someone.
- Hide someone's tools or clothes.
- 'Watch and beset' or picket someone's home or place of work (NB it is not unlawful to picket peacefully at your own place of work).
- Follow someone in the street, with two others, in a disorderly manner.

But this applies only if you do any of these acts with the intention of compelling the person not to do something he or she has a legal right to do (for example, the right to use the highway to go to work) or to do something he or she has a legal right not to do (for example, the right not to join the picket). Persuasion, even vigorous persuasion, will not amount to an offence unless it crosses into the realm of compulsion.

For offences connected with picketing see p. 10. For offences connected with meetings see p. 11. For offences of stirring up racial hatred see p. 207.

Highway obstruction

You commit an offence if, without lawful authority or excuse, you wilfully obstruct the free passage of the highway.

This is a widely drawn offence. It is often seen in practice as a police licensing power over public gatherings. The police use it to remove sit-down demonstrators, to prevent protesters outside South Africa House in Trafalgar Square from straying outside the barrier positions agreed with police, to keep marchers from leaving the agreed police route, to control pickets, and in every conceivable public order context on the highway. The offence does not require violence or the threat of violence.

When cases reach court, prosecutors commonly agree to offer no evidence if the defendant agrees to be bound over (see below). Often the police will give a warning to move before making an arrest, although there is no legal requirement to do so. Nevertheless, a failure to give a warning may be relevant to the reasonableness or otherwise of the use of the highway.

The test of reasonableness is always objective. Was there an actual obstruction? If there was, how long did it last? Where was it? What was its purpose? The police often decide to make an arrest on the basis that other people are prevented from passing along the highway or going into shops or business premises. But it is a question of fact in each case and the test of reasonableness can very often be argued successfully in demonstration cases, particularly where the police have taken no action in the past, or where the place of protest is a regular post or where the obstruction was trivial. It is often helpful to have photographs which show just how extensive a particular obstruction was.

The offence can only be tried in the magistrates' court. The maximum penalty is a fine of £400. There is no power to send a person convicted of highway obstruction to prison.

Breach of the peace

There is no offence of breach of the peace. But if a police officer sees a breach of the peace or reasonably believes that a breach of the peace is about to be committed or that a renewal of a breach of the peace is threatened, he or she may arrest, disperse or detain those involved and, if necessary, take them before a magistrates' court to be bound over.

There is a breach of the peace whenever harm is actually done or is likely to be done to a person, or in his or her presence to his or her property, or a person is in fear of being so harmed. If a breach of the peace occurs, one or more of the public order offences of threatening behaviour, disorderly conduct, assault or criminal damage (see above for these offences) is likely to have been committed. In such a case, the police can choose whether to charge an offence or go before the magistrates for a bind-over order.

Bind-overs

The magistrates' court may bind you over to keep the peace or be of good behaviour for a specified period in a number of different circumstances:

- You may be brought before the court for a breach of the peace (under the Justices of the Peace Act 1361).
- You may be brought before the court on a complaint made by any person at the court.
- In a criminal case, a witness or a defendant (even if acquitted) may be bound over.

A bind-over order is not a conviction or a penalty. It is an undertaking as to future conduct. Its purpose is to prevent offences being committed in the future. The order will bind you over to keep the peace for a period of time for a specified sum, say £200 for twelve months. If you breach the order and are brought back to court, you will have to pay up to the whole amount. Sometimes sureties are taken, in which case the person who has put up the surety would have to forfeit some or all of the amount of their surety too. If you refuse to be bound over in the first place, you can be sent to prison for up to six months. You should always be given the opportunity to say in court why you should not be bound over, if you wish to, or why you are not in breach of the order.

Bind-over orders are often used against demonstrators and protesters. Sometimes a charge, such as obstruction of the highway, is dropped by the prosecution if the defendant agrees to be bound over and the court also agrees. In some cases, unions will advise their members who have been picketing not to accept bind-overs if they wish to return to the picket line. A bind-over cannot of itself prevent someone returning to the picket line (see the right to bail, p. 169) but it is an inhibiting factor.

Some people believe that the bind-over order is an outdated form of justice and that it is wrong to give the courts the power to send somebody to prison for refusing to be bound over, particularly when no offence has been committed.

Fine levels
Fine levels for offences tried in magistrates' courts are updated from time to time. The current amounts of maximum fines for adults were set in October 1992:

Level	£
1	200
2	500
3	1,000
4	2,500
5	5,000

Where the statute gives no specific level the maximum fine is £400.The maximum fines for juveniles are:

young person (14–16)	£1,000
child (10–13)	£250

For offences which can be tried in the Crown Court or in the magistrates' court the maximum fine in the magistrates' court is £2,000. For offences which are tried in the Crown Court there is no limit on the fine which can be imposed.

In fixing the amount of the fine the court must take into account the means of the offender. The court may give the offender time to pay, for example, within three months, or at so much a week. If the court imposes a sentence of imprisonment in default and the fine is not paid, the court may send the offender to prison, but only after a careful means enquiry (for criminal compensation orders see p. 110).

1.5 Stop Press

The Criminal Justice and Public Order Bill which was going through Parliament in January 1994 will restrict the right to protest.

In particular it will limit the right to protest by criminalising some forms of trespass. If a person trespasses on land with the intention of intimidating others or disrupting or obstructing the activities of others a criminal offence will have been committed. The bill also creates a new criminal offence of disobeying the orders of a police officer who has directed a person to leave land in such circumstances.

These provisions will not only affect hunt saboteurs but also environmental campaigners who trespass by mistake, trades unionists involved in peaceful picketing but who are perhaps technically trespassing on land belonging to their employer or consumers picketing outside shops (but perhaps on the land belonging to the shop).

Another clause provides a new power to ban assemblies. Breach of a ban will also become a criminal offence. Even incitement to breach the ban will be an offence. The police are also to be granted another new power allowing them to stop persons on their way to such assemblies.

Other clauses give powers to police officers to ban 'raves', to prevent people attending them and to confiscate sound equipment.

If these provisions are not stopped they will probably become law by the end of 1994.

1.6 Further Information

It is often useful to talk to people who are experienced at organising protest events to get ideas on ways to get the most impact from the available resources and, in the event of unexpected arrests, on ways of supporting defendants and their legal teams.

Bibliography

J. Cooper, *Public Order Review*, Legal Action.
I. McShane, *How To Use the Media*, Pluto, 1979.
J. Marston, *Public Order*, Fourmat, 1987.
A.T.H. Smith, *Offences Against Public Order*, Sweet and Maxwell, 1987.
P. Thornton, *Public Order Law*, Blackstone Press, 1987.

2

The right of free expression

This chapter deals with:

- The right to speak freely?
- Defamation – libel and slander.
- Obscenity and indecency.
- Blasphemy.
- Racial hatred.
- Contempt of court.
- Secrets and confidentiality.
- Copyright.
- Controls on broadcasting, films, video and cable.
- Whose freedom?
- Further information.

2.1 The right to speak freely?

Surely we can say what we like? It's a free country, isn't it? American lawyers can answer these enquiries with reasonable confidence by pointing to their Bill of Rights. Its first clause (and the First Amendment to the American constitution) prohibits the US Congress from making any law which would infringe freedom of speech or the press. The English Parliament passed a Bill of Rights after the 1688 revolution. It guaranteed freedom of speech – but only for Members of Parliament. There was not then, and there never has been since, a British equivalent of the First Amendment promising freedom of expression for all.

The right of free expression in the European Convention on Human Rights

The closest that Britain has come to a constitutional guarantee of free speech is in ratifying the European Convention on Human Rights. Article 10 of the Convention provides:

1. Everyone has the right of free expression. This right shall include freedom to hold opinions and to receive and impart information and ideas without interference by public authority and regardless

of frontiers. This Article shall not prevent states from requiring the licensing of broadcasting, television or cinema enterprises.

2. The exercise of these freedoms, since it carries with it duties and responsibilities, may be subject to such formalities, conditions, restrictions or penalties as are prescribed by law and necessary in a democratic society, in the interests of national security, territorial integrity or public safety, for the prevention of disorder or crime, for the protection of health and morals, for the protection of the reputation or rights of others, for preventing the disclosure of information received in confidence, or for maintaining the authority and impartiality of the judiciary.

Even here then, the initial promise of free expression is hedged and circumscribed by exceptions and provisos, but the European Court of Human Rights (see p. 112), which is the ultimate arbiter on disputes as to the Convention's meaning, has not allowed paragraph 2 to drain paragraph 1 of all meaning. It has given the right of free expression a special status to which only limited restrictions are permissible.

British restrictions on free speech have often failed the European test. The law on contempt of court (see p. 42) for instance, has had to be changed several times because it did not match up to Article 10.

Yet the European Convention is still a very inferior means of protecting free expression when compared with the American First Amendment. The Convention is a treaty. It binds the governments in international law. It has a better system of enforcement than many treaties in that the European Court was created to decide disputes and individuals can make use of the complaint procedure. In addition, British judges should use the Convention in resolving ambiguities in British law. But these are the limits of its usefulness. The Convention has not been adopted by Parliament in a British statute. British judges cannot use it to override an unambiguous British law. The victim of an unjustified restriction on freedom of expression must start the European complaint procedure and have the patience to wait several years before reaching the European Court and, if successful, before British law is changed to bring it into line with the Court's decision.

The negative approach

Without a First Amendment and without Article 10 as part of British law, 'the right of free expression' has only the limited legal meaning that a person is free to say anything which is not prohibited. Hence, this chapter will largely be concerned with things that cannot be said. However, the position is not quite as bleak as this statement suggests. Thankfully, the popular understanding of the right of free speech, however ill-defined or shifting, defines it as being more than a purely negative proposition. This is important because many of the restrictions which we shall examine are only brought into play if the government takes the initiative. It may choose not to do so if it perceives such action being criticised as contrary to the popular notion of 'free speech'. Of course, on other occasions (for instance, the *Spycatcher* litigation) it will carry on regardless but whatever the courts say such obduracy may carry a political price.

The role of the jury in 'free speech' cases

The principle of free speech has more than purely negative connotations in other respects as well. The conflicts between the government and the press in the seventeenth and eighteenth centuries demonstrated the importance of the jury. The right of the jury to acquit – whatever the weight of the evidence in favour of the Crown – was established in 'free speech' cases. That right has not been altered even though it has meant in recent years that the government's ability to prosecute successfully under the Official Secrets Act has been severely curtailed.

In libel cases, both criminal and civil, it is for the jury to decide whether the publication was against the law. In turn, this means that juries have been preserved in libel cases although they have been abolished in almost all other types of civil litigation. This has not always been to the advantage of the press which has been ordered to pay huge sums in damages by libel juries. More importantly, the courts are extremely reluctant to issue an injunction to prevent publication of something that is said to be libellous. If the publisher (or broadcaster) swears an affidavit that it is true, the judges regard it as a matter for the jury at the trial to decide the dispute and will not prevent publication (or transmission) in advance. Unfortunately, this judicial self-restraint does not apply outside libel, and injunctions are all too readily granted against the media to prevent disclosure of something which is said to be in breach of confidence.

The following sections give an outline of the principal restrictions that limit the right of free expression.

2.2 Defamation – libel and slander

Libel and slander are intended to protect reputations and provide compensation for injury to them. Libel is used if the damaging words take a permanent form (books, magazines, films, etc., and broadcasts have been included in this category by Parliament); slander is used if they do not. We refer to 'words' but pictures, signs and any other expression can be defamatory. Collectively these wrongs are known as 'defamation'. This distinction between libel and slander is largely historical, but a difference of continuing importance is that a plaintiff must show financial loss to succeed in slander; this is not necessary for libel. For certain types of slander even this distinction dissolves: accusations of imprisonable crime; that the plaintiff carries a contagious disease; that the victim is unfit for his or her office, business or profession; slanders on the credit of tradespeople; and the imputation of unchastity or adultery to a woman or girl. Here, as with all libels, damage is presumed and need not be proved.

Meaning and defamation

Words are defamatory if they damage the reputation of the victim in the eyes of 'right-thinking' members of society. This definition has the ring of ancient clubland quarrels and indeed this type of litigation is still the prerogative of the rich since, uniquely, legal aid is not available to bring (or defend) actions for defamation. However, the definition does also contain important limitations. Mere vulgar abuse is not defamatory because no one would think the worse of its object. The words may be untrue or hurtful, but they are still not defamatory if they do not impinge on a person's reputation. In addition, damage to a person's credibility amongst the more heretical members of society is immaterial. In one case a person wrongly accused of being a police informer failed in a defamation for this reason.

There are two remedies which might help a person who is angered by a false publication which is not defamatory. Firstly, 'false attribution of authorship' may be relied on when a publisher fabricates quotations. Secondly, if it can be shown that the words were spoken or written maliciously and that they have caused financial loss, then, even though they are not defamatory, the victim can claim damages for 'malicious falsehood'. The bar on legal aid does not apply to these remedies and so, for instance, a claim for malicious falsehood can be publicly funded even though the same publication might also constitute a libel.

In addition, complaints about the unethical behaviour of newspapers and magazines can be made to the Press Complaints Commission (PCC). The behaviour need not have resulted in a libel or any of the other legal wrongs considered above; the PCC is not a court but a voluntary body set up by the newspaper industry. It cannot award damages or any other redress other than a decision vindicating (or rejecting) the complaint. Its decisions are usually well publicised. It is likely that recent criticism of its performance will lead to changes in the way complaints against newspapers are dealt with.

Publication

To return to defamation, the words must have been 'published' by the person sued. This expression has a much wider meaning than its colloquial one. It covers any means of communication even if only to one other person.

Because 'publish' is defined so broadly, distributors and even shops can find themselves sued for libel. They do have a special defence that, having taken all reasonable care, they had no reason to believe that their wares contained defamatory material. For this reason, distributors will sometimes insist that magazines obtain an opinion from a barrister that nothing defamatory is included in the publication. On the other hand, publishers, printers, writers, editors and broadcasters are all responsible for what they put out and cannot argue for immunity because they took every precaution. They are responsible also in the sense that they will be liable for repeating what others have said. Untrue allegations in a published reader's letter can cost a magazine dear. For the same reason it is usually no help to attribute a defamatory remark to a source, to put it in quotation marks or to preface it by 'allegedly' if the net effect of the publication is still to damage the reputation of the person spoken of in the eyes of 'right-thinking' readers.

Identification

At least one person to whom the words are published must be able to identify the victim as the object of the attack. However, direct identification is not essential and the anonymous victim of an attack can sue if there are sufficient clues in the piece pointing to his or her identity. Sometimes the reference to the victim is unintentional, for instance, the character in a novel who, unwittingly, is given the name of a real person. Publishers have a defence in these circumstances, although the conditions which surround it mean that it is rarely relied upon.

Who can sue?

This is not to say that defamation actions can be brought only by individuals. Companies can and do sue if their trading reputation is damaged. Groups without a legal identity cannot complain of libel. Thus blacks or Jews can get no help from the law of libel for the outrageous lies published about them. For the same reason an unincorporated club cannot sue for libel, whatever the damage to its reputation. The same rule applies to trade unions. Public corporations, such as local authorities, cannot sue for defamation. If they can prove malice and likely financial damage, they may have a claim for malicious falsehood. If there is an express or implicit attack on a particular councillor or officer, the individual would be able to sue for defamation. Similarly, while there is no remedy generally for group libels, there are some cases where the words can be read as libelling every member of the group; all the crime reporters who covered the Old Bailey once obtained damages for a story which implied they were all drunk.

Only the living can sue for defamation. Thus, historians have considerably greater freedom of expression than current commentators, but even they must be careful that the things they write about the dead do not in some way damage the reputation of the living.

The defences of truth, fair comment and privilege

The law does not elevate the protection of reputations above all else. There are three important defences which limit the incursion which actions for defamation make on free speech; truth, fair comment and privilege.

Truth (or justification) is simple to state. If a publisher can show that the words were true, the plaintiff's claim fails. The only exception to this principle concerns defendants whose convictions have become 'spent' under the Rehabilitation of Offenders Act 1974 (see Chapter 7 p. 170). Publication of the details of these old convictions can lead to damages for libel, but only if the plaintiff can show that the publisher acted 'maliciously'.

The position is less clear-cut when a criminal prosecution for libel is brought. These cases are rare: the libel (slanders are not criminal) must be serious and, in the case of a newspaper or periodical, permission to bring the action must first be obtained from a High Court judge, who must be persuaded that the evidence is strong and that criminal charges are in the public interest. Historically, criminal libel was intended to prevent breaches of the peace (for example, caused by speakers at public meetings) and it was in this context that truth was recognised as being an aggravating feature of the publication. Justification is a defence, but here the defendant must show that the words were true and that their publication was in the public interest. Criminal libel is an anachronism and the Law Commission has recommended that it be abolished.

In civil actions for damages, these complications are stripped away and truth on its own is a complete defence. The simplicity is beguiling. The court assumes that the plaintiff is of good character. The publisher has to prove, by admissible evidence, that the words were true. This can be difficult if there are 'reliable sources' but they are not prepared to testify in court. Like all other aspects of libel litigation, this defence will also only benefit the publisher who can afford to do battle through the courts. There are insurers who will cover such legal costs as well as any damages which are ultimately ordered, but the premiums are considerable and the insurance company will insist on taking over or reviewing closely the progress of the litigation.

Critics and reviewers do not have to prove the truth of their opinions in order to defend a libel action; they have the easier defence of fair comment. This covers any comment on a matter of public importance, however trenchantly expressed or misused, as long as it is honestly held.

The plaintiff can undermine the defence only by showing that the comment was written with 'malice'. This is not the same as spite or ill-will, but rather it means abusing the commentator's position. Expressions of honestly held opinions are safe.

Privilege is the general name given to the wide variety of occasions on which the law thinks it preferable that people should be able to speak freely even though reputations may suffer. No distinction is made between fact and comment. There is, though, an important difference between occasions which carry 'qualified privilege' and those where the privilege is absolute. When the privilege is qualified, it is lost if the speaker or publisher acts through malice (as with fair comment, above). If the privilege is absolute, the speaker is protected from a libel action even if he or she has acted maliciously.

Absolute privilege is relatively unusual. It is confined to cases such as proceedings in Parliament or the courts where, such is the priority given to free speech, it is considered undesirable to allow even the possibility of a libel action. Reports of parliamentary proceedings in newspapers or court reports are absolutely privileged if they are fair, accurate and contemporaneous.

Qualified privilege is more common. It covers not only reports of parliamentary proceedings and non-contemporaneous court reports, but a wide range of other official sources. These include fair and accurate reports of: Commonwealth Parliaments; conferences of international organisations of which Britain is a member or is represented; proceedings of international courts; proceedings of British court martials outside Britain; Commonwealth courts; public enquiries set up by Commonwealth governments; extracts from public registers; and notices published by judges or court officers.

Fair and accurate reports of the following are also subject to qualified privilege, but only if the victim is granted, on request, a reasonable right of reply: findings or decisions of any association or committee of associations formed in the UK and empowered by its constitution to exercise control over or adjudicate on matters relating to art, religion or learning; and trade, business, industry or profession, or persons connected with games, sports or pastimes and who are contractually subject to the association (for instance, the decision of the Law Society to discipline a solicitor or of the General Medical Council to strike off a doctor); proceedings at any lawful public meeting (whether or not admission is restricted) which is called to discuss any matter of public concern; proceedings of any meeting open to the public within the UK of a local authority or its committees; Justices of the Peace acting in non-judicial capacities; committees of enquiry appointed by statute or the government; local authority enquiries; bodies constituted under Acts of Parliament; general meetings of public companies and associations; and any notices or other matter issued for the information of the public by or on behalf of any government department, officer of state, local authority or Chief Constable.

Qualified privilege also applies where the person who publishes the words has a duty or interest in communicating them and his or her audience has a duty or interest in receiving them. The press argued unsuccessfully that they had such a duty of informing their readers of matters of public interest. The courts would not extend the privilege that far, but it does protect, for instance, employers providing references or complaints made to the proper authority.

2.3 Obscenity and indecency

Commercial dealings in obscene items, or possession of them for these purposes, is an offence. With or without a prosecution, the items can be seized under a magistrate's warrant and, after a hearing to determine whether they contravene the statute, can be forfeited. The statute is the Obscene Publications Act 1959 (as amended in 1964).

The test of obscenity – 'deprave or corrupt'

The 1959 Act adopted as the core of its test of obscenity the famous phrase of Lord Chief Justice Cockburn in 1868: does the article have a tendency to deprave or corrupt the persons who are likely to read, see or hear it? Courts have since interpreted 'deprave or corrupt' as implying a powerful and corrosive effect. There must be more than an immoral suggestion or persuasion or depiction; it must constitute a serious menace. Despite this, the deprave and corrupt test is essentially nebulous. It is difficult to predict in advance whether juries or magistrates will be persuaded that it has been satisfied. This in turn can lead to incompatible decisions in different parts of the country.

However, the 1959 Act did not simply mimic the previous law. There had been a tendency for earlier prosecutors to focus on purple passages and to invite juries to consider them in isolation. The state now requires courts to have regard to the effect of the item taken as a whole (where the article, for instance in a magazine, consists of two or more distinct items, they can be viewed separately). Again, what matters is the likely audience, and a publisher is entitled to rely on circumstances of distribution which will restrict those into whose hands the article might fall. The prosecution's case is not made by showing that the odd stray copy might be read by a more impressionable person; it is necessary to show that it would have the tendency to deprave or corrupt a significant proportion of the likely audience.

Defence of merit

The most important change introduced by the 1959 Act was a new defence that publication (in the case of magazines and books) is in the interests of science, literature, art or learning, or of other matters of general concern. A similar but rather narrower defence (the interests of drama, opera, ballet or any other art, or of literature or learning) applies to plays and films. The use of this defence was demonstrated in the first major case under the 1959 Act when the publishers of D. H. Lawrence's *Lady Chatterley's Lover* were acquitted at the Old Bailey in 1960.

Obscenity – drugs and violence

Obscenity cases do not necessarily involve sex. There have been occasional prosecutions and forfeitures of books which advocated the taking of prohibited drugs. In 1968, while allowing the appeal of the publishers of *Last Exit to Brooklyn*, the Court of Appeal said that the encouragement of brutal violence could come within the test of obscenity. In recent years video 'nasties' have also been dealt with under the Act.

Children

There are special and much more rigorous offences to try to stop the taking or distribution of indecent photographs of children.

Indecency offences

Obscenity is concerned with the harmful effect of the article on its reader or audience; another group of offences regulates indecency where the complaint is more that the material is offensive to public susceptibilities – a nuisance rather than a danger. No easy definition of indecency exists. The courts have said that this is something that 'offends against the modesty of the average man ... offending against recognised standards of propriety at the lower end of the scale'. It depends on the circumstances and current (and in some cases, local) standards. This vagueness is dangerous. Posters for causes such as animal rights which are deliberately intended to shock their audience have sometimes had to contend with indecency prosecutions.

There is no general crime of trading in indecent articles (as there is with obscene ones) but a number of specific offences incorporate the indecency test. Thus, it is a crime to send indecent matter through the post, or to put it on public display unless entry is restricted to persons over eighteen and payment is required, or the display is in a special part of a shop with an appropriate warning notice. The indecency offences do not apply to television broadcasts (although, as we shall see, both the BBC and private TV companies operate under internal prohibitions on indecent matter – see p. 51), to exhibitions inside art galleries or museums, to exhibitions arranged by or in premises occupied by the Crown or local authorities, or to performances of a play or films in licensed cinemas.

In addition to these offences, local councils can now adopt powers to regulate sex shops and sex cinemas in their areas. Council licences always prohibit the public display of indecent material and licences can be revoked if breaches of these conditions occur. Similarly, the music and entertainment licences granted by local authorities will often be conditional on the licensee ensuring that no indecent display takes place. Breach of this condition is both an offence and a ground for withdrawing the licence.

Customs regulations also prohibit the importation of indecent articles. The bookshop Gay's the Word was prosecuted under these provisions for importing books concerned with homosexuality. However, these restrictions have been substantially undermined by an unlikely source – the EEC provisions on free trade. A cardinal principle of the EEC is that one member state should not set up trade barriers to goods from another member state if there is a legitimate internal market in the same goods. In the case of the UK there is a legitimate market in indecent (but not obscene) articles as long as the traders observe the restrictions noted above. Consequently, Britain cannot discriminate against the importation of the same indecent books from other EEC countries: European law prevails over the British customs regulations. For these reasons the Gay's the Word prosecution was dropped.

2.4 Blasphemy

Blasphemy is another anachronistic relic of the common law of libel. It applies to outrageous comment or immoderate or offensive treatment of the Christian faith. Consequently, opponents of Salman Rushdie's *Satanic Verses* were unable to start a blasphemy prosecution – the book was about Mohammed and Islam, not Christ or Christianity. More particularly, it protects only the sensibilities of the followers of the Church of England. The intentions of the publisher are irrelevant. Moderate or reasoned criticism of Anglican doctrine is not a crime and the court must consider the likely audience in order to decide whether the publication would produce the necessary outrage.

For newspapers and periodicals there are the same procedural protections as with criminal libel. Consequently, the prosecutor must first get permission to bring the case from a High Court judge who must be persuaded that the evidence is clear 'beyond argument' that the offence is a serious one and that the public interest would justify a prosecution.

There has only been one prosecution for blasphemy since 1922, and that a private one (brought by Mrs Mary Whitehouse) of the magazine *Gay News* for a poem on the homoerotic musings of the centurion guarding the body of Christ. It has been argued that the crime can no longer be justified in our pluralistic society, and that the alternative of extending the offence to all religions (taken by Lord Scarman in the *Gay News* case) would seriously curtail freedom to criticise and ridicule some of the more bizarre cults which style themselves as religions.

2.5 Racial hatred

The offences of inciting or stirring up racial hatred have been progressively expanded since they were first introduced in 1965 (see also p. 207). They are currently contained in the Public Order Act 1986. In brief, they prohibit the use of threatening, abusive or insulting words, behaviour or displays with the intention of stirring up racial hatred or where racial hatred is likely to be stirred up.

The acts do not have to be done in public, but they are not crimes if done in a private dwelling and cannot be seen or heard from the outside. The inadvertent use of words which are threatening, abusive or insulting is not an offence. Only since the Public Order Act 1986 have the police had a limited power of arrest without a warrant for the offence. There are other offences of publishing or distributing material; presenting or directing a play; distributing, showing or playing visual images or sounds; broadcasting a TV programme (except programmes transmitted by the BBC or IBA; for further controls on broadcasting see p. 51); or distributing a cable programme with the same characteristics (i.e. threatening, abusive or insulting) and which is either intended to stir up racial hatred or likely to have this effect. In addition, it is an offence to possess racially inflammatory material unless ignorant of its contents. The police can obtain a search warrant for such material and magistrates can order its forfeiture.

Very few prosecutions have been brought for racial hatred offences. One of the reasons for this is that no prosecution can be brought without the consent of the Attorney General and successive Attorneys General have expressed their reluctance to authorise prosecutions giving the reason that unsuccessful prosecutions do more harm than good to racial equality.

2.6 Contempt of court

Contempt of court covers a multitude of sins, but all of them share the common feature that they are regarded by the courts as a threat to the administration of justice.

The most obvious example is disobedience to a court's order or the failure to observe an undertaking given to the court. Publication of a secret document in defiance of an injunction prohibiting its disclosure would thus be punishable as contempt. Until 1987, it was thought that orders of this kind only affected the immediate person to whom they were directed (and their servants or agents). Third parties, it was thought, would only be in contempt if they aided the defendant to break the court's order. However, one of the most serious encroachments on press freedom in the *Spycatcher* litigation was the decision of the Court of Appeal that other publishers, acting on their own behalf, could be in contempt of court by publishing the same material. Because this would frustrate the court's intention to keep the material secret it is a contempt.

Judge-made law

The *Spycatcher* litigation further illustrates a general problem of the law of contempt: it has been developed almost exclusively by the judges who have tended to pay only nodding respect to other values (such as freedom of expression) which have to be balanced against the preservation of the administration of justice. Thus, by using this branch of contempt, the courts have invented offences of disclosing the identity of blackmail victims who had remained anonymous in court, day-by-day re-enactments on television of court hearings, and (in certain circumstances) of disclosing details of a jury's deliberations. These were matters more properly left to Parliament. Parliament did subsequently enact restriction to jury disclosures, ironically much more severe than the judge-made law. It is now an offence to disclose any details of a jury's deliberations or votes taken, other than to give their verdict at the end of the trial.

Another type of contempt is the deliberate interference with current proceedings. Understandably, there is no freedom to intimidate or threaten reprisals against witnesses. A more controversial question is whether it is permissible to put pressure on a party to abandon a law suit. *Private Eye,* in its own special way, castigated Sir James Goldsmith for his various suits against the magazine. The magazine was held not to be guilty of contempt because nothing of what they published was likely to have any effect on the outcome of the proceedings. In the early 1970s, the *Sunday Times* campaigned for compensation on behalf of the victims of the drug thalidomide and urged Distiller's, its UK distributor, to reach a generous settlement with the plaintiffs. The Attorney General successfully obtained an injunction to stop further stories on the grounds that they would be in contempt of court. The principal basis for the decision has now been reversed by legislation, but two of the Law Lords suggested that it was contempt to pressurise a party into settling. The current position is probably that fair and temperate appeals are not prohibited, but that abusive or misrepresentative articles would run the risk of contempt proceedings.

It is still said that it is contempt to do any act or publish anything which is calculated to bring a court or judge into contempt or lower his or her authority. 'Scandalising the court' was one of the weapons used against John Wilkes, the eighteenth-century radical. It was revived in the early twentieth century to punish various affronts to judicial dignity, including a communist paper which dared to suggest that the judges were class biased. This type of contempt has been used occasionally in Commonwealth countries but it has lain dormant in the UK for the last fifty years. The present attitude is that judges must tolerate even misplaced criticism and that only serious allegations of corruption or other impropriety could possibly prompt a prosecution.

Strict liability – the sub judice rule

The manifestation of contempt which most frequently restricts what the papers can say is that known as 'strict liability contempt'. For specified periods before and during the time that a case is going through the courts, the media are liable if they publish anything that would cause a substantial risk of serious prejudice to the proceedings. During these periods, the case is 'active' although the older phrase sub judice is still used.

Criminal proceedings are active from the time an arrest takes place or a warrant or summons is issued. Civil proceedings do not become active until a date is fixed for the hearing. The degree of restriction that this imposes depends on the court or tribunal which will hear the case. If it is to be tried by a jury, nothing should be written or broadcast which might prejudice the jury against the defendant; in particular, no past misdeeds should be referred to and care should be taken that reports do not assume the defendant's guilt. At the other end of the spectrum are cases on appeal. These will be heard by professional judges who are trained to exclude extraneous considerations such as press reports. Consequently, it will be very rare for a publication to be in contempt of such proceedings. However, the Court of Appeal banned Channel 4 from broadcasting a dramatic re-enactment of the appeal of the Birmingham Six until after the case was over.

Defences to strict liability contempt

There are two important special defences to charges of strict liability contempt. The first is that a discussion in good faith of public affairs or other matters of general public importance will not be contempt if the risk of prejudice is merely incidental to the discussion. Thus Malcolm Muggeridge was free to write about the issues of terminating medical support to deformed babies even though a doctor was on trial at the same time for the killing of a Downs Syndrome child. Muggeridge focused on a by-election in which the issues of principle had been raised and did not mention the trial. The House of Lords held that the newspaper could rely on the public interest defence.

A second important defence is that it is not generally contempt to publish a fair, accurate, good faith and contemporaneous report of legal proceedings held in public. This is important because things are sometimes said in trials which might reflect adversely either on participants in those proceedings or in other active cases. However, the media's freedom to report is subject to the power of the court to make a postponement order. These can delay full reporting until the end of either the proceedings in question or the others which are at risk of prejudice.

Postponement orders are a real headache for the media. Usually, none of the parties has any interest in full publicity and too often, it is felt, orders are made with insufficient regard to the principles of open justice, an integral part of which is the ability of the press to carry full reports. However, it is now accepted that the media should be permitted to make arguments against gagging orders. These can be made to the judge before the order (if the media learn of the application in time), after the order in an effort to persuade the judge to set it aside, or to the Court of Appeal.

Other restrictions on court reporting

These powers are in addition to restrictions on reporting which apply without the need for a specific order. Only very attenuated reports can be carried, for instance, of proceedings in a magistrates' court of a case which might eventually be sent to trial by a judge and jury at a Crown Court. Newspapers can name the parties, their lawyers and whether bail was granted, but very little else until the trial is over. A defendant has the right to have these restrictions lifted, but if co-accused differ in their attitude to publicity, the bench decides.

In sex offence cases the victim must remain anonymous unless the court orders otherwise. Until 1988, the defendant was given the same protection (unless convicted). The press (unlike the rest of the public) have a right to attend juvenile court hearings, but are prohibited from identifying defendants or witnesses, or from publishing their photographs. Young people do not have automatic anonymity in other courts, but the courts can make orders in specific cases.

In civil cases the problem is not so much that reporting is prohibited (though this is so in certain cases involving children and others to do with trade secrets), but that journalists (and other members of the public) frequently do not have the right to be present and so cannot learn what has transpired unless one of the parties involved is willing to talk. This restriction may be acceptable in disputes over custody or access to children. It is wholly unjustifiable in a large and important category of cases heard in the judge's private chambers.

Before a civil dispute comes to trial it is common for there to be initial skirmishes or interlocutory applications. The most important are where one party wants a court order pending trial. Classic examples are injunctions against the press to prevent disclosure of an allegedly secret document, or orders prohibiting industrial action. If the plaintiff has chosen to bring the case in the Chancery Division of the High Court, these applications are heard by a judge in public (subject to any special orders to preserve legitimate confidences). However, if the case is brought in the Queen's Bench Division of the High Court, the applications are heard in chambers and the press are excluded. Plaintiffs are generally free to choose in which division to bring their case and can thus effectively select the degree of publicity they prefer.

These cases apart, it is very unusual for courts to depart from the principle of open justice. There is a statutory power to do so in particular cases (for example, official secrets prosecutions) and a general power where the public's presence would defeat the ends of justice. The courts have repeatedly stressed that it is only exceptional circumstances which will justify excluding the public or restricting reporting.

The public may be present in court, but sketching and photography is prohibited. In 1981, Parliament permitted the limited use of tape recorders in court with the judge's leave. There are administrative directions that applications should be treated sympathetically. Taping can be used only as an aid in compiling an accurate record of what was said: public reproduction is banned.

Tribunals

In addition to the regular criminal and civil courts, there is a bewildering array of 'courts', tribunals and enquiries. It is impossible to generalise about when the public have a right of access. If they do, there will usually be a qualified privilege to protect the publisher of a fair and accurate report from libel actions. The 'strict liability contempt' provisions will only apply if the body is 'exercising the judicial power of the state'. By way of example, licensing authorities act administratively and therefore their proceedings are never 'active' (see p. 45). Industrial tribunals, on the other hand, do exercise a statutory judicial jurisdiction – their proceedings will be active from the time a hearing date is set, but of course there will be no contempt unless the publication poses a serious threat to the integrity of the proceedings.

Enforcement

Prosecutions under the strict liability rule can be brought only with the Attorney General's consent. This was intended to ensure that some consideration was given to the public interest before prosecutions were brought. However, while private parties cannot prosecute, they can, if they would suffer particularly from a publication which offended against the rule, seek an injunction to stop it. This development has therefore considerably undermined such protection to freedom of expression as the Attorney General's veto had offered.

2.7 Secrets and confidentiality

Secrecy, it is sometimes said, is the British disease. The scope of the law for preventing and punishing the disclosure of private and governmental confidence represents one of the most important restrictions on free speech. We will look at the criminal and civil dimensions in turn.

The Official Secrets Acts

The Official Secrets Act 1911 slipped onto the statute book in a single day, borne along on a wave of anti-German spy fever (although its gestation had taken much longer). While it does provide punishment for spies, it has become notorious for its section 2 which was intended to curb civil service leaks and their publication in the press. On one occasion in 1978 the government did try to turn the big guns of section 1 (the spying charge, carrying a maximum of fourteen years' imprisonment) on journalists investigating signals intelligence and its disturbing implications. This trial, known as the ABC case after the initials of the defendants, was notable for the judge's round denunciation of the section 1 charges as 'oppressive'. The defendants were convicted under section 2 but the journalists were given conditional discharges. While the government has on rare occasions (such as Tisdale and Ponting) prosecuted their sources, it has not, since the ABC case, tried again to prosecute the media itself under these Acts.

Official Secrets Act 1989

Section 2 was replaced in 1989 by another Official Secrets Act. Instead of a broad catch-all provision of the 1911 vintage there is now a series of offences prohibiting disclosure of information relating to intelligence, security, defence and crime. Those at the heart of the security establishment are still prevented from disclosing any information. Other Crown servants and government contractors are restricted only from disclosing information which is 'damaging' (although this qualification does not apply to information relating to telephone tapping or criminal investigations). This is less than the full 'public interest' defence for which civil libertarians had argued, but it will give defendants some scope for argument. Journalists, the media and others outside government will commit offences if they publish information which they know has been leaked in breach of the Act and whose publication would be damaging.

The right to jury trial

The critical fact that anyone charged with most official secrets offences can elect for a jury trial has a real effect in curbing the impact of the Act. Whatever the law may say, if the information leaked was already public knowledge or if its disclosure is in the public interest (as in the case of Clive Ponting's memorandum on the government's policy on the sinking of the *Belgrano*), convictions are far from certain. Even if a conviction is achieved, it will be at the price of attracting considerable press attention to the prosecution and the 'secret' at its centre will attract substantial press coverage. By now the reputation of the Acts has become so tarnished that the government cannot be certain of convictions in any case outside their proper espionage sphere. The very width of their application has become their weakness. The attitude of juries to the 1989 Act has yet to be tested and no doubt the government will try to select its first test case with care.

Other secrecy offences

Apart from the Official Secrets Acts, there are dozens of specific statutory offences of disclosing information in the hands of the government. Frequently, they are imposed where a government department has powers to acquire information under compulsion. These 'mini' Official Secrets Acts also lack a public interest defence.

The civil law of confidence

Increasingly, the government has abandoned the use of the criminal law to protect its secrets in favour of the civil law of breach of confidence (see p. 56). This law was originally intended to protect trade secrets (such as the formula for Coca Cola) or the business development plans of companies. It was extended to afford some privacy to an individual's confidential documents or papers. This was first done for Prince Albert and Queen Victoria whose sketchings were about to be published without their permission.

Unlike the criminal law, the civil law of confidence will generally only protect material which is still confidential. It was the widespread publication of *Spycatcher* which powerfully influenced the House of Lords to refuse a final injunction to the government.

In the public interest

None of the civil law was thought to be relevant to public secrets until the Labour government tried to use the law of confidence to stop the publication of Richard Crossman's diaries in 1976. It failed because the Cabinet meetings and other private encounters which Crossman described had happened too long ago. Yet the principle was established that the government could rely on the law of confidence to stop a publication if it could show a public interest that still needed protection.

The public interest is also material as a defence. It used to be said that only crime or iniquity would justify the breach of a confidence, but now the test is more open and the court must strike a balance between the interest in preserving confidence and the interest in publication.

Pre-trial injunctions
If the plaintiff can find out in advance that publication of a leak or other alleged breach of confidence is planned, and is willing to go to court, then the inevitable first step will be an application for an injunction to stop publication until trial. The test which the courts apply in deciding whether to grant such injunctions is extremely favourable to plaintiffs. Usually the judges will grant an injunction, unless there is clear evidence of public interest, and in the case of the *Spycatcher* pre-trial injunction even that was not sufficient. The argument for this 'balance of convenience test' is that at the pre-trial stage, the evidence is incomplete and the court is often required to make a hasty decision because publication is imminent. The objection is that the time between injunction and trial is usually so great that the story will have gone cold by the time that full argument on the merits is heard. This in turn means that the defence is not pursued and there never is a full hearing of the case.

2.8 Copyright

Writers, broadcasters and artists have an ambivalent attitude towards copyright law. On the one hand it grants them the exclusive use to exploit (and thus profit from) their works. On the other hand it can seriously hamper the creative process by giving other copyright owners a power of veto over the incorporation of their words or images in some new work. The use of 'sampling' technology to produce highly original and very profitable 'hit' records has led to copyright litigation between record companies. The collage artist, the scratch video-maker, the popular songwriter, the cartoonist, and the journalist in possession of a leaked memorandum can all encounter copyright obstacles in creating their work, yet none of them would want others to be free to plagiarise their final product.

Meaning of copyright
Copyright, in brief, gives the owner of the work the right to stop others reproducing it without his or her consent. The Copyright Act 1988 is one of the most bewildering statutes (which its recent revamping by Parliament has done little to simplify). It creates several different categories of 'work' in which copyright can exist. The most important are original (but not necessarily distinguished) literary, dramatic,

musical and artistic works (including photographs); sound recordings (notably records, tapes and CDs); films, television and sound broadcasts; and cable programmes.

Copyright does not exist in ideas as such, although the law of confidence has recently been developed to protect those who provide well-worked-out and practicable suggestions for others to develop and exploit. The law of copyright does not operate until the ideas have been reduced to some material form and then it is generally the reproduction of that form which is restricted. This means, for instance, that newspapers do not have a monopoly even in their 'exclusive' news stories. They can stop others using their photographs, their text (or a substantial part of it) or a imitation of their work, but the information conveyed is not theirs to control.

Defences

Copyright is not infringed if the owner consents to the copying. This sounds simple, but it can be a complicated business finding out who the owner is. In some works (a television play, for instance) it is possible for different people to own the copyright in the script, the photographs, the sound track, the dramatic screenplay, the film recording, the play and the broadcast. Even if the owners can be identified there is generally no obligation on them to sell reproduction rights.

In the absence of the owner's licence, the media have two important defences to claim for infringement of copyright. The first is fair dealing. This includes the fair use of another's work for the purpose of criticism or review, or the reporting of current events. The originator of the work must be acknowledged in a criticism or review and in the print media's news reporting. In an important case concerning a critical book about Scientology, which made use of unpublished internal Scientology documents, the courts confirmed that the fair dealing defence could apply, even though the work had not previously been published and even though the criticism was directed at the contents of the work rather than its style.

The second important defence is public interest. This does not appear in the statute, but the courts have said that, just as they will not stop publication of confidential information which is in the public interest (see p. 48), so, too, they would not prohibit the infringement of another's copyright where the public interest in publication outweighed the private right of property.

Cut-price copies

The purpose of many of the recent changes in the law of copyright has been to strengthen the rights of copyright owners. The making of unauthorised copies of films, cassettes and videos for sale at cut-rate prices has been perceived as a major threat to the entertainment industry and led to substantial increases in the penalties that can be imposed for the criminal offences that are involved. The civil courts have also been prepared enthusiastically to grant to copyright owners what in practice are private search warrants.

'Moral rights'

The 1988 Act introduced new 'moral rights' for the authors of copyright works. Subject to complex limitations and qualifications, authors of copyright works have the right to be identified as such and the right not to have their works subjected to derogatory treatment. A new right of privacy was also introduced to limit the use of photographs commissioned for private and domestic purpose, for example, wedding photographs, etc.

Passing off

In addition to copyright protection, the law will prevent one trader passing off its goods as those of another. These commercial disputes often have little to do with free speech, but their over-zealous application (or the minimal investigation of a plaintiff's claim on an application for an interlocutory injunction) can lead to the suppression of parody, spoof and satire.

2.9 Controls on broadcasting, films, videos and cable

The poet Milton campaigned in 1644 against 'prior restraint', the suppression or censorship of material in advance of publication. Court injunctions can still prevent the press from adopting a 'publish and be damned' posture, but, these apart, the press is generally free of prior restraint. For broadcasters the position is very different. The BBC, by its charter, is intended and expected to 'censor' the programmes it transmits. The Independent Broadcasting Authority (the IBA) had similar duties in relation to commercial broadcasting. The IBA's successors, the Independent Television Commission (ITC) and the Radio Authority, are intended to regulate with a lighter touch, but their powers to penalise their licensees and ultimately to revoke licences mean that they wield considerable influence.

The ITC regulates through its Code of Practice. This requires that commercial television programmes do not offend against good taste or decency and are not likely to encourage crime or lead to disorder; that news is presented with due accuracy and impartiality and that due impartiality is preserved in regard to matters of political or industrial controversy or relating to current public policy.

Unlicensed broadcasters are prohibited. A radio transmitter is still one of the cheapest ways to reach a large audience, but the radio pirates have to keep one step ahead of the Department of Trade Inspectors, who can forfeit equipment as well as prosecute for infringements. The government has a power to direct that certain matters should not be broadcast. It used this power in 1988 to ban spoken comment by or in support of Sinn Fein, the UDA or any of the organisations proscribed under the anti-terrorism laws.

Unlike newspapers which can openly propagate their own views, the TV companies cannot editorialise on matters (other than broadcasting issues) which are politically or industrially controversial or relate to current public policy. Subliminal messages are prohibited and religious broadcasting is specifically controlled.

There are limits to these duties. Thus the Court of Appeal has accepted that in judging whether all the constituent parts of a programme satisfy the 'good taste' canon, the ITC can take account of the purpose and character of the programme as a whole. The duties set out above have also to be reconciled with the Commission's other duties, for instance to secure a wide showing of programmes of merit. Channel 4 was deliberately created to provide programmes 'calculated to appeal to tastes and interests not generally catered for by ITV', and 'to encourage innovation and experimentation in the form and content of programmes'. Inevitably, this can only be done in some cases at the risk of causing offence to those with mainline tastes. The requirement of impartiality in non-news programmes can be satisfied over a series of programmes and a tradition has developed of allowing more latitude to 'personal view' programmes that are 'balanced' by others.

The courts have discouraged legal challenges to the ITC and its predecessor, the IBA for vetting programmes, and their decisions on individual programmes can (generally) only be quashed if they are so perverse as to be unreasonable. The BBC has accepted similar restraints to those imposed on commercial television, but the legal position of the restraints remains uncertain.

The Obscene Publications Act now applies to television and radio broadcasts, although no prosecutions have yet been brought (since 1990). A further tier of regulation is provided by the Broadcasting Standards Council which was set up by the government to monitor sex and violence on radio and television. (see Chapter 5 on the right to complain p. 105)

The Broadcasting Complaints Commission

Radio or television programmes put out by the independent broadcasters or the BBC can be reviewed by the Broadcasting Complaints Commission. This was created by Parliament in 1981 to consider complaints of unjust or unfair treatment or unwarranted infringements of privacy in, or in connection with, the obtaining of material included in sound or television broadcasts. Any complaint must be made by a person affected. Complaints cannot be made in connection with someone who has died more than five years previously, but within this period a member of the family, a personal representative or someone closely connected can complain.

The Commission cannot order the payment of any money to the complainant, but they can insist on the responsible body publishing the Commission's findings and, more significantly, can insist on an approved summary being broadcast at a stipulated time.

The British Board of Film Classification

The British Board of Film Classification (BBFC) is a hybrid system. There is no general requirement that a film must have a BBFC certificate before being shown, but this position is achieved indirectly by the power of local councils to licence cinemas. Most licenses have a condition attached that only films with a BBFC certificate will be shown. Like television and radio programmes, films can be prosecuted under the Obscene Publications Act (see p. 39) although feature films (not less than 16 mm) can only be prosecuted or forfeited with the approval of the Director of Public Prosecutions.

The BBFC has been given an enlarged role in relation to video cassettes. Here it is a censor in law as well as in practice and it is an offence to supply an unclassified video or to breach any restrictions which have been imposed by the BBFC (as to minimum age, type of supplier, etc.). Videos concerned with sport, religion, music and education are exempt, but not if they show or are designed to encourage human sexual activity (or force or restraint associated with it), or mutilation, torture or other gross acts of violence towards humans or animals. Videos are not exempt either if they show human genitalia or human urinary or excretory functions. The BBFC has to consider whether videos are suitable for viewing in the home. There is an appeal structure for those who submit videos to the BBFC, but the sizable fees charged by the Board and the delays that the process necessarily entails can cause grave difficulties for producers.

Cable

Cable programming is still in its infancy but the regulatory framework has been established on a similar model to that for broadcasting. Thus, the ITC has the power to license operators. It must do all that it can to see that its licensees do not include in their programmes material which offends against good taste or decency or is likely to encourage or incite to crime or lead to public disorder or to be offensive to public feeling. Subliminal images are, again, banned. News must be presented with due accuracy and impartiality, but only if it originates in the UK.

Non-news programmes are considerably less inhibited than in broadcasts; instead of a requirement of 'balance' there is only the duty to see that undue prominence is not given to the views and opinions of particular persons or bodies on religious matters, matters of public controversy or issues relating to current public policy. Editorialising on religious, political, industrial controversy or current public policy is, as with broadcasting, prohibited.

The ITC has the ultimate sanction of withdrawing an operator's licence if these or the other conditions are broken.

2.10 Whose freedom?

It might be thought that the restrictions we have examined are of relevance only to the wealthy, for surely only they have the practical and legal freedom to publish what they will. But publishers or media organisations are not necessarily large, wealthy and dependent on large audiences. A radical bookshop, a community radio station or a local video project could be as much affected by the restrictions on free expression discussed here as the multinational media organisation.

It is true, though, that the laws we have examined are concerned mostly with what cannot be said, not with what must be said. There are generally no rights to be heard, broadcast or published. The exceptions are few.

A right of reply

We saw, for instance, that certain types of qualified privilege were dependent on the victim being given a right of reply. During an election, one candidate cannot appear in a programme about the constituency without the other candidates' consent (so that, in effect, all have the right to appear on or to veto the programme). The broadcaster's duet of balance can again effectively mean that one party to a current controversy can insist on the opportunity to put their view. Under threat of a libel action, some publishers will prefer to offer a reply to the person they attacked. This, though, like readers' letters columns or the television 'video box' is a matter of negation or marketing policy rather than a legal right of access.

On several occasions MPs introduced private members' bills to give a legal right of reply to correct misstatements of fact or to offer alternative views. These attempts have been generated by the blithe indifference to truth or any notion of journalistic standards in some part of the media. Yet the problems created by a legal right of reply would be formidable. Resolving whether a statement is true or false can be no easy task. As long as the press (unlike broadcasters) are free to be partisan, there are real difficulties in insisting that equal – and as prominent – space be given to the papers' adversaries.

The right to receive information and ideas

Accepting the inequality of access to the media, the rights and restrictions considered in this chapter are still important for those unable to be publishers themselves. The corollary of freedom to communicate, as the European Convention recognises, is the freedom to receive information and ideas. The Peter Wright *Spycatcher* litigation was not just about the right of the *Sunday Times* to serialise the book or of the *Independent* and other papers to print its allegations, but also, and more importantly, the right of the public to read them.

2.11 Further information

Useful organisations

Campaign for Freedom of Information
88 Old Street
London EC1V 9AR
Tel: 071 253 2445.

Campaign for Press and Broadcasting Freedom
8 Cynthia Street
London N1 9JF
Tel: 071 278 4430.

National Union of Journalists
314 Gray's Inn Road
London WC1X 8PD
Tel: 071 278 7916.

Newspaper Society
Bloomsbury House
Bloomsbury Square
74–77 Great Russell Street
London WC1 3DA
Tel: 071 636 7014.

Bibliography

G. Robertson, *Obscenity*, Weidenfield and Nicolson, 1976.
G. Robertson and A. Nicol, *Media Law: The Rights of Journalists and Broadcasters*, Penguin, 1992.

3

The right of privacy

This chapter deals with

- Confidential information.
- Telephone tapping and the interception of mail.
- Bugging and surveillance.
- Intrusion or harassment by neighbours and others.
- Unwanted letters and telephone calls.
- Power of officials to enter your home.
- Privacy and the media.

There is no right of privacy as such. The English courts have refused to follow the pioneering course of their American counterparts who have spelt out from the common law and the American constitution general principles which protect an individual's right to be left alone.

Article 8 of the European Convention on Human Rights follows a similar model to Article 10 (freedom of expression), i.e. it begins with a ringing declaration, in this case of the right of a person to be free of interference from the state in his or her private and family life, correspondence and home. This is then qualified with an acknowledgement that intrusions are permitted if they are prescribed by and necessary in a democratic society in the interests of national security, public safety and the economic well being of the country; for the prevention of disorder or crime; for the protection of health or morals; or for the protection of the rights and freedom of others.

We shall see in this chapter that although there is no general right of privacy, a collection of rights and obligations from different sources cover much of the same ground.

3.1 Confidential information

The law of confidence has its origins in the commercial world of trade secrets and confidential lists of business contacts. However, it has grown far beyond this. Three main elements have to be proved before the courts will grant an injunction to preserve a secret:

- The information must be confidential.
- The person with the information must be under a duty to keep it confidential.
- The proposed use must be incompatible with that duty.

The duty can be a promise contained in a contract. Members of the Royal households, for instance, have to promise never to reveal what they learn in the course of their employment. But many secrets are shared by people who never think in terms of contracts. The courts have been willing to recognise that duties of confidence can be owed between spouses and even friends. As importantly, third parties who acquire information and who know or learn of its confidential character can also be required to respect the confidence. This means that a newspaper to whom a secret is sold or given can be ordered not to publish it. The courts have enthusiastically enlarged the categories of people who owe duties of confidence. Secret documents which are accidentally sent to third parties must be returned. The language of 'duty of confidence' is even applied to a thief who steals private papers.

The requirement that the information must be confidential is loosely applied. The court will not refuse an injunction because the information has leaked out to a limited extent. However, there will come a point (as in the *Spycatcher* saga) when it is plainly silly to pretend that there is any secret left to be preserved.

There is obvious potential for a clash of interests here: between the original confider who wants the secret kept and the press who appeal to the principle of freedom of expression. Although there is a public interest defence to breach of confidence, the balance between these two interests is still unsatisfactory (see Chapter 2 on freedom of expression).

Most breach of confidence cases take the form of applications for injunctions, but if publication takes place before the plaintiff can act, the courts can still award damages or order the defendant to account for any profits made as a result of the disclosure.

3.2 Telephone tapping and the interception of mail

The Interception of Communications Act 1985 makes private telephone tapping and mail interception an offence. We add the qualification 'private' because the Act perpetuates the system that is as old as the Post Office itself for the interception of mail (or telephone calls) on the warrant of the Home Secretary. Warrants ought to be confined to cases involving national security, serious crime or the economic well being of the UK, but the scope for investigating the propriety of an official tap or intercept is extremely limited. There is a tribunal which can investigate whether there was a warrant and, if so, whether it was properly issued. However, the complainant will not be told the government's story or have a proper chance to test it.

Where it is found that a warrant has been improperly issued, the tribunal has power to order compensation and the destruction of the intercepted material. If the interception took place without a warrant the only sanction is a criminal prosecution (to which the Director of Public Prosecutions must consent).

There is no offence if the interception is with the consent of either party and there is nothing to prohibit one party to a telephone call making a recording of it, even if the other party is unaware of what is being done. An offence is not committed if a third party does not interfere with the telephone line itself but instead listens in by placing a bug on or near the telephone.

3.3 Bugging and surveillance

The person who owns or rents property on which a bug is placed without permission will have a claim for trespass. This will be of limited use if the person who planted the bug cannot be traced, but the apparatus can at least be disabled.

The Security Service (MI5) was given legal recognition in 1989. Burglary and other interferences with property can only be authorised by the Home Secretary personally. The intrusion must be necessary to obtain information for one of MI5's functions. These are broadly defined as the protection of national security and safeguarding the economic well being of the UK against threats posed by persons outside the country. As with telephone tapping there is a complaints procedure (a senior judge who is appointed to act as Security Service Commissioner in the case of intrusions into property, and another tribunal in the case of other MI5 activities). However, if the intrusion is skilfully done, the victim will be ignorant of it. The tribunal and the Commissioner's powers are limited, and again the process denies the complainant a proper opportunity to hear the case against him or her.

The Intelligence Services Bill being considered by Parliament at the time of writing will set up a similar complaints procedure for the Security Intelligence Service (MI6 – responsible for the foreign secret services) and the Government Communications Head Quarters (GCHQ – the government's listening centre). The Bill will also set up a parliamentary committee to oversee the work of all three security services. Unfortunately, this is unlikely to provide any significant level of accountability.

If the surveillance (whether by the government, the press or by others) does not involve physical intrusion, there are even fewer restrictions. Snooping which employs radio transmitters will be an offence under the Wireless Telegraphy Act 1949 which prohibits the use of unlicensed transmitters (or receivers). Other listening devices and the use of long-range telephoto lenses are not barred by law, although there have been increasingly loud demands for their use as a means of intruding on personal privacy to be prohibited.

Surveillance in public places (whether overhearing conversations or taking photographs) is treated only as a public order issue. If no breach of the peace is threatened there will usually be no offence. The law of confidence would not protect conversations which occur in public places.

3.4 Intrusion or harassment by neighbours and others

Property is a concept which English law can understand. The right to keep others out is one of the defining characteristics of property ownership. Those who are fortunate enough to own or rent their home are entitled to injunctions to prevent intrusion and damages to compensate for trespass. Harassment of tenants by their landlords for the purpose of encouraging the tenants to leave can be particularly expensive for landlords. The tenants can claim the additional value which the house or flat has for the landlord with vacant possession. Harassment of this kind can also be a criminal offence which can be prosecuted by local authorities.

Neighbours who do not physically intrude may nonetheless make life intolerable in a variety of ways. Their unreasonable use of their land can be the tort of private nuisance. Again such behaviour can be restrained by injunction or lead to a claim in damages.

People who come to your door to sell goods, ask you to give to a charity, persuade you to support a particular religion or political party or ask questions for a market research survey have no right to enter your home. You can refuse to talk to them and they must leave when you ask them to.

3.5 Unwanted letters and telephone calls

It is a criminal offence to telephone grossly offensive messages or make indecent or obscene or menacing telephone calls or calls which cause annoyance, inconvenience or needless anxiety (Telecommunications Act 1984). If the perpetrator is known and is persistent in making calls the courts are increasingly willing to grant injunctions to prevent this type of harassment. They have even made these orders at the request of a relative of the property owner. 'Nuisance', the legal category into which these claims fall, may thus be moving away from being exclusively an aspect of property ownership and more openly a means of protecting domestic privacy.

Hate mail is usually anonymous, but if it can be traced the sender can be prosecuted under the Malicious Communications Act 1988. This makes it an offence to send a letter or other article which contains an indecent or grossly offensive message or a threat or which contains information known to be false and the purpose of the letter is to cause distress or anxiety.

Inertia selling used to be common before the Unsolicited Goods and Services Act 1971. The technique was to send goods to customers who were then charged for them if they did not go to the trouble to return them. The 1971 Act allows recipients of unsolicited goods to keep them as free gifts after six months (thirty days if the recipient writes to the sender asking for them to be collected). The 1971 Act also makes it an offence to send obscene or indecent books, magazines, leaflets or advertising material describing or illustrating human sexual techniques (see p. 39 for more on obscenity).

3.6 Power of officials to enter your home

A house on fire, or infested with rats, or with a gas leak, or where building works have been carried out in a dangerous manner, is something which concerns the whole community. To cope with problems such as these, many officials are given the right to enter your home whether you like it or not.

There are, in fact, tens of thousands of officials in the UK who have the power, in certain circumstances, to enter private premises, but most of them only have the power to enter business premises and are not dealt with here. This section describes the most important powers of entry which may involve officials entering your home. (The powers of the police to enter and search private premises are dealt with in Chapter 6.)

Each type of official is subject to different rules of procedure because each is governed by a different Act of Parliament and there is no general code which covers their conduct. Quite commonly, however, the procedure is that the official must produce evidence of identity and authority before entering and may not insist on entering without first giving you at least twenty-four hours' notice. If, after such notice, you refuse to let him or her in, the magistrates' court may give authority to enter without your consent, by force if necessary.

In general, if someone asks to come into your home, claiming to be an official, you should:

- Ask to see the caller's identity card.
- Ask the caller what authority he or she has to enter your home.
- If in doubt, refuse entry and contact the office from which the official claims to come in order to check his or her credentials.

If you have a complaint to make about the way an official behaves, you should approach the appropriate authority. For example, in the case of a local authority official, you should complain to your local councillor; in the case of a gas or electricity official, the gas or electricity company; in the case of a VAT inspector, the collector in charge of VAT at the local office; or, in the case of a tax inspector, the Commissioners for the Inland Revenue. There may also be the possibility of a complaint to an official regulator or an ombudsman (see Chapter 5 on the right to complain).

Fire brigade

A member of a local authority fire brigade who is on duty or a police officer may enter any premises where a fire has broken out, or where there is reason to believe a fire has broken out. Other premises, such as neighbouring houses, may also be entered if this is necessary for fire-fighting purposes. The fire officer can force entry, if necessary. The permission of the owner or occupier does not have to be obtained. It is an offence to obstruct or interfere with any member of a fire brigade who is involved in fighting a fire; the maximum penalty is a fine of level 3 – see p. 29 (Fire Services Act 1947).

Gas and electricity boards

An official of a gas or electricity company may enter your home if:

- You agree to let the official enter.
- A magistrate has given the official a warrant authorising the official to enter.
- There is an emergency and the official has reason to believe that there is danger to life or property.

A gas or electricity board official is entitled to ask to enter your home, or to apply to a magistrate for a warrant, in order to:

- Inspect the meter or any other fittings.
- Disconnect the supply in certain circumstances.

In order to obtain a warrant, the official must show that:

- You have been given at least twenty-four hours' notice; *and*
- He or she has asked to be admitted and you have refused; *or*
- The premises are unoccupied.

Entry must be at a 'reasonable' time and the official must leave the house as secure against trespassers as it was when he or she arrived, and make good any damage caused.

It is a criminal offence to obstruct a person who has a warrant or who asks to be admitted in an emergency; the maximum penalty is a fine of level 3 (see p. 29). It is not an offence to refuse to let the official enter if there is no emergency and the official does not have a warrant (Rights of Entry (Gas and Electricity Boards) Act 1954).

Water companies

An authorised official of a water company may enter any premises at a 'reasonable' hour in order to:

*   Inspect water meters.
*   Ascertain whether there has been any contravention of the law relating to water supplies.
*   Detect waste or misuse of water.

In the first two cases (But not the last), twenty-four hours' notice must be given. Entry can be obtained in an emergency or under a warrant.

Housing

An official authorised by the local authority may enter any house in the area at any 'reasonable' time in order to:

*   Make a valuation or survey, where a compulsory purchase order is being considered or has been issued.
*   Examine the premises and make a survey where a notice requiring repairs, a demolition order, a closing order or a clearance order has been issued.
*   Measure the rooms, etc., to determine whether there is or has been overcrowding.
*   Ascertain whether there is or has been a contravention of the Housing Act regulations.

The official must have a written document of authority and must give at least twenty-four hours' notice. It is an offence to obstruct the official, providing the official is authorised and has given notice; the maximum penalty is a fine of level 2 – see p. 29 (Housing Act 1985).

Planning

An authorised local authority official may enter premises at any 'reasonable' time for various planning purposes, including:

*   Preparing or approving development plans.

- Dealing with applications for planning permission.
- Making a valuation in connection with compensation.
- Making a survey in connection with a compulsory purchase order.

The official must give twenty-four hours' notice. The local authority must also pay compensation for any damage caused. It is an offence to obstruct the official, provided that proper notice has been given; the maximum penalty is a fine of level 2 – see p. 29 (Town and Country Planning Act 1990).

Rating

A local assessor may enter any property in the area in order to carry out a survey or make a valuation for the purposes of drawing up rating valuation lists. The official must give three days' notice. It is an offence to obstruct the official provided that proper notice has been given; the maximum penalty is a fine of level 2 – see p. 29 (Local Government Finance Act 1992).

Social security

An inspector may enter business premises at any 'reasonable' time in order to interview employers, employees and self-employed people about their contributions' record. It is an offence not to produce National Insurance Certificates or other relevant documents. It is also an offence to refuse to answer the inspector's questions, except that you are not obliged to give information which will incriminate yourself or your spouse – this does not include a common law husband or wife (Social Security Act 1986). The maximum penalty for either offence is a fine of level 3 (see p. 29) and a fine of £40 for each day that the offence continues.

An investigator (such as an official trying to find out if a person is cohabiting) does not have a right to enter your home. If the official forces entry, or refuses to leave after you ask him or her to do so, he or she is committing a trespass and you may be able to take legal action.

Tax

A tax inspector can obtain a warrant from a circuit judge if he or she reasonably suspects that an offence involving serious fraud in relation to tax has been committed. The warrant authorises the inspector to enter and search private premises and remove documents. Any application for a warrant must be made with the approval of a Commissioner for the Inland Revenue (Taxes Management Act 1970).

VAT

A VAT official may enter any premises at a 'reasonable' time for any purposes connected with administering value added tax. The official may enter without a warrant, and may also inspect goods which are liable to tax. If the official has reasonable grounds for suspecting you of an offence related to VAT, he or she may apply to a magistrate for a warrant authorising him or her to:

- Enter, by force if necessary, at any 'reasonable' time within fourteen days of the warrant being issued.
- Seize any documents relating to the investigation.
- Search any people on the premises (but a woman can only be searched by another woman).

Obstructing a VAT official could amount to an assault for which you could be prosecuted.

Mental health

An approved social worker may at all 'reasonable' times, after producing identity if requested, enter and inspect any premises in which a mentally disordered person is living if there is reasonable cause to believe that he or she is not being properly cared for.

Magistrates have the power to issue a warrant authorising a police officer to enter premises (by force, if necessary) if they have reasonable cause to suppose that a mentally disordered person is being ill-treated there, or is unable to look after him or herself. The police officer must be accompanied by a social worker and a doctor.

Infectious diseases and illness

In the case of 'notifiable diseases' (for example plague and cholera) a magistrate may make an order for the compulsory medical examination of suspected sufferers and carriers and for the removal to and detention in hospital of anyone suffering from such a disease where it appears that proper precautions are not being taken to prevent the spread of the disease (Public Health (Control of Diseases) Act 1984). AIDS is dealt with similarly to notifiable diseases, but slightly less stringently; there is no provision for compulsory examination provided the suspected sufferer or carrier is already receiving treatment from a doctor (Public Health (Infectious Diseases) Regulations 1985).

On a certificate from the appointed local authority officer, the local authority may serve notice on an occupier to disinfect or destroy articles likely to retain infection within a fixed period, if doing so would tend to prevent the spread of any infectious disease. The occupier has twenty-four hours to inform the local authority that he or she will comply, failing which the local authority has the right to enter and to do the necessary work. The occupier can be forced to reimburse the local authority and the provision for compensation for articles destroyed is not very satisfactory. Where an infectious disease occurs in a house, the local authority may also, at their own cost, remove persons from the premises, acting with a magistrates' warrant if there is no consent. This is not limited to the notifiable diseases mentioned above.

Magistrates also have the power to issue a warrant authorising an officer of a local authority to enter premises to remove to hospital persons who are so chronically ill or old as to be unable to look after themselves, and who are not being properly looked after by others. Seven days' notice to the person of such an application must be given (National Assistance Act 1948).

Pests and vermin

The occupier of land is under an obligation to notify the local authority if rats or mice in substantial numbers live or resort to the land. The local authority may serve notice on the owner or occupier (or both) of land (including buildings), requiring them to take specified steps within a specified time to keep the land free of mice or rats.

Where premises are so filthy or unwholesome as to be prejudicial to health, or are verminous, the local authority may require corrective measures, including, for example, disinfection or the removal of wallpaper. If necessary, the notice may require the occupiers of infested premises (and neighbouring premises which might be affected) to vacate the premises while gas is employed to destroy vermin. In such a case, the local authority must provide temporary alternative accommodation at its own expense.

It is an offence to disobey the notice (maximum penalty level 1, or level 3 in the case of a mice or rat notice – see p. 29 for fine levels). In the event of disobedience, the local authority also has the power to enter the land to do the work itself (Public Health Act 1936, Prevention of Damage by Pests Act 1949).

Foster homes

A local authority can authorise someone (for example, a social worker) to inspect any home where a child is being fostered. The inspector must produce an official document, showing that he or she has the right to enter. It is an offence to refuse to allow the inspector to enter; the maximum penalty is a fine of level 3 – see p. 29 (Children Act 1989).

The Anton Piller order

Over the past ten years, the courts have developed a form of civil search warrant called an 'Anton Piller' order (called 'Anton Piller' after a case of the same name). This is usually issued in cases involving 'pirate' goods, such as unauthorised video copies of popular films, but it can be issued in any case where the court is persuaded that the defendant is the sort of person who might destroy relevant evidence in his or her possession if the order is not made. Strictly speaking, an Anton Piller order is not a search warrant because it does not directly empower the holder to enter or search premises. What the order does is to instruct the person in charge of the premises to let the holder in. But since it is a contempt of court to refuse to let him or her in, the order has much the same effect as a search warrant.

The order must be served by a solicitor, but it will usually allow him or her to be accompanied by others. If you are served with an Anton Piller order, the person serving it will give you an opportunity to take legal advice. In view of the seriousness of the matter, it would be sensible to do so. It would, however, be a very rare case in which your lawyer would advise you not to comply with the order. Nearly all Anton Piller orders contain a provision forbidding you to tip off others (apart from your lawyer) about their existence. In fact, the plaintiff often has means of telling whether others have been tipped off; he or she may have persons watching for such activity and, if you were caught arranging for others to dispose of inconvenient evidence, you would risk prison for contempt of court.

The solicitor serving the order is under a strict duty to behave responsibly. In one case where it was held that the solicitor acted oppressively, he was ordered to pay substantial compensation.

Bailiffs

Bailiffs are officers of the court, although they may be employed by private companies, and their job is to seize property. Courts can make a variety of orders which are enforced by bailiffs. Their rights to enter your home are complex and will depend on the order made by the court. In virtually all cases they are entitled to enter your home but only in a few cases, such as eviction orders, are they entitled to force their way in. They can, however, climb through unlocked windows and break down internal doors and will obviously put pressure on you to invite them in.

If they are employed by the court following a judgement debt they can seize any goods or possessions belonging to the debtor but cannot seize anything needed *personally* for his or her job (for instance tools, books and vehicles) or used for basic needs (clothing, bedding, furniture, household equipment and food). Thus they can take stereo equipment, televisions, video recorders, etc. Baliffs cannot seize property belonging to people other than the debtor.

The goods are then usually impounded for a short period (five days) before being sold by auction. Often the goods are left on the premises until sold. This is known as 'taking walking possession'.

Customs and excise

Approximately 40,000 travellers each year are stopped and bodily searched at customs points throughout the country. The nature of the search may take a number of forms, from a 'pocket search' to a full strip or intimate body search. Most people find such searches distressing and humiliating, and frequently ask the question 'Why me?'

When you may be searched

A customs officer may ask to search you or anything you have with you if he or she reasonably suspects that you are carrying:

* Any item which is liable to excise duty or tax which has not been paid; for example, perfume, alcohol, cigarettes, in excess of the duty-free allowance.
* Any item which is prohibited or restricted from being imported or exported; for example, illegal drugs.

A request to search you does not mean that you are under arrest; it means that you are to be detained whilst a search is carried out. If you are placed under arrest, you will be told.

Length of detention

How long you may be detained for will depend on the circumstances, but in all circumstances the length of detention must be reasonable and not exceed the time taken for the actual search, which is usually completed in under ten minutes. If you decide to leave before being searched, the customs officer may let you go or you may be arrested (see below). You may also (exceptionally) be charged with the offence of obstructing or impeding a customs officer.

What amounts to reasonable suspicion?

A customs officer does not have to be certain that you are carrying an unlawful item in order to justify a search. But there must be some concrete basis for the officer's suspicion which relates to you. The mere fact alone that you have arrived from a particular destination, that you are dressed in a certain way or that you are carrying particular items such as condoms, cigarette papers or petroleum jelly, which could be associated with drug use or drug trafficking, is not in itself sufficient justification. However, a combination of these or other factors, such as suspicious behaviour, an unusual quantity of luggage, unexplained journeys abroad, etc., may give rise to enough reasonable suspicion to justify your being searched.

What you must be told

The customs officer must tell you what you are suspected of. For example, 'I have reasonable grounds to suspect that you are carrying illegal drugs.' Although you should ask why you are suspected of a particular offence, the customs officer does not, in fact, have to tell you.

If you are asked to submit to a 'rub-down' search (see below), you must be told that you have the right to go before a senior customs officer if you do not agree with the search. In the case of a strip or intimate search (see below), you must be told that you have the right to be taken before either a senior customs officer or a magistrate who will then decide whether or not the search should take place.

Going before a senior customs officer or magistrate

If you decide to exercise your right to go before a senior customs officer or a magistrate, you are entitled to be present to hear the reasons why you should submit to a body search and have the opportunity to say why you disagree. If you wish someone to speak on your behalf, you should say so.

If you decide that you wish to go before a magistrate there may be some delay, but arrangements should be made to ensure that a magistrate is available at all times. It would not be reasonable to expect you to wait more than a couple of hours. If you are told or if it appears that the delay will be any longer than this, you should ask to see the most senior officer in attendance at the airport or port so that you may make an official complaint. If you decide to leave because of the unreasonable delay, you should ensure that the customs officer knows that this is the reason. As mentioned above, you do run the risk of being arrested if you decide to leave prior to the search taking place.

After hearing the evidence from both the customs officer requesting the search and yourself, the senior officer or magistrate (depending on whom you request to be taken before) will then direct whether or not the search is to take place and the form that the search may take.

What form may the search take?

The nature and extent of the search depends on what you are suspected of carrying and where. It may take any of the following forms:

- A 'pocket search' (i.e. removal of all items from pockets).
- A 'rub-down' (i.e. the body is frisked).
- A search of outer clothing (i.e. removal of outer coat, jacket, hat or gloves).
- A strip search (see below).
- An intimate search (see below).

Customs officers are instructed to ensure that any person searched is treated courteously and considerately. All 'rub-down' and strip searches can be carried out only by a person of the same sex as the person being searched. (For those who may carry out an intimate search see below.)

Strip search

A strip search is essentially a visual search of your body. You will be accompanied by two customs officers of the same sex as yourself to a private room and asked to remove your clothing. Customs officers are under a duty to make every reasonable effort to reduce to the minimum the embarrassment that you may experience. For example:

- You need not be completely naked at any time. It will usually be possible for the top and bottom halves of the body to be unclothed and reclothed separately. If this is not suggested to you, you should ask that you be allowed to undress in this way.
- If you are required to be naked, a blanket or other suitable covering should be provided. Again, if this is not offered to you, you should request it.

An intimate search

An intimate search consists of the physical examination of one or more of your body orifices (i.e. mouth, nose, ears, anus and genitalia) and may only be done if an officer of at least the rank of senior executive officer authorises it. The reason why it is thought necessary must be explained to you. The examination may only be carried out by a doctor or a nurse. No person of the opposite sex to yourself who is not a doctor or nurse should be present, nor should anyone whose presence is unnecessary. An intimate search of a juvenile (i.e. under the age of seventeen) or of a person who is mentally ill or mentally handicapped may only take place in the presence of an appropriate adult (for example, a relative or social worker) who is of the same sex as the person being searched – unless the juvenile requests otherwise and the adult agrees.

If you do not consent to an intimate search, it is most unlikely that the doctor or nurse will agree to carry it out. However, you must remember that you run the risk of being arrested if you do not consent, particularly if the search has been authorised by a magistrate.

If you are arrested

A customs officer may arrest you if he or she has reasonable grounds to suspect that you are committing, or have committed, an offence as described above. You must be informed of why you are being arrested. The customs officer has the same powers to search you as described above if you are not under arrest and you have the same rights to be taken before a senior officer or a magistrate (see above). In addition, if you are under arrest, customs officers have the power to request that you submit to an intimate search if they believe you have an article on you that may cause a physical injury to yourself or others whilst in detention.

A customs officer of the same sex as yourself may carry out this search but only where a senior officer has authorised that it is not practicable for a doctor or nurse to do so. If you are under arrest, you may be detained for longer: up to twenty-four hours, or if it is alleged that you have committed a 'serious arrestable offence', up to thirty-six hours and to a maximum of ninety-six hours if a magistrate authorises further detention.

During detention you have the right:

- To inform someone of your arrest.
- To consult a solicitor in private.

But exercising these rights may be delayed by thirty-six hours if you have been arrested for a 'serious arrestable offence'. You are entitled to a copy of your custody record (see p. 143).

An intimate body sample such as urine or blood can only be taken with your consent in writing.

If you wish to make a complaint
If you feel that you have been unreasonably subjected to a body search or have any objections to the way in which it was carried out, you may complain in writing to the Collector (the person in overall charge of the airport or port) at the address of the airport or port at which the search took place. You may also take up the matter with your MP and request that your complaint be referred to the Paymaster General at the Treasury (the minister responsible for Customs and Excise).

3.7 Privacy and the media

The laws about breach of confidence, trespass, nuisance, surveillance, etc., apply equally to the media. Libel may restrict some intrusions on private life but only if the words are defamatory (see p. 34), and in reality it only helps the wealthy because legal aid is not available for libel actions.

'Malicious falsehood' is a growing cause of legal action. It was used against a newspaper which photographed a famous footballer who was recovering in hospital from brain surgery. The court said that the remarks which the patient had made were wrongly portrayed as a voluntary and exclusive interview. Malicious falsehood can also be pursued even though the published material is at the same time a libel. The ban on legal aid does not apply to malicious falsehood. However, the ingredients are difficult to establish: the victim must show that the words are false, that they were published maliciously (i.e. for some improper purpose), and that they have either caused financial loss or, in some cases, were likely to cause such loss.

Copyright can also be used as way of preventing publication of private papers or pictures, but working out who owns copyright (and who is therefore the right person to bring an action) can be a complicated matter. Additional protection is given to a person who commissions photographs for private or domestic purposes. Even if copyright is owned by the photographer, the commissioner can prevent their publication.

If the makers of television and radio programmes intrude on a person's privacy, a complaint can be made to the Broadcasting Complaints Commission. The complaint will only be upheld if the intrusion was 'unwarranted' which allows the BCC to assess the nature of the intrusion against the public interest in the programme. The BCC can also consider complaints of unjust or unfair treatment which may overlap with intrusions on privacy but goes far wider. The complaint must relate to a programme which has been broadcast, but the BCC can insist on reviewing material which was filmed or recorded but not used. The BCC has no power to ban a programme in advance and cannot award compensation. However, it can insist that its findings are published and/or broadcast.

The BCC is a statutory body. There is no equivalent legislation for the press, but there is a Press Complaints Commission which has been set up by the industry itself. The PCC has drawn up a code of conduct which prohibits intrusions into an individual's private life unless this is justified in the public interest. The PCC publishes its own findings. There is no obligation on a newspaper which is found to have breached the code to report the findings or to give it any particular prominence, although rival titles may be quick to report PCC criticism.

The PCC replaced the previous Press Council in 1991 after a report by the Calcutt Committee in 1990 condemned the inadequate protection for individual privacy. Three years later, Sir David Calcutt QC again reviewed the performance of the press and considered that it was still lamentable in its disrespect for privacy. He proposed a range of new measures including a statutory tribunal with the power to order compensation and publication of its adjudications on privacy matters. He also recommended that there should be new criminal offences of trespass on private property or the use of surveillance devices for the purposes of obtaining personal information. Calcutt considered that there should be public interest defences, but only in tightly defined situations. His proposals caused concern not only in the press itself, but amongst others who feared that the new rights would be used to spike stories of real public interest which did not fit neatly into the proposed defences. There was also concern that his suggestions might lead to new grounds for granting injunctions before trial and that the usual cautious approach of the courts to injunctions at that stage (where priority is given to preserving the status quo) would mean that even stories within his categories of public interest would not see the light of day.

The government has now proposed that there should be a statutory right to privacy which would allow individuals to sue for compensation in specific circumstances. In response, the newspaper industry in January 1994 appointed an ombudsman, Professor Robert Pinker, to deal with complaints.

3.8 Further information

Useful organisations
Consult your telephone directory for local addresses and telephone numbers of the following organisations:

- Law centres
- Citizens' Advice Bureaux

Bibliography
'Report of the Committee on Privacy and Related Matters', HMSO Cmnd. 1102, 1990.
Sir David Calcutt, 'Review of Press Self-Regulation', HMSO Cmnd. 2135, 1993.

4

The right to know

This chapter describes the rights you *do* have, to see:

- Computer records.
- Credit reference agency records.
- Non-computerised records: some common features.
- Health records.
- Housing records.
- Social work records.
- School records.
- Other records.
- Changes in the pipeline.
- Other rights of access.

Many organisations, both public and private, hold files on the people they deal with. Important decisions about you may be taken on the basis of your file – often by people who have never met or spoken to you. All they know about you is what the file says. If the information is incomplete, inaccurate or unfair your rights may be at risk or you could be denied a benefit or service that you need. The best safeguard is a right to see the file for yourself, so you can challenge unjustified statements, correct factual inaccuracies and make your views known before – not after – decisions are taken. Several laws passed in the last decade allow people to see certain files held on them – though many other records remain confidential.

4.1 Computer records

The Data Protection Act 1984 gives you the right to see personal data about yourself held on computer. The Act applies to computerised information held by anyone, including government departments, public bodies, the NHS, the police, private sector and commercial organisations, employers and even individuals such as a GP or college lecturer.

However, even the most highly computerised organisation usually has at least some information on paper too. There is no right to see

73

these 'manual' files unless they are covered by one of the specific rights described later.

The exemptions

The Data Protection Act allows certain information to be withheld. One of the weaknesses of the Data Protection Act is that you need not be told if exempt information has been withheld – so you don't know whether you have been given the full file or only an edited version. You may even get a deliberately ambiguous reply to your request, such as 'We hold no data on you which we are required to disclose to you.' This either means there is no file on you or that there is a file, but it is regarded as totally exempt.

Nevertheless, it is worth asking if anything has been held back: it may be difficult for the person involved to evade a direct question. If you suspect you have been refused access to information which is not genuinely exempt you can ask the Data Protection Registrar to investigate. The following are the main exemptions.

National security

The Act does not apply to data which a cabinet minister has certified needs to be exempted to safeguard national security. Neither the courts nor the Data Protection Registrar, who enforces the Act, can challenge a ministerial certificate.

Law enforcement

Personal data held for the purpose of preventing or detecting crime, apprehending or prosecuting offenders, or assessing and collecting any tax or duty are exempt from access, but only if disclosure would prejudice one of those purposes.

The exemption is not restricted to bodies like the police or Inland Revenue. For example, information about suspected fraud held by a bank or a social security office would also be covered.

Not all law enforcement information is necessarily exempt. For example, if you are the victim of a crime you should be able to see what is held about you without much risk of prejudicing the purpose for which the record is held. But if you are the suspect, the chance of it being withheld will be much greater.

Personal information about someone else

This will not be released to you without that person's consent. However, if the information can be disclosed to you in a way that does not identify the individual – for example by deleting the name – then it must be.

The 'data user' (the person using the computer) is not required to ask someone who is referred to in your file for consent to let you see the information. But if you think you know who may be mentioned

– for example, a family member – you can ask if they will sign a letter of consent which you can include with your application.

Details that would identify someone who has supplied information about you

These are exempt – though the information they have provided is not. Only identifiable individuals, not organisations, are protected.

Intentions

The intentions of the data user towards you are exempt. A note in your employment file saying your employer intended to promote or make you redundant could be withheld. However, opinions about you must be disclosed.

Word processing

The text of a document which is being written or stored on a computer does not have to be disclosed. A journalist writing an article on a computer does not have to let someone mentioned in it see it. But if the computer is used to process or analyse the data in any way – for example to identify people with particular characteristics – then it is accessible.

Other exemptions

These apply to data used purely to calculate pay or pensions or for business accounting purposes or for managing an individual's personal or family affairs; to some kinds of club membership records; to information kept solely for statistical or research purposes and published anonymously; and to lawyer–client communications. Additional exemptions, described later in this chapter, apply to medical and social work records.

Applying

To apply to see a file, write to the organisation which holds the data, saying that you are applying under section 21 of the Data Protection Act for access to any personal information about yourself held on computer. If the data user has different offices or branches and you're not sure which to write to, telephone first and ask. Alternatively, contact the Data Protection Registrar's office (see p. 77) for the address. Data users must register under the Act and provide an address for 'subject access' requests in their register entry. Sending your request by recorded delivery will help avoid any later dispute about whether or not it was received.

The data user is entitled to ask you for proof of your identity and for information needed to locate any file on you. It may help if you say what your relationship to the organisation is (for example, customer, employee, student, patient), give any relevant dates or reference numbers and say which of its offices or branches you have dealt with – but don't volunteer any information which you regard as sensitive. You do not need to say why you want the information. The data user cannot refuse access because you might use the data to criticise it, complain or take legal action.

Fees

You may have to pay a fee. At the time of writing the maximum is £10, though some organisations charge less or nothing.

Unfortunately, the charge can sometimes exceed this. If the data user has more than one register entry, for example if data is held for different purposes, a separate application fee can be charged for each entry applied for. For instance, an application to the Metropolitan Police for information about you held on computer files about vehicle owners, disqualified drivers and stolen cars is covered by a single £10 application fee. But you would have to pay a second fee if you also wanted a search of records on parking tickets or traffic offences. Checking the files on pedal cycles and licensed taxi cabs would involve another £10 apiece. If the data user has an application form, this may explain the different register entries and help you narrow your request down.

The data user must give access within forty days of receiving your request and any supplementary details needed. He or she can supply either a print-out or a typed copy of the information. Any unintelligible terms, such as computer codes, must be explained.

Parents and children

The Act has no minimum age limit for applicants. Except in Scotland, children can apply for their own records provided they are capable of understanding the nature of the request. A parent or guardian can only apply on the child's behalf if:

- The child has given consent; *or*
- The child is too young to understand the nature of the request *and* access is in the child's interests (initially this is decided by the data user, but ultimately the Registrar or the court decides – see enforcement below).

A parent concerned about a small child's health probably would be able to see the medical record. But a parent wishing to defend him or herself against allegations of child abuse, or looking for evidence to support a custody claim, probably would not.

In Scotland, a child must be sixteen to apply on his or her own behalf. A child's guardian, normally the parent, would exercise the right on behalf of an under-sixteen year old.

Inaccurate information

If you find that computerised data about yourself is factually incorrect or misleading, you are entitled to have it corrected or erased. Opinions cannot be challenged unless they are based on wrong facts. If you have been damaged by inaccurate data, you are entitled to ask a court to award you compensation.

Disclosures to others

The Data Protection Act gives you little control over what is done with your details. It does say that information must be obtained 'fairly' and the Registrar interprets this to mean that when you are asked for information you must be told to whom it might be disclosed – unless it is obvious, or the disclosure is required by law or for law enforcement purposes. Once you have been told that the information may be used for, say, mailing list purposes, you have no specific right to know which organisations have bought a list which includes your details.

The data user's register entry must state in general terms the kinds of organisations to whom it may want to disclose data, but need not give the names of the specific organisations. For example, it may tell you that disclosures will be made to local authorities – but not which ones. You can get a copy of the entry from the Registrar's office.

Enforcing the Act

If a data user fails to comply with any of the Act's requirements – for example, if it withholds information which is not exempt, fails to respond to your request within forty days, or refuses to correct demonstrably inaccurate information – you can complain either to a court or to the Data Protection Registrar. The Registrar is usually preferable as this costs you nothing.

You can also complain to the Registrar if a data user has failed to comply with the Data Protection Principles laid down in the Act. Briefly, these require organisations to obtain and process personal data fairly and lawfully; to hold, use and disclose it only for specified purposes which they have identified in their register entries; to ensure that the data is accurate, up to date, relevant to and not excessive for the purpose for which it is held and not kept longer than necessary; and is protected against improper disclosure.

You can contact the Registrar at:

Office of the Data Protection Registrar
Wycliffe House
Water Lane
Wilmslow
Cheshire SK9 5AF
Tel: 0625 535777

4.2 Credit reference agency records

When you apply for a loan, credit card, bank account or mortgage the chances are that the company involved will run a check on you with a credit reference agency. These agencies check the electoral register to confirm that people live where they say they do and report on bad debts, bankruptcies and perhaps on how well people keep up repayments of existing loans. If any of the information about you is wrong, it could be extremely damaging.

When they supply information about you, credit reference agencies may also include information about other people who live or used to live at your address. Following a legal ruling by the Data Protection Tribunal, agencies now can only supply information about other people if they are family members living in the same household. But this still means you could be refused credit because someone else in your family is a bad credit risk.

Under the Consumer Credit Act 1974 you have the right to know whether a lender has consulted a credit reference agency, and if so which one. If you are refused credit, ask the lender to give you these details. Whether or not you have been refused credit, you are entitled to see what a credit reference agency holds about you.

To apply, write to the agency enclosing a £1 application fee. Give your full name and address and any other addresses you have lived at during the past six years. The information must be sent to you within seven days.

If the file contains mistakes, the agency must correct them and tell you in writing what it has done within twenty-eight days. If it refuses, or you aren't satisfied with the amendment, you can send it a note of correction of up to 200 words which it must add to your file and send out whenever information about you is supplied in future.

There are four main credit reference agencies:

CCN Systems Ltd
Consumer Affairs
PO Box 40
Nottingham NG7 2SZ
Tel: 0602 868172

Credit Data & Marketing Services
Nationwide Securities
PO Box 105
Bolton
Lancashire BL3 4YA
Tel: 051 949 0214

Equifax
Spectrum House
1a North Avenue
Clydebank
Glasgow G81 2DR
Tel: 041 951 1100

Infolink Ltd
Coombe Cross
2/4 South End
Croydon CR0 1DL
Tel: 081 686 7777

Enforcement

If you have a complaint about a credit reference agency, write to:

Director General of Fair Trading
Field House
Bream's Building
London EC4A 1PR
Tel: 071 242 2858

4.3 Non-computerised records: some common features

A series of individual laws, most resulting from private members' bills sponsored by the Campaign for Freedom of Information, provide rights of access to manually held health, social work, housing and school records. The laws generally have a number of common features, which are given here to avoid repeating them in each of the following sections:

- Applications must be in writing.
- Only information recorded after the law came into force is accessible. In general, earlier information can only be seen on a voluntary basis, if the record holder agrees.
- There is a very limited exception to the above: some earlier information is accessible if, in the record holder's opinion, it is necessary to understand information to which the right of access does apply. This is most likely to apply if recent information explicitly refers back to something recorded before the right came into force.
- You can be charged a £10 fee for applying for your records. Unfortunately, the government has refused to rule out 'double' payments. This means you can be charged one fee for asking for your com-

puterised social work records, say, and another £10 for access to the manual record. Fortunately, some record holders reduce or waive these fees.

- You are entitled to inspect the records and get photocopies, on payment of copying and postage costs.
- You have the right to have factually inaccurate information corrected. If the record holder does not accept that it is inaccurate you can either appeal against the decision and/or insist that a statement setting out your views about the disputed information is added to the record.
- Information about another identifiable individual, and any details which will identify someone who has supplied information about you is exempt.
- Information that is likely to cause 'serious harm' to your or someone else's health is exempt.
- Information held for law enforcement purposes can be withheld if disclosure would prejudice those purposes.
- The record holder can withhold information about his or her intentions towards you.
- For certain records (housing records and medical reports to insurers and employers) you have to be told if exempt information has been withheld from you. But you have no right to know when information has been withheld from health, social work or school records.

4.4 Health records

- If your health records are held on computer, you are entitled to see them under the Data Protection Act (see above).
- If your records are held manually (i.e. on paper), you have the right to see any information recorded after November 1991.
- There is no right to see information recorded manually *before* November 1991 – but it's worth asking, as some doctors allow access on a voluntary basis.
- You have the right to see a report which your doctor sends to an employer or an insurance company.

Access to health records

The Access to Health Records Act 1990 allows people to see information about their physical or mental health which has been recorded manually by or on behalf of a 'health professional' who has treated them. It applies both to NHS and private medical records.

The health professionals whose records can be seen are doctors, dentists, opticians, pharmacists, nurses, midwives, health visitors, chi-

ropodists, dieticians, occupational therapists, orthoptists, physio-
therapists, clinical psychologists, child psychotherapists, osteopaths,
speech therapists, art or music therapists employed by a Health Service
body and scientists who head Health Service departments. Other kinds
of health records – for example, those held by various kinds of psychotherapists or alternative practitioners – are not accessible.

Applications must be made to the holder of the record, usually the
GP, health authority or board or NHS trust. In private practice, applications should go directly to the health professional. You must be given
access within forty days. If all you want is information added to your
file in the last forty days, you must be given it within twenty-one days.
This reduces delays for someone who only wants to see a recent entry
about a current health problem.

You can inspect your record in person or authorise someone to look
at it for you. Unintelligible terms must be explained.

Although a £10 application fee can be charged, there is no fee if information has been added to your record in the last forty days. This
should allow free access – to the whole file, however many years back
it goes – to anyone who has recently been seen by a health professional.

Children can apply for their own records. Parents normally require
their child's consent before they can see the child's records. If the child
is incapable of understanding the nature of the request, the parent can
have access only if the record holder is satisfied that access is in the
child's best interests. Even then, parents will not be allowed to see information which the child has provided in confidence – for example, about
contraception or problems in the home.

The relatives of someone who has died have no right to the deceased's
records. The only exception is if the death may have been caused by
negligence. The Access to Health Records Act allows someone who might
be entitled to compensation – usually a dependent – to get records
relating to the cause of death.

Exemptions
There are two main exemptions to the Access to Health Records Act.

'Serious harm'
Information likely to cause serious harm to the patient's or someone
else's physical or mental health is exempt. Doctors argue that this is
necessary – but it inevitably provokes suspicion in patients. Its purpose
is to allow information to be withheld from, for example, someone
with a mental illness whose condition could be seriously aggravated
by seeing the record. It is not, however, a blanket exemption for psychiatric patients – or any other class of patients. Studies have shown
that most psychiatric patients benefit from seeing their medical records,

provided they have been written in the knowledge that they might be seen and someone is available to help explain them.

Note that the exemption refers to 'serious harm' and not, for example, to distress. It is not intended to allow doctors to withhold possibly upsetting news from a patient, particularly one who could be helped to come to terms with it by suitable support and counselling.

This decision must be based on the advice of a health professional, normally the doctor treating the patient. A similar exemption applies to requests for computerised health records under the Data Protection Act.

Information about or provided by another identifiable individual
This information, other than that provided by a health professional, is exempt. Your GP does not need a consultant's permission before showing you a report on you written by the consultant.

Enforcement
If a record holder does not comply with the Act you can enforce your rights in the courts. Where NHS records are involved you can also complain under NHS complaints procedures.

Access to earlier information
There is no right to see information recorded before November 1991. However:

*   Some doctors voluntarily allow patients to see pre-1991 records. The NHS Management Executive has issued guidance encouraging Health Service bodies to make 'informal, voluntary arrangements' for access, which could allow access to earlier records.
*   If you think you have been injured as a result of a medical mistake and could be entitled to compensation, your solicitor will be able to obtain your pre-1991 medical records. But unless you are eligible for aid, you may have to pay some legal expenses.

Insurance and employment medical reports
If your doctor writes a report on your health for an insurance company or an employer you have the right to see it before it is sent under the Access to Medical Reports Act 1988.

Any doctor who is or has been involved in your medical care is covered. But a report by an independent doctor, who has never treated you, but acts solely for the insurer or employer will not be accessible.

An employer or insurer cannot contact your doctor unless it has your written consent and has informed you of your rights under the Act.

You must be given the chance to say whether you want to see the report before it is sent. If you say yes, the doctor is supposed to wait for twenty-one days before sending the report to the insurers or employers to allow you time to arrange to see it. Get in touch with your doctor straight away and ask to be contacted as soon as the report is ready. No charge can be made if you just inspect the report; if you want a copy you can be charged a 'reasonable fee'.

If information has been withheld under an exemption (for example, for 'serious harm') you are entitled to be told.

If you see the report and are unhappy with it – for example, if you feel it involves an unacceptable breach of your privacy, or misrepresents the true picture – you have the right to stop it being sent. But if you do, the employer or insurer may not be willing to offer you the job or insurance policy, so do not take this step lightly.

The doctor is required to keep a copy of the report for six months after sending it and you have the right to see it during this period. You may want to do this if you are unexpectedly refused insurance or employment.

Enforcement

If you believe that a doctor, employer or insurance company has breached the Act you can apply to a court for an order requiring compliance. If a doctor has sent a report without your consent, this may be a breach of medical confidentiality and you may have grounds for a complaint to the General Medical Council.

4.5 Housing records

If you are or have been a local authority tenant, have applied to be one, or have bought your council home, you have the right to see the council's housing records on you. Regulations under the Access to Personal Files Act 1987 entitle you to information recorded after April 1989 (or, in Scotland, after August 1992). Access must be given within forty days.

Information likely to cause you or someone serious harm and information about or provided by someone else can be withheld – but not if the person is a member of your family living with you or a housing officer or a health professional. If information about someone else is on your file, the authority is obliged to contact the person and ask if they will let you see it – a requirement which does not apply to other types of records. For further details see the Access to Personal Files (Housing) Regulations 1989 and the Access to Personal Files (Housing)(Scotland) Regulations 1992.

There is no right of appeal to the courts. The regulations say that complaints must be considered either by a group of councillors who were not involved in the original decision to deny access to a file or by the full council. You may also be able to complain to the local government ombudsman who investigates complaints about councils' 'maladministration'.

4.6 Social work records

Other regulations under the Access to Personal Files Act 1987 give you the right to see information about yourself recorded after April 1989 in a local authority's social work records.

The exemptions are generally the same as for housing records (above). The main differences are:

- You can only see information about *yourself* – not other members of your family.
- Information about identifiable social workers or people paid by the social services department for doing related work (for example, a foster parent or child minder) cannot be withheld.
- Information which would be likely to cause serious harm to your or someone else's physical or mental health *or emotional condition* can be withheld. The Department of Health's guidance says that only in the 'most exceptional' circumstances should information be withheld on any of these grounds.
- You have no legal right to be told if exempt information has been withheld.
- Appeals must be heard by a committee of three councillors, no more than one of whom may be a member of the social services committee.

Children
Children are entitled to apply for access to their own records and parents cannot normally see information about them unless:

- The child consents; *or*
- The child is too young to understand the nature of the application *and* access is in the child's best interests (initially this is decided by the council and on appeal by the committee – see above).

There is no exemption for information relating to child abuse as such. Disclosures likely to identify an informant who has reported suspected abuse can be withheld, but not if the person is a social worker or health professional. Information likely to expose the child or anyone else to serious risk is exempt. Unless it is in the child's 'best interest', parents will probably not be able to see information which the child has provided to social workers in confidence, or anything likely to expose the child to pressure to withdraw allegations, risk of reprisals or continued abuse. But parents should normally be able to see information about themselves – as opposed to the child – such as a social worker's notes of an interview with the parent in the child's file.

For further details see the Access to Personal Files (Social Services) Regulations 1989, the Access to Personal Files (Social Work) (Scotland) Regulations 1989 and the guidance contained in Department of Health Circular LAC(89)2.

4.7 School records

Parents and older pupils have the right to see information recorded in school records after September 1989 or, in Scotland, after October 1990. Local education authority (LEA) maintained schools, grant maintained schools and all special schools are covered, but records of independent schools are not.

The parents of a pupil under eighteen can see the records, as can a pupil who is sixteen or above. Access must be given within fifteen school days of a request and – unlike most other kinds of records – it is free, though the costs of any copies supplied can be charged.

Any material in a pupil's educational record produced by a teacher, an education welfare officer or an employee of the LEA is accessible, but information supplied by others is not. A teacher's private notes, kept purely for his or her personal use are exempt – but not if they are available to other teachers. Other exemptions apply to information likely to cause serious harm to the pupil or anyone else, information relating to potential child abuse and references about a pupil sent to employers, colleges or universities. There is no right to be told when exempt information has been withheld. Appeals are dealt with by the school governors.

For further details see the Education (School Records) Regulations 1989 and the School Pupil Records (Scotland) Regulations 1990 and Department of Education and Science Circular No 17/89.

4.8. Other records

There is no right of access to other kinds of manually held records, for example to police, social security, immigration, banking or employment records.

If you are dismissed and bring a tribunal complaint, you may be able to get your employment records during the case. But these are not available otherwise – nor are job references. There is little you can do if you think your job prospects are being harmed by an unfair or inaccurate reference.

Some organisations do have access policies and let people see their files on a voluntary basis. Even in the absence of a policy you may occasionally get access, if the person holding the record feels you have a good case and the request is made in a non-confrontational manner.

4.9 Stop press

In July 1993, the government announced that it intended to create a new statutory right of access to personal records in the public sector. The proposals are described in the White Paper on 'Open Government' (Cm 2290). At the time of writing no timetable for the legislation has been announced. The precise scope has not been decided but the government has said the right *might* extend to records held by government departments and agencies, the NHS, local authorities, police forces, educational and other public bodies.

The new right will not apply to information held by the courts, to immigration records, to employment records or to records held by private sector bodies – and it will not apply to information recorded before the new law comes into force.

However, a new European directive may cover these records. At the time of writing the European Commission has published a draft directive on data protection which, if accepted, would require Britain to strengthen the Data Protection Act and extend it to manual as well as computerised records, in both the private and public sectors. At the time of writing, no firm timetable for introducing the changes was available.

4.10 Other rights of access

This chapter has only dealt with access to personal files. There are also rights to other information. For example, the Local Government (Access to Information) Act 1985 allows the public to attend meetings of local authorities and their committees and sub-committees and to see agendas, reports, minutes and background papers – subject to a series of exemptions. The Environmental Information Regulations 1992, which implement a European directive, provide a general right of access to information about environmental pollution held by public bodies, again subject to broad exemptions.

The Open Government White Paper proposes a new legal right to health and safety information, though no date for the legislation has been announced. But it says disclosure of other information should be based on a new Code of Practice supervised by the ombudsman, which is due to come into force in April 1994. The Code has a number of serious defects. It would be voluntary: the government could refuse to act on the ombudsman's recommendations. People would be charged for information. The exemptions are extremely broad. Many important areas are excluded from its scope altogether, including foreign relations, immigration, policing, the security services and the nationalised industries. Finally, the government is only promising to release 'information' – in other words, to answer questions – but not disclose copies of actual documents. People are likely to get only a highly edited version of the facts, rather than the full story.

There are also many laws which forbid the disclosure of information. The best known of these is the Official Secrets Act 1989, which makes it an offence to disclose official information in certain areas without authorisation. The government has rejected calls for a 'public interest defence' to this Act, so a defendant cannot argue that he or she was justified in releasing information which revealed serious wrong-doing.

Many countries now have freedom of information laws, giving the public an enforceable right of access to government records. These include the USA, Canada, Australia, New Zealand, France, Denmark, Holland, Norway, Greece and Sweden – which has had a freedom of information act since 1766. Until Britain follows suit secrecy will too often still be the norm.

4.11 Further information

Useful organisations

Campaign for Freedom of Information
88 Old Street
London EC1V 9AR
Tel: 071 253 2445

You can find the addresses and telephone numbers of the following in your telephone directory.

- Law centres.
- Citizens' Advice Bureaux.

Bibliography

Patrick Birkinshaw, *Government and Information: The Law Relating to Access, Disclosure and Regulation*, Butterworths, 1990.

Campaign for Freedom of Information, *Secrets newspaper*, available from the CFI, 88 Old Street, London EC1V 9AR, £12.50 annually.

Duncan Campbell and Steve Connor, *On the Record: Surveillance, Computers and Privacy*, Michael Joseph, 1986.

Data Protection Registrar, *Annual Reports*, available from HMSO.

Data Protection Registrar, *Data Protection Act, Guidelines 1 to 8*, available without charge from the Office of the Data Protection Registrar, Wycliffe House, Water Lane, Wilmslow, Cheshire SK9 5AF.

5

The right to complain

This chapter contains information on:

- Government departments.
- Local government.
- Health services and care services.
- The police.
- Courts and legal services.
- Financial professions.
- The media.
- Public utilities.
- Transport and travel agencies.
- Miscellaneous complaints.
- Compensation for the victims of crime.
- Complaints and European law.
- The Citizen's Charter.
- Further information.

5.1 Government departments

If you wish to complain about the way that your case has been handled by a department of central government, or by some non-departmental bodies (a list of which can be obtained from the address below) the Parliamentary Commissioner for Administration (PCA or parliamentary ombudsman) exists by law for this purpose. The PCA has the power to investigate complaints of injustice or loss arising from maladministration, a term which includes such faults as delay, bias and arbitrary decision making. These powers include making government departments show investigators all relevant documents. Regular reports are also made to Parliament and the PCA has a committee of MPs who can follow up reports. The PCA cannot award you damages, but in the past recommendations that money be paid back or compensation be given have been accepted by the departments concerned. The PCA cannot go to court on your behalf, and the decision whether to take up a complaint and make an investigation is entirely up to the Commissioner.

If you feel that you have a good complaint in that you have lost out in some way because of maladministration, you cannot complain directly to the PCA but must do so via an MP (any MP). You should first have complained to the department and used up all internal tribunals and appeals. There is no charge for the PCA's services and any expenses you incur during the investigation can be reimbursed. You can contact your own MP locally or write to him or her or any other MP at the House of Commons. The PCA's address is:

The Parliamentary Commissioner for Administration
Church House
Great Smith Street
London SW1P 3BW
Tel: 071 273 6450

There are some areas in which the PCA cannot act: national security, civil service employment and government contracts being among them. The decision reached is not legally binding on the department involved but is usually followed.

Northern Ireland has its own Commissioner, whose address is:

Office of the Northern Ireland Parliamentary Commissioner
33 Wellington Place
Belfast BT1 6HN
Tel: 0232 233821

5.2 Local government

There are different ombudsmen for local government, but they exist to carry out the same sort of investigation. You can complain direct to the relevant ombudsman's office about maladministration by any local body such as the local authority or police authority, but only once you have exhausted all the procedures used by the body you are complaining about. The Commissioner for Local Administration can look into a local education authority but cannot examine matters relating to the direct provision of teaching. Investigations into local health authorities may also be undertaken, but in some areas specialist bodies exist (see below). England has three Commissioners for different regions and Wales and Scotland have one each. Their addresses are:

London and the South
21 Queen Anne's Gate
London SW1H 9BU
Tel: 071 222 5622

Midlands
The Oaks
Westwood Way
Westwood Business Park
Coventry CV4 8JB
Tel: 0203 695999

The North
Beverly House
17 Shipton Road
York YO3 6FZ
Tel: 0904 630151

Scotland
23 Walker Street
Edinburgh EH3 7HX
Tel: 031 225 5300

Wales
Derwen House
Court Road
Bridgend
Mid Glamorgan CF31 1BL
Tel: 0656 661325

5.3 Health Services and care services

The way to complain about matters connected to the provision of state healthcare depends on the profession of the person about whom you wish to complain and which aspect of their work you wish to complain about. You should consider all the options below before taking any action. Advice and assistance in all Health Service complaints is available from your local Community Health Council (see your telephone book) who can help write letters and present cases.

Complaints against general practitioners

These fall into two categories; those about breach of the GP's conditions of employment and those relating to behaviour.

Complaints about a GP not meeting his or her contractual obligations to the NHS as his or her employer, as well as complaints about dentists, chemists and opticians go to the Family Health Services Authority. The address of your local FHSA will be in your phone book and it is also on your medical card. Complaints should be made in writing to the General Manager. The FHSA can formally investigate such matters as failure to come to a call-out outside surgery hours. There is a time limit on complaints of thirteen weeks from the event causing the complaint (thirteen weeks from finding the cause or six months from the treatment in the case of dentists). You can make a complaint for someone else who is unable to do so.

Informal complaints can cover any aspect of the service provided by a surgery but only breaches of the GP's contract with the NHS can be formally investigated by a committee of medical and lay members. At this hearing, you can put your own case or have a friend's help. You will receive a copy of the findings and if your complaint is proved, the GP may be disciplined. You cannot receive compensation from the committee – you would have to go to court for this – but you can claim back expenses. The decision can be appealed to the Secretary of State for Health and the Health Service Commissioner can investigate how the FHSA handled your case (see below).

Complaints about hospitals

Initially, if you are dissatisfied with your treatment in hospital, you should speak to the ward sister. Under the Patient's Charter, you are allocated a named nurse whose name you should be told and who is responsible for your care. If this does not solve the problem, go to the Unit General Manager (hospital manager) or District General Manager or the Chair of the District Health Authority. If the hospital is an NHS trust, complain to the Chief Executive.

If you are still unhappy, you can go to the Health Service Commissioner (ombudsman) at:

Church House
Great Smith Street
London SW1P 3BW
Tel: 071 276 3000

The ombudsman cannot investigate matters of clinical judgement. You should complain in writing within a year and you must have complained to the health authority first. The Commissioner has powers similar to the PCA and covers all hospital services such as ambulances, but not GPs. Ombudsmen exist also for Scotland and Wales. They can be contacted at:

Second Floor, 11 Melville Crescent
Edinburgh EH3 7LU
Tel: 031 225 7465

Fourth Floor, Pearl Assurance House
Greyfriars Road
Cardiff CF1 3AG
Tel: 0222 394621

Complaints about nurses and midwives

These professions are covered by a national council which may take action on a complaint of conduct which brings the profession into disrepute. Its address is:

UK Central Council for Nursing, Midwifery and Health Visiting
23 Portland Place
London W1N 3AF
Tel: 071 637 7181

Complaints about doctors

If your complaint is about improper behaviour by a doctor (such as sexual harassment or fraud) address it to:

The General Medical Council
44 Hallam Street
London W1N 6AE
Tel: 071 580 7642

The GMC is the governing body for doctors and may discipline its listed doctors, including disqualifying them from practice. It does not investigate complaints of medical negligence or incompetence. Leaflets exist to help you make a complaint – see your Community Health Council.

Complaints of negligence

In this case you should first go to the appropriate consultant. If this does not work, complain to the Regional Medical Officer at the Regional Health Authority, who may organise an investigation by specialists.

If this does not work, or you seek monetary damages, you could consider going to court in a private action for negligence. Be careful, as the law tends towards the doctor, although it is better than it used to be. Advice on this matter can be sought from a solicitor, from your Community Health Council or from:

Action for the Victims of Medical Accidents
Bank Chambers
Forest Hill
London SE23 8TP
Tel: 081 291 2793

Complaints about community care

Write first to the Director of Social Services. This may lead to informal problem solving, registering a complaint or a formal review by a panel which reports to the local authority. Leaflets telling you who to complain to in social services and the DSS are available from Citizens' Advice Bureaux and other advice centres. If the complaint is of mal-administration, it could go to the Commissioner for Local Administration.

If your complaint is about social security payments, you should go to your local office of the Benefits Agency, the address of which will be in the phone book. They have procedures for dealing with complaints and appeals, which include a system of tribunals.

5.4 The police

If you are dissatisfied with your treatment by the police, the first thing to do is to get as many details as possible about the officer(s) who dealt with you: their names, numbers, car number and so on, as well as details of any witnesses. Such information will be important. Write down what happened as soon as you can, this again will help later.

Before making a complaint you should consider the following points:

- The law imposes a time limit for making a complaint. Complaints must be made within one year of the incident. If you are worried or uncertain, always take advice first. Do not allow yourself to be pressurised by the police or anyone else into making your complaint on the spot.
- Your complaint must be about a particular officer or officers, not about general police practice or policy. If you have a general complaint concerning policing practice, you should raise the matter with your MP and the Home Office. Complaints about local policing policy can be taken up through your Police Consultative Committee or Police Authority (or Home Secretary for the police in London).

Before making your complaint against the police, it is a good idea to get advice from a solicitor, law centre or Citizens' Advice Bureau (CAB). If you do not have much money, you should consult any solicitor who does legal aid work and ask for Green Form Advice. This advice will be free, or virtually free, depending on your income and savings. For more information, see p. 101.

How should a complaint be made?

A complaint can be made verbally at a police station but your views will be more accurately recorded if you submit your complaint in writing and retain a copy for yourself. Your initial complaint should be brief, stating what happened and why you are complaining. At this stage, you need only give sufficient detail for the incident to be identified. As this is the only statement which the officer(s) concerned are entitled to see and on which a libel or slander action could be brought (and not any statement made during the formal investigation), it is important to keep it as factual and as accurate as possible.

If you do not want to contact the police yourself, you may ask someone else to put your complaint forward for you, for instance, a Citizens' Advice Bureau, law centre, solicitor, your employer, trade union representative or a friend. You will need to give them written consent to do so.

If you decide to complain, write to the police officer's Chief Constable or, if in London, to the Metropolitan Police Commissioner. Give as many details as you can and be honest and accurate, because the police could take legal action if they are falsely accused of wrongful conduct. The complaint must be registered by the police.

In some cases the police may need to take action as soon as a complaint is received to get evidence which might not be available later. For example, if you complain about an assault while you are in custody, the police would normally ask a police doctor to examine you then and there but only if you are willing. Nobody can compel you to be examined.

It may be decided to try to settle the matter informally, with an officer of at least chief inspector rank mediating. This can only happen if you agree to it. Informal resolution is quicker and simpler than formal investigation. If you do not agree to informal resolution, if attempts at informal resolution do not work or if your complaint turns out to be more serious than originally thought, it can be formally investigated instead.

How does informal resolution work?

An officer of the rank of chief inspector, or at least of the rank of the officer(s) concerned, will be appointed to oversee the procedure. He or she must ask you and the officer(s) concerned for your views of the incident under investigation. Although the procedure is meant to be informal, you may still want to give your views in writing or have someone else with you when you are interviewed about your complaint. If there were witnesses to the incident who would support your complaint, you should ask the officer in charge to interview them. The officer should take any other appropriate steps, but no specific procedure is laid down. The appointed officer can apologise to you on behalf of the officer(s) concerned if that officer(s) admits the misconduct; even without the officer's admission, it is possible that an apology on behalf of the Chief Constable, or the force generally, will be made, but there is no power to require the police officer(s) to take part. If you are asked to attend a meeting to discuss your complaint, you can insist that it take place away from police premises and that you have someone to accompany you.

If you are not satisfied by the informal resolution, you can request that your complaint be formally investigated instead (minor complaints are rarely upheld using the formal procedure, however).

If a complaint is informally resolved, there will be no formal entry in the personal record of the officer(s) concerned. A record will be kept, however, and you are entitled to a copy if you request it within three months of the complaint having been resolved.

What is the Police Complaints Authority and how does it work?

Investigation of all complaints is conducted by the police themselves. In certain cases, however, their investigation will be supervised by the Police Complaints Authority (PCA).

The PCA is a civilian body whose members are not, and never have been, members of the police. The chair is appointed by Her Majesty, and no fewer than eight other members are appointed by the Home Secretary. Members are appointed for a maximum of three years at a time. The Home Secretary appoints two of the members to the position of deputy chair.

The PCA must supervise any complaint alleging that the conduct of a police officer:

- Resulted in death or serious injury to another person; *or*
- Constituted assault causing actual bodily harm, or constitutes a 'serious arrestable offence'.

In addition, the Chief Constable or Commissioner may ask the PCA to supervise the investigation of any other complaint.

What happens when a complaint is formally investigated?

If the investigation is to be formal, the Chief Constable or Commissioner must appoint an investigating officer of at least the rank of chief inspector and not lower in rank than the officer(s) concerned. The investigating officer must be from a different sub-division or branch and can be appointed from a different police force.

The officer(s) you have complained about will be informed of your complaint and cautioned that any statement he or she (or them) makes may be used in disciplinary proceedings. The officer(s) and any police witnesses will be interviewed and statements taken. Then you and your witnesses will be asked to meet the investigating officer to give full statements.

The investigating officer will then report to the Chief Constable or Commissioner who may:

- Refer to the Director of Public Prosecutions (DPP) if the officer has committed a criminal offence.
- Not refer but notify the Police Complaints Authority of the possibility that there was a criminal offence and of any disciplinary action taken.
- Notify the Authority of any disciplinary charges made against the officer(s).
- Notify the Authority that he or she will take no action.

The Authority can order the Chief Constable or Commissioner to refer to the DPP or to bring disciplinary charges, even if he or she has said he or she does not intend to. Serious investigations may (and if very serious must) be supervised by the Authority who will consider the report itself.

When does a complaint involve prosecution by the DPP?

If the investigation report indicates that a criminal offence may have been committed, the Chief Constable or Commissioner will probably refer the complaint to the DPP. It remains for the DPP to decide whether the officer(s) should be prosecuted. But in fact very few officers are ever prosecuted.

What are the disciplinary charges and when can they be brought?

The Chief Constable or Commissioner must also consider whether disciplinary charges should be brought and must inform the PCA whether or not they intend to bring disciplinary proceedings. The PCA may recommend that the officer(s) be charged, and if the Chief Constable or Commissioner refuses to comply with this recommendation, the PCA can direct him or her to do so.

Under the Police and Criminal Evidence Act of 1984, the police discipline code has been expanded. For example, failing without good cause to follow the Codes of Practice established under the 1984 Act becomes an offence, as does racially discriminatory behaviour.

An officer(s) against whom disciplinary charges are brought must face a disciplinary hearing; if the charge is upheld, a punishment will be awarded. Disciplinary hearings are conducted by the Chief Constable or Commissioner of the officer's own force, or by the Deputy Chief Constable or Commissioner to whom responsibility may be delegated. In some cases a Chief Constable from another force might take their place. If the officer(s) involved has already been prosecuted by the DPP, no disciplinary charge may be brought for an offence which is 'in substance' the same as the criminal offence, whether or not the officer(s) was acquitted or convicted.

What is the complainant's role at the disciplinary hearing?

If the officer(s) denies the charge, you will be expected to attend the disciplinary hearing to give evidence although it is likely that this is the only part of the hearing you will be allowed to attend. You may be accompanied by a friend but you cannot be legally represented by a lawyer. The police officer(s), however, is entitled to be legally represented at the disciplinary hearing in all serious cases and in other cases only at the discretion of the Deputy Chief Constable.

You will normally be called as the first witness. You should be told what the officer(s) has been charged with and whether he or she admits or denies it. You will be allowed to question the officer(s) but you will not be allowed to ask questions which are considered to be irrelevant, including any questions concerning previous disputes between yourself and the same officer(s).

If found guilty of a disciplinary offence, the police officer(s) can be punished in a variety of ways, including a reprimand or caution, a fine, a reduction in rate of pay or rank, a requirement to resign, or dismissal.

The officer(s) can appeal to the Home Secretary against both the finding of guilt and the punishment. The Home Secretary can appoint a three-member panel to enquire into the matter before deciding the appeal, and must do so if the officer(s) has been punished with the loss of either job or rank. In this case the complainant may have to give evidence again.

Bringing a complaint against senior officers

If your complaint concerns the conduct of an officer above the rank of chief superintendent, your complaint will be directed to the police authority for the officer's area (except in London where the Commissioner also deals with complaints about senior officers – other than those against him or herself and the Deputy Commissioner, in which instance the Home Secretary takes over). The police authority is an organisation made up of magistrates and local councillors and is responsible for the efficiency of the police.

The decision to deal with minor complaints against senior officers by informal resolution is at the police authority's discretion, and your consent to your complaint being dealt with in this way is not a legal requirement for this procedure to be pursued. If your complaint is to be investigated by the police authority, the officer appointed on behalf of the authority must be of at least the same rank as the officer about whom you have complained. The role of the PCA in supervising the investigation applies equally to complaints against senior officers (see 'The Police Complaints Authority' above).

Disciplinary charges against senior officers are drawn up by an independent solicitor and are heard by a single person appointed by the police authority or commissioner from a list provided by the Lord Chancellor.

Note: a senior officer cannot be suspended by a police authority whilst a complaint is being investigated unless the PCA approves the suspension.

Conclusion

Proving complaints is difficult for the burden of proof is against the complainant with the general assumption that the police have acted appropriately in the line of duty.

If you wish to contact the Police Complaints Authority direct you may do so at:

10 Great George Street
London SW1P 3AE
Tel: 071 273 6450

Taking legal action yourself

Suing the police – civil action

You may bring a civil action against the police and seek damages to compensate you for your injuries and loss if your case falls into one of the categories under which the police can be sued:

- Assault and battery or the use of excessive force in arrest or detention.
- False imprisonment or restricting your liberty unlawfully (for example, detaining you without justification or for too long without charge).
- Trespass or searching property without proper authority.
- Malicious prosecution or bringing a prosecution without any good reason – which then fails.

• Negligence or failure to meet the standard of care which the police should show for the safety of people forseeably affected by their actions.

Many civil cases succeed where formal complaints fail. Under such circumstances, you should ask a lawyer as soon as possible to advise you on your chances of success and how much you might hope to receive. Legal aid is usually available if you do not have much money.

An advantage of a civil action is that if you do not know the name of the police officer(s) involved, you can sue the Chief Constable or Commissioner of the force.

If you are considering a civil action, it is usually best not to make a detailed statement in support of a complaint as this may put you at some disadvantage. If you have already made a complaint, refer the investigating officer to your solicitor. Be prepared for a considerable wait as civil cases are rarely completed in less than a year.

Prosecuting the police – criminal action
If you believe that there is good evidence to show that the police officer(s) has committed a criminal offence, for example by assaulting you, you can bring a private prosecution. Normally you should wait to see if the DPP will prosecute since the outcome would be the same (see 'When does a complaint involve prosecution by the DPP?' on p. 97). If the officer(s) is convicted he or she would be sentenced and could be ordered to pay some compensation to you.

You must get legal advice before bringing a private prosecution since you will need strong evidence if you are to have any chance of success. Under these circumstances there is no legal aid available and a private prosecution can be very expensive, especially if the officer(s) elects for trial by jury. It is important to realise that the odds are against your winning.

How are major incidents involving the police dealt with?
The Home Secretary can set up an independent enquiry into any matter concerning the police in England and Wales – not only misconduct by individuals or groups of officers but also as a result of police instructions and policing policies which result in serious conflict with members of the public. Such enquiries, however, are rarely held.

Police authorities can require chief police officers to report on any matter concerning the policing of their area; this is another way in which major incidents can be investigated.

Because the scope of public enquiries and reporting to police authorities is much wider than individual complaints, a campaign of public pressure is often needed before action is taken. If there has been an incident which needs to be examined in a public way, you should take up the matter with Liberty, with relevant local organisations, your MP and elected members of the police authority and with the press.

Complaints about local policing practice

If you are not happy with the way the police are carrying out their responsibilities in your area – for example, if you think that their priorities are wrong, or that they are harassing certain sections of the community – this can be addressed by a Police Consultative Committee.

Almost all police authorities have set up Police Consultative Committees in their areas. Each committee covers quite a small area (in London they are based on boroughs). Their members are appointed by the police authority. They tend to meet quarterly, although in some areas it is more frequent, and at least part of each meeting is usually open to the public so that issues of concern may be raised. Details of meetings may be obtained from your town hall.

However, the committees are merely consultative in function and have no power actually to change police practice. They are just a forum for the police to meet the public, not a mechanism for investigating or rectifying complaints.

Useful organisations

Police Complaints Authority
10 Great George Street
London SW1 3AE
Tel: 071 273 6450

Law Centres' Federation
18–19 Warren Street
London W1P 5DB
Tel: 071 387 8570

5.5 Courts and legal services

This subject area includes the courts and the legal professions, and each has its own system for dealing with complaints.

Going to court

Before taking any complaint as far as court, you should always seek legal advice. This may be available free through a law centre or by going to a solicitor, many of whom now offer a free initial interview. Beyond this, if you are eligible, the Legal Aid Green Form Scheme covers pre-hearing advice given to you and the writing of letters and preparation of a written case. Advice is valuable because in some cases you could stand to pay both sides' costs if you lose.

For people on a low income, legal aid may be available to cover the costs of going to court. Obtaining full assistance has become more difficult after recent changes in the system, and the current limit for full aid is around £60 per week disposable income (allowances are also given for dependents). If your disposable income is over this limit, you will have to pay some of the costs of the case, worked out on a sliding scale. Legal aid is payable for the majority of criminal and civil cases, but not if you are bringing a defamation action or if your case will be decided in a tribunal. There are exceptions to the rule and you can check your situation by getting detailed advice.

If your case relates to a money claim of under £1,000 you can use the small claims procedure in the County Court. You can make such a claim without needing a solicitor and your local court has leaflets on how to submit a claim. There is an initial fee, but this is recoverable if you win. The case is heard by the judge in chambers – that is to say not in a court room – and the procedure is designed to be quicker and easier than a full trial. You can apply to have judgement entered for you in fourteen days if no defence is put up. Sums of over £1,000 can be dealt with at the judge's discretion by referral to arbitration. If in doubt, ring your local court and ask; the number is under 'courts' in the Yellow Pages.

In cases where you are claiming compensation for negligence causing injury or loss, for breach of contract or for a civil offence such as assault, you must go to the County Court or, in some cases, the High Court. This will require a lawyer.

The magistrates' court usually deals with criminal matters where the police have summonsed or charged someone. They also deal with cases involving the poll tax (community charge) and the council tax.

The above is only an outline of the court system and before getting involved in your case you should get advice, which may often be free. Many complaints are not heard by courts as such but at tribunals like industrial tribunals which can deal with the matter in a less formal way. The rules on tribunals are varied and uneven, and you should seek advice on whether or not you can be represented and on how the tribunal in your case will work.

Complaints about the courts

If you are dissatisfied with the way the court system works (although not with the result of your case, which is a legal matter), for example, if you have been kept waiting excessively or you have not been given information by the court which you should have received, your rights as a complainant are now in the Courts' Charter which is available from the Court Service Secretariat at:

The Lord Chancellor's Department
Trevelyan House
30 Great Peter Street
London SW1P 2BY
Tel: 071 210 8832

At a local level, the name of the Chief Clerk, to whom all complaints should be addressed, and the complaints procedure must now be on display in all court buildings.

Complaints against solicitors

If your complaint is about the way your lawyer has handled your case or how he or she has acted towards you, there are several ways to proceed. If your grievance is over the professional conduct of a solicitor, for example if you were not told how high the fees would be beforehand (you should be told this) or if your case has taken much too long to be dealt with, you should first complain directly to the solicitor concerned. If this does not produce a solution, go to the senior partner at the firm where your solicitor works. If this fails, you should address complaints to:

The Director
Solicitors' Complaints Bureau
Victoria Court
8 Dormer Place
Leamington Spa
Warwickshire CV32 5AE
Tel: 0926 820082

The SCB may pass the matter to an Investigation Committee who will see whether the conduct complained of is below the standards set for solicitors by the Law Society (their governing body). The profession has self-regulating disciplinary measures, which can include striking a solicitor off the list of those qualified to practise.

If you are complaining that a solicitor acted negligently and so caused you to lose out, after complaining to the firm direct you would have to go to court and sue. It is far from easy to succeed in this and can only work in limited circumstances. The Solicitors' Complaints Bureau has a Negligence Panel which can examine your complaint and tell you if, in their opinion, you have a case. If you go to court and win, you will be paid compensation.

If you are unhappy with the way that your complaint is dealt with, you can complain, within three months, to the Lay Observer at:

The Royal Courts of Justice
The Strand
London WC2A 2LL
Tel: 071 411 1220

Complaints against barristers

You cannot sue a barrister for negligence in the way he or she presents your case in court although you may be able to sue for negligent advice. If you are dissatisfied with your barrister's professional conduct, for example if your instructions have been ignored, you should complain to the profession's governing body at:

The General Council of the Bar
3 Bedford Row
London WC1R 4DB
Tel: 071 242 0082

This body may impose disciplinary sanctions on barristers.

5.6 Financial professions

The professions which deal with your financial affairs have regulatory bodies set up and run by these professions. You should complain to the company involved first and then to the appropriate regulator.

The Banking Ombudsman
Citadel House
5–11 Fetter Lane
London EC4A 1BR
Tel: 071 583 1395

Corporate Estate Agents' Ombudsman
PO Box 1114
Salisbury SP1 1YO
Tel: 0722 333306

The Insurance Ombudsman Bureau
City Gate One
135 Park Street
London SE1 9EA
Tel: 071 928 7600

Investment Managers' Regulatory Organisation (IMRO)
Broadwalk House
5 Appold Street
London EC2A 2LL
Tel: 071 628 6022

The Investment Ombudsman
6 Fredrick's Place
London EC2R 8BT
Tel: 071 796 3065

Pensions Ombudsman
11 Belgrave Road
London SW1V 1RB
Tel: 071 834 9144

5.7 The media

If you are upset by something shown on television or in the press or
covered on radio, or feel that you personally have been misquoted or
wrongly represented, you can complain directly to the organisation
involved and/or to the regulatory bodies.

For the press, the Press Complaints Commission is the current
official watchdog. Initially, they operate a telephone helpline which
can give you the name and address of the relevant editor so you can
complain directly. You can call this on 071 353 3732. Beyond this, the
PCC upholds a code of practice which penalises inaccuracy and intru-
siveness. Complaints should be in writing to:

The Press Complaints Commission
1 Salisbury Square
London EC4Y 3AE
Fax: 071 353 8355

The newspaper industry with the PCC in January 1994 appointed an
ombudsman, Professor Robert Pinker, to deal with complaints against
newspapers.

For radio and television, you should first complain to the programme's
producer. Further to this you may also address complaints to the
appropriate senior manager or directly to:

The Director-General
BBC Broadcasting House
London W1A 4AA
Tel: 071 580 4468

Complaints should be sent to the Programme Controller in the case of a commercial station. Beyond this, you may contact:

The Broadcasting Complaints Commission
PO Box 333
London SW1W OBQ
Tel: 071 630 1966

The Broadcasting Standards Council
5–8 The Sanctuary
London SW1P 3JS
Tel: 071 233 0544

The Broadcasting Complaints Commission (BCC) and the Broadcasting Standards Council (BSC) both deal with complaints against BBC1 and 2, Channel 3 and 4 and the radio stations. The BCC is a statutory body set up by Parliament in 1981. Its aim is to regulate the media by making decisions on complaints made by members of the public. Allegations of unfair treatment and invasions of privacy by radio and television programmes may be made to the BCC. It has legal powers to demand transcripts and explanations from broadcasters and to order its verdicts to be published by the offending station in such a way as to rectify the mistake.

The BSC was established in 1988 as a watchdog to monitor the levels of sex and violence on television. The BSC draws up codes for broadcasters and deals with complaints from listeners and viewers. For independent TV the umbrella body is:

The Independent Television Commission
33 Foley Street
London W1P 7LB
Tel: 071 255 3000

As from 1993, the ITC deals with matters of complaint against the commercial television companies, i.e. Channel 3 and 4, cable and satellite. It punishes the commercial companies that infringe the more detailed codes issued by the BSC or are regularly subject to complaints upheld by the BCC. It can impose heavy fines or revoke licences in serious cases or ensure that an apology is broadcast.

If your complaint is directed at the content or tone of an advertisement in any medium, you should complain to:

The Advertising Standards Agency
Brook House
2–16 Torrington Place
London WC1E 7HN
Tel: 071 580 5555

If you feel that you have been personally defamed by the media, you may wish to bring a civil action for defamation. You should again seek legal advice before acting although legal aid is only available for advice and not for representation. Starting such an action cannot occur simultaneously with the complaints procedures described above.

5.8 Public utilities

Since the privatisation of the gas, electricity, water and telephone companies, the government has created watchdog bodies for each industry. If a complaint to the company itself at a local or regional level (addresses will be in the phone book) does not lead to a solution, you should complain to the regulator. Such complaints may be about standards of service or matters relating to billing. Below are the relevant general addresses. If a local office exists, it will be listed in the phone book.

Telecommunications

OFTEL
Export House
50 Ludgate Hill
London EC4M 7JJ
Tel: 071 822 1650

The Secretary
Welsh Advisory Committee on Telecommunications
First Floor Caradog House
St Andrew's Place
Cardiff CF1 3BE
Tel: 0222 374028

The Secretary
Scottish Advisory Committee on Telecommunications
43 Jeffery Street
Edinburgh EH1 1DN
Tel: 031 244 5576

The Secretary
Northern Ireland ACT
Chamber of Commerce and Industry
22 Great Victoria Street
Belfast BT2 7PU
Tel: 0232 244113

The Secretariat
Independent Committee for the Supervision of Standards of
Telephone Information Services (ICSTIS)
Third Floor Kingsbourne House
229–231 High Holborn
London WC1V 7DA
Tel: 071 837 4483

Electricity
OFFER – the regional office will be listed in the phone book or available
on request from the electricity company.

Water

OFWAT
Centre City Tower
7 Hill Street
Birmingham B5 4UA
Tel: 021 625 1300

River and Canal complaints to The National Rivers' Authority (see phone
book for local office) or:

Rivers House
Waterside Drive
Aztec West
Almondsley
Bristol BS12 4UD
Tel: 0225 444066

Gas
You should complain to your local office of the Gas Consumers'
Council, the address of which will be in the phone book or available
from the local gas company office. The national office of the council
is at:

Abford House
15 Wilton Road
London SW1V 1LT
Tel: 071 931 9151

You can also complain to the regulator whose national office is at:

OFGAS
Sixth Floor Stockley House
130 Wilton Road
London SW1V 1LQ
Tel: 071 828 0898

Complaints about the Post Office

For complaints about counter service, look under Post Office Counters Ltd in your phone book. For complaints about the letters service, look under Royal Mail in your phone book. This will include a freepost address. For complaints about the parcels service, look under Parcelforce in your phone book.

5.9 Transport and travel agencies

Complaints about public transport should be made first at a local level and then to the appropriate body set up to deal with complaints.

British Rail

You should complain first to the station manager and if this does not work to the regional manager. You now have set rights to compensation under the Passengers' Charter, a copy of which must be available on request at any staffed station. Beyond this, contact your regional Transport Users' Consultative Committee (see your phone book for the address).

If, as seems likely, privatisation strikes here too, your address to complain to will depend on location and the area of the service about which you wish to complain.

Buses

After deregulation, you must complain to your local Passenger Transport Executive. The address to contact will be in the phone book. If your complaint is that negligence by a transport company caused you to be injured, the appropriate course of action might be to sue in the civil courts. You should take advice.

Complaints against travel agents

The travel business has several regulatory bodies to whom you can complain if your dealings with the travel company have not reached a satisfactory conclusion. This only applies if the company is a member of the organisation – all good travel agents are, so you should check for membership before booking. If you then have to make a complaint, contact the appropriate organisation at the address below:

The Association of British Travel Agents (ABTA)
55–57 Newman Street
London W1P 4AH
Tel: 071 637 2444

The International Association of Travel Agents (IATA)
Sceptre House
75–81 Staines Road
Hounslow
Middlesex TW3 3HW
Tel: 081 569 5230

The National Association of Independent Travel Agents (NAITA)
46 Oxford Street
London W1N 9FJ
Tel: 071 323 3408

5.10 Miscellaneous complaints

Complaints about many consumer issues should be taken to the appropriate section of your local authority, or county council such as
environmental health and trading standards. They may also be able
to advise on housing complaints against private landlords, but specialist
advisers in this field exist at Citizens' Advice Bureaux, law centres and
such organisations.

5.11 Compensation for the victims of crime

If you are the victim of a criminal act, there are three ways in which
you could obtain compensation from the offender:

* A compensation order made by the court as part of a guilty verdict.
  This is not an award you can apply for, and it is important that
  the prosecution at the trial knows as much information as possible
  which might persuade the judge to make such an order.
* A civil action suing for damages. Seek advice from a solicitor or a
  Citizens' Advice Bureau before attempting this.
* An application to the Criminal Injuries Compensation Scheme
  which exists by law to award compensation to those injured by
  crimes of violence. You may apply for an award even if the
  offender has not been arrested, as long as you have not been
  awarded any compensation by either of the first two methods above.

Information on the latter scheme is available from:

The Criminal Injuries Compensation Board
Blythswood House
22 West Regent Street
Glasgow G2 4SW
Tel: 041 221 0945

The scheme will not pay compensation assessed at under a certain amount (about £1,000) and will not accept claims made if the offence has not previously been promptly reported to the police or if any information is held back from them. Claims made later than three years after the event are also inadmissible. The Board can take other factors into account in deciding whether to award and how much to award, including whether or not they consider the injuries to be your fault. Unfortunately, they can also refuse or reduce the compensation if you have a criminal record or if you 'associate with criminals'. Different rules also apply to situations where the victim making the claim is in the same family as the offender.

If your claim arises from a road traffic offence, unless it was a deliberate attempt to run you over, you should claim from the offender's insurance company. If the offender is uninsured, payments can be made by the Motor Insurers' Bureau, an organisation funded by the insurance companies. Their address is:

Motor Insurers' Bureau
City Gate One
135 Park Street
London SE1 9EA
Tel: 071 928 7600

Victims may also receive advice and counselling from Victim Support, a national charity which is in contact with the police and will contact those it feels it can offer assistance to. You can contact the organisation through the local police's community involvement unit or phone Victim Support directly at their local address which will be in the phone book.

Other organisations exist to assist victims of crimes such as rape and they can be found in the phone book or by asking the police.

5.12 Complaints and European law

European law is increasingly affecting UK law and in addition to opening up new courts to complain to, it has already brought in grounds for complaint. There are two major European Courts each of which is based on a different organisation. The first is the European Court of Justice which is part of the European Union (formerly the 'EEC' currently comprising twelve countries). It exists to rule on questions of European Community law put to it by national courts, and also to hear cases between member states and against Community institutions. If you feel that you have such a case, you should seek expert legal advice as the law is often complex.

The European Commission and Court of Human Rights

The second system is based on the Council of Europe (composed of nearly thirty countries). The United Kingdom is bound by many international treaties which oblige it to respect human rights. One of the most important of these is the European Convention for the Protection of Human Rights and Fundamental Freedoms (ECHR). This treaty offers the possibility of redress where a person's civil liberties have been infringed and no remedy can be obtained from the British courts or government.

The Convention was drawn up under the auspices of the Council of Europe, an organisation of West European countries which is based in Strasbourg, France, and is quite separate from the European Community. The Convention was adopted on 4 November 1950 and came into force on 3 September 1953. Its provisions guarantee most, but not all, civil liberties, including the right to life, freedom from torture, freedom from arbitrary arrest, the right to a fair trial, the right to privacy, freedom of religion, freedom of expression, and freedom of assembly and association. The rights guaranteed by the Convention have been expanded on several occasions by the adoption of 'protocols' (i.e. additions) but the UK has yet to accept the fourth, sixth and seventh protocols (see p. 124). The Convention's principal shortcoming remains, however, the absence of any general prohibition of discrimination; at present it only prohibits discrimination affecting the enjoyment of the rights and freedoms set out in the Convention and protocols. The text of those rights and freedom is set out on p. 118.

The enforcement of the Convention is entrusted to the European Commission and Court of Human Rights, together with the Committee of Ministers of the Council of Europe. The Commission and Court each consists of one person nominated by each of the countries belonging to the Council of Europe. These persons act in their individual capacity and cannot be government officials. The Committee of Ministers consists of the foreign ministers (or their deputies) of the member states of the Council of Europe.

There are two ways in which alleged breaches of the Convention's provisions by the UK can be brought to the attention of these bodies. The first is through a complaint made by one of the other countries which are also bound by the Convention. It was as a result of a complaint by the Republic of Ireland that certain interrogation practices used in Northern Ireland were held to amount to inhuman and degrading treatment. Countries are, however, reluctant to bring cases against each other and will only do so in the most extreme cases or where their own interests are affected.

The second method of complaint – by the person whose rights have been infringed – is used much more frequently and with greater effect. Any person, non-governmental organisation or group of individuals (whatever their nationality) can complain about a country bound by the Convention where it has declared that it is prepared to accept such complaints. The UK has allowed complaints by individuals since 1966. The complaints can be about the law, acts of governmental bodies or the decisions of courts. They will be dealt with first by the European Commission of Human Rights and may go later to either the European Court of Human Rights or the Committee of Ministers.

During 'war or other public emergency threatening life of the nation', governments can derogate from their obligations under the Convention. This enables them to restrict the exercise of some of the rights and freedoms, but only insofar as what is necessary to deal with the emergency. The UK has, in the past, used this provision in Northern Ireland and one is in force now which allows the police to detain people under the terrorism laws for up to seven days. No derogation is ever possible in respect of the right to life (other than in respect of deaths resulting from lawful acts of war), freedom from torture and slavery and the prohibition of retrospective penalties.

Using the Convention

The procedure for making a complaint where you believe that any of your rights under the Convention have been violated is relatively straightforward. It is not, however, a speedy process (a case can take five years to be resolved) and the delays are undoubtedly exacerbated by the many complaints that do not fall within the ambit of the Convention or do not comply with its requirements which are rejected at the early stages. It is important, therefore, to check whether the subject matter of your complaint has previously been considered and to ensure that you have complied with the admissibility requirements set out below. It is not essential to be represented by a lawyer but it is better to get advice from a solicitor experienced in this type of case or Liberty. Although the UK's legal aid scheme does not cover complaints under the Convention, limited legal aid may be provided by the Commission (but only towards the end of the examination of a complaint's admissibility and not before it is lodged) and legal costs are recoverable where a complaint is successful. There are no fees payable to the Commission and Court and there is no liability to meet the costs of the government in any event.

Making a complaint

A complaint does not have to be started on a special application form although you will eventually be asked to complete one. Complaints should be directed to:

> Secretary of the Commission of Human Rights
> Council of Europe
> F–67075 Strasbourg Cedex
> France
> Tel: 010 33 88 41 2000 (for urgent cases only – see p. 115)

The following information will be required and should, therefore, be provided in your letter to the Commission:

- Your name, age, address and occupation.
- The name, address and occupation of anyone acting as your representative (for example, your lawyer).
- The country against whom you are complaining (for example, the UK).
- A clear and concise statement of the facts you are complaining about – it is important to describe the events in the order in which they occurred, the way in which the legislation or decision complained about has affected you and to give exact dates.
- The provisions of the Convention on which you are relying and an explanation as to why you consider that the facts involve a violation of them.
- The object of your application (for example, the repeal or amendment of certain legislation or the reversal of a decision and compensation).
- The details of all the remedies (including any appeal) which you have pursued within the country concerned and, where appropriate, an explanation as to why you have not pursued any available remedies.
- The judgements, decisions and any other documents relating to your complaint.

Liberty may also be able to assist with cases taken under the Convention.

Admissibility

The Commission then has to decide whether your application is admissible (i.e. falls within its terms of reference). The application will be referred to one of the Commission's members – the *rapporteur* – who may ask for further information from you or the government before reporting on the case to the Commission. The Commission itself may then decide to ask for further information or invite the government to make observations on whether or not the application should be admitted. You will be sent a copy of the government's observations and can in turn make observations yourself. The Commission may hold an oral hearing in Strasbourg at this stage.

All the proceedings before the Commission are confidential and you should be careful not divulge information about them to the press or anyone else. Although divulging information will very rarely lead to the application being dismissed, it can happen and you should take expert advice. The following factors will lead to a ruling that your complaint is inadmissible:

- It was anonymous.
- It was not made within six months of the final decision relating to the alleged violation of the Convention.
- It concerned a matter already dealt with by the Commission or some other international process.
- It was incompatible with the Convention, i.e. it concerned a country, period in time or territory to which the Convention does not apply, or a right not guaranteed by it.
- The domestic remedies were not exhausted (i.e. any judicial or administrative procedure within the country concerned which could have resolved your complaint – it has to be a procedure that can lead to a binding decision and so would not include any discretionary or political remedies, such as a complaint to the ombudsman).
- It was 'manifestly ill-founded' (i.e. the facts did not disclose any *prima facie* violation of the Convention).
- It was an abuse of the right of petition (for example, the primary aim was political, the Commission was misled, the confidentiality of the proceedings was disregarded, insulting or threatening language was used before the Commission or the government).

The overwhelming majority (95 per cent) of applications are found to be inadmissible by the Commission. This underlines the importance of a thorough evaluation of your case before you write to the Commission. There is no appeal against its decision. Moreover, a case that has been admitted can, on further examination by the Commission (or even the Court), be rejected as inadmissible.

It is likely to take at least a year before the Commission decides on the admissibility of a case but it will give priority to urgent cases (i.e. those where a person's life or wellbeing is immediately threatened by the action being complained about). In such cases, the Commission should be contacted by telephone, telex or fax. The Commission may then ask the government to refrain from acting until the application has been considered. Although not bound to do so, the government is likely to accede to such a request.

The later stages

If the Commission decides that your application is admissible, it will then examine the substance of your case. The Commission may hold a hearing in Strasbourg (or may have considered the merits at the same time as it considered the issue of admissibility). When it has reached a provisional opinion on the merits of the case – which will not be published – the Commission will try to reach a 'friendly settlement' (i.e. a negotiated agreement) between you and the government.

The settlement may simply involve the payment of compensation or the making of a decision (for example, the revocation of a deportation order) but it may also require a change in the law or administrative practice which gave rise to the complaint. The Commission has to be satisfied that any settlement takes account of the general interest (for example, where a complaint arose from the application of the rules restricting access by prisoners to legal advice, the settlement would require the reform of those rules as well as the payment of compensation). If a friendly settlement is agreed and approved, the Commission will prepare a brief statement of the facts and the solution reached. This is all that will be published about the case.

Where no friendly settlement is achieved, the Commission draws up a report on the case which will state whether in its opinion there has been a breach of the Convention. The report will include any dissenting views from individual members of the Commission. There is then a period of three months during which the decision whether to refer the case to the Court of Human Rights must be made. Such a decision can only be taken where the respondent state has accepted the jurisdiction of the Court (the UK has) and can only be made by the Commission or any government of a Council of Europe country involved (or whose citizen is involved) in the case; the individual applicant has no part to play in this decision (although a newly designed procedure that does give a right will be brought in as soon as it has been agreed by the governments). Cases tend to be referred to the Court where they involve problems of interpretation or where the commission is divided. A referral is unlikely where the Court has already resolved the issue in an earlier case brought against the same government.

The proceedings before the Court amount to a fresh examination of your complaint. It is likely to involve written and oral submissions by the Commission, the government and yourself. You may be represented by a lawyer for this purpose. It is also possible for the Court to allow any person, organisation or government to make submissions relevant to the case (Liberty has put in submissions in the past – particularly on issues connected with long detention periods in terrorist cases). The case will be heard either by a chamber of seven judges or (where it raises serious questions affecting the interpretation of the Convention) the full Court. The Court will issue a judgement stating whether or not the Convention has been violated. Where it considers that there was a violation, it may also (in the same or a later judgement) award you 'just satisfaction' (i.e. damages and reimbursement of your legal costs). The Court's judgement is binding on the government but it does not have any legal effect within the UK (i.e. it will not automatically overturn the legislation or decision against which you have been complaining). The government must, therefore, take the necessary steps to implement the judgement and the Committee of Ministers is responsible for ensuring that this is done.

If the case is not referred to the Court, it will be dealt with by the Committee of Ministers. It is unlikely to require any submissions (written or oral) in addition to those already made to the Commission. The Committee can only decide that there has been a violation of the Convention by a vote of at least two-thirds of its members; in a few instances this has not been possible and the case must be left unresolved. Where it decides that the Convention has been breached, the Committee can also decide what measures the government concerned should take and may ask the Commission to make proposals regarding an award of 'just satisfaction'.

The future

Agreement was reached in principle in October 1993 for the reorganisation of the Commission and Court. The proposals are that the current part-time Commission and Court will cease to exist and a new permanent Court will take their place. The Committee of Ministers will no longer decide on the merits of cases but will continue to supervise the compliance of states with the Court's judgements.

Individuals will now have direct access to the Court, which in the vast majority of cases will sit in chambers of seven judges. Inadmissible and unmeritorious applications will be sifted out by committees of three judges. The friendly settlement option will be dealt with by the Court. In exceptional cases the chamber will relinguish jurisdiction in favour of a Grand Chamber which will decide the more important issues. All interstate cases will be heard by the plenary Court.

The text of the new draft protocol to introduce the changes is to be ready by May 1994. Inevitably ratification by states may add further delays and there will obviously have to be a transitional period before the new system is fully operational.

The value of the Convention

It is often assumed by people whose civil liberties are being infringed that 'going to Strasbourg' will provide a ready solution. In fact there are many hurdles to be overcome before a case can even be considered, the procedure is slow (it may take five years from application to judgement and a further two before its implementation by the government), and the Convention does not provide a guarantee against all infringements of civil liberties. Nonetheless, cases brought against the UK under the Convention have led to the setting aside of repressive measures and have secured important reforms in the following areas: freedom of expression, immigration, inhuman and degrading treatment, mental patients' rights, parental rights, prisoners' rights, privacy, workers' rights and the rights of gay men. It is clear that without the Convention (and the right of individuals to complain) the UK would lack a valuable safeguard for its civil liberties.

The rights and freedoms protected by the Convention are set out in Articles 2 to 18 and Protocols 1, 4, 6, and 7 (the last three are not yet binding on the UK). These articles and protocols concern the procedure for enforcing the Convention and are not included (the full text of the Convention and Protocols, together with the rules of procedure of the Commission, Court and Committee of Ministers can be found in *Council of Europe – Collected Texts* (1987)):

Article 2

1. Everyone's right to life shall be protected by law. No one shall be deprived of his life intentionally save in the execution of a sentence of a court following his conviction of a crime for which this penalty is provided by law.

2. Deprivation of life shall not be regarded as inflicted in contravention of this article when it results from the use of force which is no more than absolutely necessary:
    (a) in defence of any person from unlawful violence;
    (b) in order to effect a lawful arrest or to prevent the escape of a person lawfully detained;
    (c) in action lawfully taken for the purpose of quelling a riot or insurrection.

Article 3

No one shall be subjected to torture or to inhuman or degrading treatment or punishment.

Article 4

1. No one shall be held in slavery or servitude.
2. No one shall be required to perform forced or compulsory labour.

3. For the purpose of this article the term 'forced or compulsory labour' shall not include:
    (a) any work required to be done in the ordinary course of detention imposed according to the provisions of Article 5 of this Convention or during conditional release from such detention;
    (b) any service of a military character, or, in the case of conscientious objectors in countries where they are recognised, service exacted instead of compulsory military service;
    (c) any service exacted in case of an emergency or calamity threatening the life or wellbeing of the community;
    (d) any work or service which forms part of normal civic obligations.

Article 5

1. Everyone has the right to liberty and security of person. No one shall be deprived of his liberty save in the following cases and in accordance with a procedure prescribed by law:
    (a) the lawful detention of a person after conviction by a competent court;
    (b) the lawful arrest or detention of a person for non-compliance with the lawful order of a court or in order to secure the fulfilment of any obligation prescribed by law;
    (c) the lawful arrest or detention of a person effected for the purpose of bringing him before the competent legal authority on reasonable suspicion of having committed an offence or when it is reasonably considered necessary to prevent his committing an offence or fleeing after having done so;
    (d) the detention of a minor by lawful order for the purpose of educational supervision or his lawful detention for the purpose of bringing him before the competent legal authority;
    (e) the lawful detention of persons for the prevention of the spreading of infectious diseases, or persons of unsound mind, alcoholics or drug addicts or vagrants;
    (f) the lawful arrest or detention of a person to prevent his effecting an unauthorised entry into the country or of a person against whom action is being taken with a view to deportation or extradition.

2. Everyone who is arrested shall be informed promptly, in a language which he understands, of the reasons for his arrest and of any charge against him.

3. Everyone arrested or detained in accordance with the provisions of paragraph 1(c) of this article shall be brought promptly before

a judge or other officer authorised by law to exercise judicial power and shall be entitled to trial within a reasonable time or to release pending trial. Release may be conditioned by guarantees to appear for trial.

4. Everyone who is deprived of his liberty by arrest or detention shall be entitled to take proceedings by which the lawfulness of his detention shall be decided speedily by a court and his release ordered if the detention is not lawful.

5. Everyone who has been the victim of arrest or detention in contravention of the provisions of this article shall have an enforceable right to compensation.

Article 6

1. In the determination of his civil rights and obligations or of any criminal charge against him, everyone is entitled to a fair and public hearing within a reasonable time by an independent and impartial tribunal established by law. Judgment shall be pronounced publicly but the press and public may be excluded from all or part of the trial in the interests of morals, public order or national security in a democratic society, where the interests of juveniles or the protection of the private life of the parties so require, or to the extent strictly necessary in the opinion of the court in special circumstances where publicity would prejudice the interests of justice.

2. Everyone charged with a criminal offence shall be presumed innocent until proved guilty according to law.

3. Everyone charged with a criminal offence has the following minimum rights:
    (a) to be informed promptly, in a language which he understands and in detail, of the nature and cause of the accusation against him;
    (b) to have adequate time and facilities for the preparation of his defence;
    (c) to defend himself in person or through legal assistance of his own choosing or, if he has not sufficient means to pay for legal assistance, to be given it free when the interests of justice so require;
    (d) to examine or have examined witnesses against him and to obtain the attendance and examination of witnesses on his behalf under the same conditions as witnesses against him;
    (e) to have the free assistance of an interpreter if he cannot understand or speak the language used in court.

Article 7

1. No one shall be held guilty of any criminal offence on account of any act or omission which did not constitute a criminal offence under national or international law at the time when it was committed. Nor shall a heavier penalty be imposed than the one that was applicable at the time the criminal offence was committed.

2. This article shall not prejudice the trial and punishment of any person for any act or omission which, at the time it was committed, was criminal according to the general principles of law recognised by civilised nations.

Article 8

1. Everyone has the right to respect for his private and family life, his home and his correspondence.

2. There shall be no interference by a public authority with the exercise of this right except such as is in accordance with the law and is necessary in a democratic society in the interests of national security, public safety or the economic wellbeing of the country, for the prevention of disorder or crime, for the protection of health or morals, or for the protection of the rights and freedoms of others.

Article 9

1. Everyone has the right to freedom of thought, conscience and religion; this right includes freedom to change his religion or belief, and freedom, either alone or in community with others and in public or private, to manifest his religion or belief in worship, teaching, practice and observance.

2. Freedom to manifest one's religion or beliefs shall be subject only to such limitations as are prescribed by law and are necessary in a democratic society in the interests of public safety, for the protection of public order, health or morals, or for the protection of the rights and freedoms of others.

Article 10

1. Everyone has the right to freedom of expression. This right shall include freedom to hold opinions and to receive and impart information and ideas without interference by public authority and regardless of frontiers. This article shall not

prevent states from requiring the licence of broadcasting, television or cinema enterprises.

2.   The exercise of these freedoms, since it carries with it duties and responsibilities, may be subject to such formalities, conditions, restrictions or penalties as are prescribed by law and are necessary in a democratic society, in the interests of national security, territorial integrity or public safety, for the prevention of disorder or crime, for the protection of health or morals, for the protection of the reputation or rights of others, for preventing the disclosure of information received in confidence, or for maintaining the authority and impartiality of the judiciary.

Article 11

1.   Everyone has the right to freedom of peaceful assembly and to freedom of association with others, including the right to form and to join trade unions for the protection of his interests.

2.   No restrictions shall be placed on the exercise of these rights other than such as are prescribed by law and are necessary in a democratic society in the interests of national security or public safety, for the prevention of disorder or crime, for the protection of health or morals or for the protection of the rights and freedoms of others. This article shall not prevent the imposition of lawful restrictions on the exercise of these rights by members of the armed forces, of the police or of the administration of the state.

Article 12
Men and women of marriageable age have the right to marry and to found a family, according to the national laws governing the exercise of this right.

Article 13
Everyone whose rights and freedoms as set forth in this Convention are violated shall have an effective remedy before a national authority notwithstanding that the violation has been committed by persons acting in an official capacity.

Article 14
The enjoyment of the rights and freedoms set forth in this Convention shall be secured without discrimination on any ground such as sex, race, colour, language, religion, political or other opinion, national or social origin, association with a national minority, property, birth or other status.

Article 15

1. In time of war or other public emergency threatening the life of the nation, any High Contracting Party may take measures derogating from its obligations under this Convention to the extent strictly required by the exigencies of the situation, provided that such measures are not inconsistent with its other obligations under international law.

2. No derogation from Article 2, except in respect of deaths resulting from lawful acts of war, or from Articles 3, 4 (paragraph 1) and 7 shall be made under this provision.

3. Any High Contracting Party availing itself of this right to derogation shall keep the Secretary General of the Council of Europe fully informed of the measures which it has taken and the reasons therefor. It shall also inform the Secretary General of the Council of Europe when such measures have ceased to operate and the provisions of the Convention are again being fully executed.

Article 16
Nothing in Articles 10, 11 and 14 shall be regarded as preventing the High Contracting Parties from imposing restrictions on the political activity of aliens.

Article 17
Nothing in this Convention may be interpreted as implying for any state, group or person any right to engage in any activity or perform any act aimed at the destruction of any of the rights and freedoms as set forth herein or at their limitation to a greater extent than is provided for in the Convention.

Article 18
The restrictions permitted under this Convention to the said rights and freedoms shall not be applied for any purpose other than those for which they have been prescribed.

Protocol 1

Article 1
Every natural or legal person is entitled to the peaceful enjoyment of his possessions. No one shall be deprived of his possessions except in the public interest and subject to the conditions provided for by law and by the general principles of international law.

The preceding provisions shall not, however, in any way impair the right of a state to enforce such laws as it deems necessary to control the use of property in accordance with the general interest or to secure the payment of taxes or other contributions or penalties.

Article 2
No person shall be denied the right to education. In the exercise of any functions which it assumes in relation to education and to teaching, the state shall respect the right of parents to ensure such education and teaching in conformity with their own religious and philosophical convictions.

Article 3
The High Contracting Parties undertake to hold free elections at reasonable intervals by secret ballot, under conditions which will ensure the free expression of the opinion of the people in the choice of the legislature.

Protocol 4

Article 1
No one shall be deprived of his liberty merely on the ground of inability of fulfil a contractual obligation.

Article 2

1. Everyone lawfully within the territory of a state shall, within that territory, have the right to liberty of movement and freedom to choose his residence.

2. Everyone shall be free to leave any country, including his own.

3. No restrictions shall be placed on the exercise of these rights other than such as are in accordance with law and are necessary in a democratic society in the interests of national security or public safety, for the maintenance of public order, for the prevention of crime, for the protection of health or morals, or for the protection of the rights and freedoms of others.

4. The rights set forth in paragraph 1 may also be subject, in particular areas, to restrictions imposed in accordance with law and justified by the public interest in a democratic society.

Article 3

1. No one shall be expelled, by means either of an individual or a collective measure, from the territory of the state of which he is a national.

2. No one shall be deprived of the right to enter the territory of the state of which he is a national.

Article 4
Collective expulsions of aliens is prohibited.

Protocol 6

Article 1
The death penalty shall be abolished. No one shall be condemned to such a penalty or executed.

Article 2
A state may make provision in its law for the death penalty in respect of acts committed in time of war or of imminent threat of war; such penalty shall be applied only in the instances laid down in the law and in accordance with its provisions. The state shall communicate to the Secretary General of the Council of Europe the relevant provisions of that law.

Article 3
No derogation from the provisions of this Protocol shall be made under Article 15 of the Convention.

Protocol 7

Article 1

1. An alien lawfully resident in the territory of a state shall not be expelled therefrom except in pursuance of a decision reached in accordance with law and shall be allowed:
    (a) to submit reasons against his expulsion;
    (b) to have his case reviewed; *and*
    (c) to be represented for these purposes before the competent authority or a person or persons designated by that authority.
2. An alien may be expelled before the exercise of his rights under paragraph 1(a), (b) and (c) of this Article, when such expulsion is necessary in the interests of public order or is grounded on reasons of national security.

Article 2

1. Everyone convicted of a criminal offence by a tribunal shall have the right to have conviction or sentence reviewed by a higher tribunal. The exercise of this right, including the grounds on which it may be exercised shall be governed by law.

2. This right may be subject to exceptions in regard to offences of a minor character, as prescribed by law, or in cases in which the person concerned was tried in the first instance by the highest tribunal or was convicted following an appeal against acquittal.

Article 3
When a person has by a final decision been convicted of a criminal offence and when subsequently his conviction has been reversed, or he has been pardoned, on the ground that a new or newly discovered fact shows conclusively that there has been a miscarriage of justice, the person who has suffered punishment as a result of such conviction shall be compensated according to the law or the practice of the state concerned, unless it is provided that the non-disclosure of the unknown fact in time is wholly or partly attributable to him.

Article 4

1. No one shall be liable to be tried or punished again in criminal proceedings under the jurisdiction of the same state for an offence for which he has already been finally acquitted or convicted in accordance with the law and penal procedure of that state.
2. The provisions of the preceding paragraph shall not prevent the re-opening of the case in accordance with the law and penal procedure of the state concerned, if there is evidence of new or newly discovered facts, or if there has been a fundamental defect in the previous proceedings, which could affect the outcome of the case.
3. No derogation from this Article shall be made under Article 15 of the Convention.

Article 5

1. Spouses shall enjoy equality of rights and responsibilities of a private law character between them, and in their relations with their children, as to marriage, during marriage and in the event of its dissolution. This Article shall not prevent states from taking such measures as are necessary in the interests of the children.

5.13 Other international treaties

Other international treaties also impose minimum standards. For instance in the Council of Europe there is one on the prevention of torture, inhuman and degrading treatment and another on data protection. In the United Nations (UN) there are others on the rights of the child, discrimination, torture and refugees. These treaties do not usually allow the right of individual complaint but impose a duty on governments to report on its human rights record. In some cases they can involve spot checks.

There is also the International Covenant on Civil and Political Rights which is modelled on the ECHR but is more wide ranging. The UK government has to report on its record under this treaty every five years and the United Nations Human Rights Committee will be examining the UK's record again in 1995. Unfortunately the Government has refused to allow the right of individual petition, to allow us to complain directly to this Committee, about breaches of the Covenant.

5.14 The Citizen's Charter

Areas covered by the Citizen's Charter have now set standards which organisations must meet. You can check whether you have a valid complaint by ringing the Citizen's Charter telephone line if there is one in your area.

5.15 Further information

Useful organisations
It is vital to get advice on complaints which have legal implications. If you cannot find advice locally, the following organisations will be able to put you in contact with their nearest affiliate:

Federation of Independent Advice Centres
13 Stockwell Road
London SW9 9AV
Tel: 071 274 1839

The Law Centres' Federation
18–19 Warren Street
London W1P 5DB
Tel: 071 387 8570

National Association of Citizens' Advice Bureaux
115–123 Pentonville Road
London N1 9LZ
Tel: 071 833 2181

Bibliography
The following books may provide useful information about the European Convention on Human Rights.
Council of Europe, *Short Guide to the European Convention on Human Rights*, 1991.
J.E.S Fawcett, *The Application of the European Convention on Human Rights*, second edition, OUP, 1987.
P. Van Dyk and G.J.H. Van Hoof, *Theory and Practice of the European Convention on Human Rights*, Kluger, 1990.

6

The rights of suspects

This chapter deals with the rights of suspects up to the point when they are either released by the police without charge, bailed by the police, or brought before a court. Other people, like customs and excise (see p. 67), have similar powers but the differences cannot be detailed here. In particular this chapter deals with:

- Police powers to stop and search persons and vehicles (without arrest).
- Police powers to search premises.
- Police powers of arrest.
- Police detention.
- The rights of suspects in the police station.
- The right to make notes.
- Special powers under the Prevention of Terrorism Act.
- Further information.

This chapter uses expressions like 'reasonable grounds' or reasonable suspicion'. The use of the word 'reasonable' implies that what is or is not reasonable is a decision for the courts. The fact that the police believe that they have reasonable suspicion, for instance, is not sufficient. It implies, therefore, an objective test and not a subjective one. Unfortunately, it is difficult to define it more accurately.

There are a number of principles that apply to the rights of suspects:

- You are not under a duty to help the police with their enquiries or to make a statement to them; further, this lack of cooperation cannot be held against you at the trial.
- You can remain silent, not answer questions and it cannot be held against you.
- There are other protections that apply if you are prosecuted.

Most of the police powers and corresponding rights for suspects are to be found in the Police and Criminal Evidence Act 1984 – known as PACE – and in the Codes of Conduct issued by the Home Secretary under PACE and approved by Parliament. PACE was the product of years

of discussion about police powers. It was based on the recommendations in the Report of the Royal Commission on Criminal Procedure
(published in 1981 – HMSO Cmnd 8092), a body which had been
directed in its terms of reference to strike a balance between the
interests of the community on the one hand and the rights and liberties
of the individual suspect on the other. There has now been another
Royal Commission set up in March 1991 – this time on Criminal
Justice – and some its recommendations along with other ideas
suggested by the government, which will change defendants' rights,
are likely to be implemented in 1994.

If any of these police powers are abused:

- The abuse may make evidence obtained inadmissible in court.
- You may make an official police complaint (see p. 94).
- You may be able to sue the police (see p. 99).

6.1 Police powers to stop and search persons and vehicles (without arrest)

Part 1 of the Police and Criminal Evidence Act (PACE) empowers any
constable acting with reasonable grounds for suspicion to stop, detain
and search you or your vehicle, or anything in or on your vehicle for
certain items, which may be seized. The provisions of the Act are sup-
plemented by a Code of Practice on stop and search. The contents of
the Code must be observed by the police, although the remedy for failure
to observe it is usually to make a police complaint (or if prosecuted to
raise an objection in court) rather than to take legal proceedings
against the police.

PACE also provides some safeguards for other police powers of
search. These relate, for instance, to drugs (on reasonable suspicion of
being in unlawful possession), evidence of liability to arrest under the
Prevention of Terrorism legislation, suspected possession of firearms,
animal conservation and evidence of offences under the Sporting
Events (Control of Alcohol etc) Act 1985. For search powers on arrest,
see p. 138.

Stolen or prohibited articles or knives

The power to stop and search in PACE enables a constable to search
for stolen or 'prohibited articles' or knives (except short-bladed
penknives, see p. 26). PACE defines two categories of prohibited
article:

- An offensive weapon.
- An article made or adapted for use in connection with one of a list of offences including burglary, theft, taking a conveyance without authority (or being carried in one) and obtaining property by deception.

Virtually any article could come within this second definition but there would have to be some evidence of the use of the article or the intention of the person making, adapting or carrying it, otherwise a constable would not have reasonable grounds to search.

Where the search may take place

The PACE power of stop and search may be used by the police in most public and some private places. In law the power is limited to one of the following types of place:

- A place to which, at the time of the proposed stop and search, the public (or any section of the public) has access as a matter of legal right or because there is permission.
- Any place (other than a dwelling) to which people have ready access at the time of the proposed stop and search.

These categories are obviously very wide and can include much private property, including front gardens and car parks. Whether you have ready access might depend on whether a gate or door is locked, or whether a plot of land is fenced.

However, a constable may not search you or your vehicle if you are on land which is used for the purpose of a dwelling, without having reasonable grounds for believing that you do not reside in the dwelling and are not in the place with the express or implied permission of a person who does reside in the dwelling. There is clearly a heavy duty on the constable in such cases, since the reasonable grounds must be justified objectively. These provisions should protect people behaving normally; window cleaners, post and milk deliverers and casual visitors.

Reasonable grounds for suspicion

The power of stop and search under PACE can only be exercised if the constable has reasonable grounds for suspecting that stolen or prohibited articles or knives will be found. The Code of Practice elaborates this requirement. There must be some concrete basis for the officer's belief, related to you personally, which can be considered and evaluated by an objective third person. Mere suspicion based on hunch or instinct might justify observation but cannot justify a search.

Reasonable grounds for suspicion cannot be based on attitudes or prejudices towards certain types of people, such as membership of a group within which offenders of a certain kind are relatively common (for example, young football fans). Nor can it be based on your skin colour, age, hairstyle, mode of dress, or previous convictions.

Stopping and detaining

Any police officer, whether or not in uniform, may search you personally, but usually only a constable in uniform may stop a vehicle. A police officer may detain you or your vehicle for a search, but not in order to find grounds to justify a search. The reasonable grounds must already exist.

The detention may only last for as long as it is reasonably required to permit a search to be carried out at the place of detention or nearby. You cannot be compelled to remain with your vehicle while the vehicle is searched, but you may wish to do so.

Police officers have other powers to stop a vehicle, for example to check whether it is roadworthy or stolen, but not to search it.

Searching

In carrying out a search the police may not force you (but may request you) to remove any clothing in public (even if the street is empty) other than an outer coat, jacket or gloves. A more thorough search, involving the removal for instance of a hat or shoes, or a strip search (but not an intimate search: see below) may take place other than in public, but only at the place of arrest or nearby. Thus it could take place, for example, in a police van. The Code lays down rules for searching in the absence of members of the opposite sex and for minimising any embarrassment.

The power to search a vehicle includes a power to search anything in or on it. If an unattended vehicle is searched, a notice to this effect must be left behind (inside the vehicle if reasonably practicable) stating the police station to which the constable is attached, that any claims for compensation should be made to that police station, and that you are entitled to a copy of the search record if requested within twelve months of the search.

A constable may use reasonable force, if necessary, in the detention and conduct of the search, but force can only be necessary if you are first given the opportunity to cooperate and refuse.

A constable who discovers an article reasonably suspected to be stolen or prohibited may seize it.

It should be noted that the safeguards in PACE and in the Code of Practice do not apply to the routine searching of those entering sports grounds or other premises with their consent or as a condition of entry. Likewise, nothing in PACE or in the Code affects the ability of an officer to search you in the street on a voluntary basis provided that you are capable of understanding to what it is you are consenting. In this case it may be that none of the following safeguards apply.

Information to be given

A constable contemplating a search under any power to search (before or without arrest) must take reasonable steps to bring the following to your attention:

- If the constable is not in uniform, proof that he or she is a constable, which the Code says must be by showing a warrant card.
- The constable's name and police station.
- The object of the proposed search.
- The constable's grounds for proposing to search.
- The availability of a search record (see below) if it is practicable to make one.

The search may not be commenced until the constable gives you such information, and the information must be given even if not requested, although it is unclear how much detail must be given.

Search records

A constable who has carried out a search under any power to search (without or before making an arrest) must make a written record on the spot, or later if impracticable on the spot, unless it is totally impracticable to make a record at all because of the numbers involved or for some other operational reason.

The Code requires the search record to include a note of your ethnic origin. The record must identify the person making it and state the object of the search, the grounds for making it, the date, time and place, whether anything – and if so what – was found, and whether any – and if so what – injury or damage resulted from the search.

You are entitled to get a copy of any record made, on request, within twelve months of the date of the search.

Roadblocks

Police powers to set up roadblocks (referred to in PACE as roadchecks) do not derive from PACE but from other sources: road traffic legislation and case law. If a roadblock is for certain purposes, PACE provides that the police must follow certain procedures.

'Statutory undertakers' – other police forces

'Statutory undertakers' include bodies authorised by statute to carry on a railway, transport, dock or harbour undertaking, the larger of which employ their own police forces (for example, the British Transport Police) whose members have the powers of constables within a geographically limited area. Members of these forces have many of the same powers as members of regular police forces, subject to certain limitations. These are not the same as private security organisations which enjoy no special 'policing' powers.

A constable employed by a statutory undertaker may stop, detain and search any vehicle (but not a person) before it leaves a goods area on the premises of the statutory body. Such stops are carried out routinely and need not be justified by any suspicion nor recorded. There is no statutory limitation on what may be searched for and the Code of Practice does not apply.

6.2 Police powers to search premises

The police have powers to enter and search your premises for many reasons. Some of these powers are set out in the Police and Criminal Evidence Act 1984 (PACE) but the police also have power to enter and search under other statutes, for instance the Theft Act 1968. It should be noted that the police do not always need to have a search warrant, although they must always have a reason for the search. There is a Code of Practice stating how the police should conduct searches. (For what you should do if the police do not follow the Code see p. 129).

Search with your consent
The police may search your premises if you consent. However, the Code of Practice on searching premises provides that before seeking your consent the officer in charge should state the purpose of the proposed search, inform you that you are not obliged to consent and inform you that anything seized may be used in evidence. For the search to be lawful you must consent in writing. If you live in rented accommodation the police should not search the premises solely on the basis of your landlord's consent unless you are unavailable and the matter is urgent.

Search of premises under a magistrate's warrant
Magistrates have the power to issue search warrants under many Acts of Parliament – for example, to search for stolen goods under the Theft Act 1968, Misuse of Drugs Act 1971 and for racially inflammatory material under the Public Order Act 1986. In addition they have a power under the Police and Criminal Evidence Act to issue a warrant authorising the police to enter and search premises for evidence of a serious arrestable offence (see p. 139). They were given this power in order to fill in gaps in the earlier law. For example, magistrates did not have any power to issue a warrant to enable the police to search for a murder weapon.

Magistrates should only issue warrants under this section if there are reasonable grounds for believing that the police will not be able to obtain access to the evidence without a warrant, for example, if consent will not be forthcoming. In addition magistrates should be satisfied that there are reasonable grounds for believing:

- The material is likely to be of substantial value (whether by itself or together with other material) to the investigation of the offence.
- That it is likely to be 'relevant evidence', that is, anything which would be admissible as evidence at a trial.
- That it does not consist of or include items subject to legal privilege, 'excluded material' or 'special procedure material' (see below).

This power clearly applies to premises owned or occupied by someone who is not implicated in the alleged offence.

Material which has special safeguards
PACE gives special protection from search (but not necessarily from seizure) to some types of material felt to be sensitive. These categories are 'excluded material', 'special procedure material' and legally privileged material.

Excluded material
There are three kinds of 'excluded material':

- Personal records – examples of material which should normally be excluded are medical and psychiatric records, records kept by priests, the Samaritans, possibly school and college records, records of advice given by law centres, Citizens' Advice Bureaux and Liberty.
- Human tissue or tissue fluid.
- 'Journalistic' material – i.e. material acquired or created for the purposes of journalism. There is no need for the holder of such material to be a professional journalist.

In order to qualify as 'excluded material' the items must have been held in confidence. This is a concept which can be legally complex.

The police cannot easily obtain a warrant to search for this material. They must follow a set procedure which will normally involve a hearing before a judge who will decide, amongst other things, whether it would be in the public interest to allow the police access to the material. Only the person in possession of the material, who will not necessarily be the suspect, and the police have a right to make representations at the hearing. If the judge considers it appropriate, he or she will make an order compelling production of the material to the police.

If the person in possession fails to produce the material he or she may be in contempt of court (see p. 42) and the judge may be able to issue a warrant to the police to search his or her premises. However, in some circumstances, if the police can convince the judge that the situation is urgent, they may be able to obtain a warrant from the judge without the party in possession of the material knowing.

Special procedure material
There are two categories of special procedure material:

* Material which is not excluded material but is held in confidence by certain persons.
* Journalistic material which is not excluded material, either because it is not held in confidence or does not consist of documents.

Examples of special procedure material are company accounts or stock records held on behalf of a client by a bank, solicitor or accountant. The procedure enabling the police to obtain this material is broadly the same as for 'excluded material' (see above).

Legally privileged material
The definition of items subject to legal privilege is crucial, since these items are exempt from most powers of search. The police have no power at all to seize material which they have reasonable grounds for believing to be legally privileged. There are three categories of legally privileged material:

* Communications to do with giving legal advice.
* Communications to do with legal proceedings.
* Items connected with either of the above communications.

In each category the definition hinges on the term 'professional legal adviser', which clearly includes barristers, solicitors and solicitors' clerks. There is no requirement that the adviser should work for a firm of solicitors and, therefore, the adviser may come from a law or advice centre. Although the advice of an unqualified person will not be privileged unless acting as an agent for a solicitor or barrister, it will in most cases be 'excluded material'. This would not protect it from seizure, however (see below).

Items held with the intention of furthering a criminal purpose are not legally privileged, but clearly a letter from a solicitor advising a client of potential criminal liability if a particular course of conduct were pursued would be privileged.

Entry and search without a search warrant

The police are given powers to enter premises without a warrant by many Acts of Parliament, for example, under the Gaming Act 1968 they have power to enter licensed premises to carry out inspections. Other powers include searches for drugs under the Misuse of Drugs Act 1971, for articles under the Obscene Publications Act 1959, for illegal immigrants under the Immigration Act 1971, and for firearms under the Firearms Act 1968. In addition, they may have the right to enter premises without a warrant to deal with or prevent a breach of the peace (see p. 28). The Police and Criminal Evidence Act provides them with several other powers:

- To execute a warrant of arrest or commitment.
- To arrest someone for an arrestable offence.
- To arrest someone for various offences under the Public Order Acts 1936 and 1986 (such as riot, violent disorder, affray, threatening behaviour and disorderly conduct) and the Criminal Law Act 1977 (offences relating to trespass).
- To recapture a person who has escaped from lawful custody.
- To save life or limb or prevent serious damage to property.

The police officer need not be in uniform unless entering in connection with the Public Order Acts or the Criminal Law Act. He or she has a power to search the premises but this is only to the extent that is reasonably required for the purposes of entry. Any further search may be unlawful and may be the subject of a complaint or civil action (see p. 99).

Search of premises on arrest

The Police and Criminal Evidence Act 1984 (PACE) provides the police with clear authority to enter and search premises after an arrest. If you have been arrested for an 'arrestable offence' (see above) the police may search premises occupied or controlled by you for evidence of that offence or of some other arrestable offence connected with or similar to that offence. The police officer conducting this search should normally have with him or her written authorisation on the Notice of Powers and Rights (see below) for the search by an officer of at least the rank of inspector.

If you have been arrested for any offence (not just an 'arrestable offence') the police may enter and search any premises you were in at the time of the arrest or immediately before it for evidence of the offence for which you were arrested. Again, in both cases the police are only permitted to search to the extent reasonably required to find the evidence sought and if the search is excessive you may have the remedy of a police complaint or a civil action against the police.

Conduct of searches of premises

The conduct of searches is governed by the Police and Criminal Evidence Act and the Code of Practice (see p. 128). A search warrant may authorise anyone to accompany the constable who is executing it. Entry and search must be within one month from the date of the warrant's issue. You have a right to see the warrant and to be supplied with a copy. You also have a right, unless it is impracticable, to a notice in the standard form setting out police powers and occupiers' rights (Notice of Rights and Powers). You are also entitled to see the police officer's warrant card as a means of identification if he or she is not in uniform and in any case, the police officer should identify him or herself. If you are not present but someone else who appears to the police to be in charge of the premises is available then they have the same rights as you. A warrant authorises entry on one occasion only.

The police have a right to use force if necessary to effect an entry or search, but only such force as is reasonable. All searches should take place at a reasonable hour, unless the constable conducting the search believes that the purpose of the search would be frustrated by waiting until such time. You are entitled to have a friend or neighbour to witness a search (although you do not have a right to delay a search unreasonably while you find a witness) unless the officer in charge has reasonable grounds for feeling this would seriously hinder the investigation.

The warrant must be endorsed afterwards by the police to show the following:

- Whether articles or persons specified in the warrant were found.
- Whether any other articles were seized.
- The date and time of the search's execution.
- The names of the officers who executed it except where the investigations are linked to terrorism in which case warrant numbers and duty stations should be shown.
- Whether a copy was handed to the occupier or left at the premises.

The occupier of the premises which have been searched has a right to inspect the search warrant (which should have been returned to the magistrates' court) within twelve months.

Seizure of property

When the police are lawfully on any premises (which includes being there with your consent) they have wide powers to seize anything on the premises if they have reasonable grounds for believing that:

- It has been obtained as a consequence of the commission of an offence.

- It is evidence in relation to any offence.
- It is necessary to seize it in order to prevent it being seized, lost or damaged, altered or destroyed.

'Anything' includes fingerprints. The police may require computerised information which comes within these categories to be produced in a form in which they can remove it. 'Excluded material' and 'special procedure material' (see above) are not protected from seizure once the police are lawfully on the premises. No power of seizure, however, authorises the seizure of material reasonably believed by a constable to be legally privileged.

If you request it, the police must provide a record of seized items within a reasonable time. Lawfully seized articles may be retained so long as is necessary, for example, for production in court, but the articles cannot be kept for use as evidence in a trial or for forensic examination if a photograph or copy would suffice.

6.3 Police powers of arrest

The police may arrest with or without a warrant. There are many powers of arrest under a warrant issued by a justice of the peace or judge and the rules governing each of them is set out in the statute creating the power. This section deals with police powers of arrest without a warrant.

The powers of arrest without a warrant are governed by the Police and Criminal Evidence Act 1984 and can be grouped into the following categories:

- Arrest at common law for breach of the peace.
- Summary arrest for an 'arrestable offence'.
- Arrest subject to conditions.
- Arrest under specific powers.
- Arrest for the purpose of fingerprinting.

Arrest at common law for breach of the peace
A breach of the peace is not in itself a criminal offence but the police and any other person have a power of arrest where there are reasonable grounds for believing a breach of the peace is taking place or is imminent.

Summary arrest for 'arrestable offences'
PACE uses the phrase 'summary arrest' to mean arrest without a warrant and lists the arrestable offences for which the police can arrest without a warrant. The following are arrestable offences:

- Offences for which the sentence is fixed by law (including murder – life imprisonment).
- Offences carrying a maximum sentence of imprisonment for five years or more (these include serious offences of violence and dishonesty, but also some relatively minor offences such as shoplifting and minor criminal damage).
- Various statutory offences including offences under the Customs and Excise Management Act 1979, under the Official Secrets Acts 1920 and 1989, under the Sexual Offences Act 1956 and under the Theft Act 1968 (including taking a motor vehicle without the consent of the owner and going equipped for theft) and under the Football (Offences) Act 1991.

This power of arrest may be carried out by anyone – either a police officer or any other person (a citizen's arrest) – in the following circumstances:

- Anyone actually committing or whom he or she reasonably suspects to be committing an arrestable offence.
- Where an arrestable offence has been committed, anyone who is guilty or whom he or she reasonably suspects to be guilty of the offence.

A police officer may arrest in the same circumstances as any person (above), and also:

- Anyone who is or whom he or she reasonably suspects to be about to commit an arrestable offence.
- Where he or she reasonably suspects an arrestable offence has been committed, anyone whom he or she reasonably suspects to be guilty of the offence.

'Serious arrestable offences'

There is a further concept in PACE described as the 'serious arrestable offence'. The definition of a 'serious arrestable offence' does not affect the powers of arrest, but the more draconian police powers under PACE relating to the detention of a subject can be invoked where the offence is a 'serious arrestable offence' – such as detention without charge for up to ninety-six hours, denial of access to a solicitor and delaying notification of detention to a friend for up to thirty-six hours, the authorisation of roadchecks, etc.

The following are serious arrestable offences:

- Treason, murder, manslaughter, rape, kidnapping, incest or intercourse with a girl under thirteen, buggery with a boy under sixteen or a person who has not consented, indecent assault constituting gross indecency, causing an explosion likely to endanger life or property, certain offences under the Firearms Act 1968, causing death by dangerous driving, hostage taking, torture and many drug-related offences, aeroplane hijacking.

- Any other arrestable offence if its commission has led or is intended to, is likely or threatened to lead to any of the following consequences: serious harm to the security of the state or to public order, serious interference with the administration of justice or with the investigation of offences, the death or serious injury (including disease and impairment) of any person, or a substantial financial gain or serious financial loss to any person.
- For the purposes of denial of access to a solicitor and notification of detention, certain offences under the prevention of terrorism legislation.

Arrest subject to conditions

Often, in a minor case, an arrest should be unnecessary. The alleged offender can be summonsed by post to attend court on a particular date and there is no need to go to a police station at all.

However, PACE also gives the police a power of arrest for all offences, no matter how trivial, petty or minor, which do not carry a power of arrest under the previously discussed powers. The power of arrest can only be used where:

- A constable has reasonable grounds for suspecting that you have committed or attempted, or are committing or attempting to commit an offence (but not where it is suspected that an offence will be committed in the future).
- It appears to the constable that service of a summons is impracticable or inappropriate because any of the general arrest conditions (see below) is satisfied.

Thus, the assumption is that the police should proceed by way of summons for minor offences and the power of arrest ought to be used only if this is impracticable or inappropriate. The impracticability or inappropriateness of the summons must arise from one of the general arrest conditions, which are as follows:

Name and address

- If your name is unknown to, and cannot be readily ascertained by, the police (you cannot be made to wait while your name is ascertained or confirmed, but might agree to do so to avoid being arrested).
- If the police have reasonable grounds for doubting that you have given your real name.

- If you have failed to furnish a satisfactory address for the service of a summons (i.e. one at which, it appears to the constable, you will be for a sufficiently long period to be served or at which some other specified persons will accept service of a summons).
- If the police have reasonable grounds for doubting whether an address furnished is satisfactory.

Prevention

- If the police have reasonable grounds for believing that an arrest is necessary to prevent you causing physical injury to yourself or to somebody else, or suffering physical injury, or causing loss of or damage to property (including your own), or committing an offence against public decency, or causing an unlawful obstruction of the highway (see p. 27).

Protection

- If the police have reasonable grounds for believing that arrest is necessary to protect a child or other vulnerable person (undefined) from you.

If you have been arrested under this power and are on the way to the police station, you must be released if a constable is satisfied that there are no longer any grounds for keeping you under arrest – for example, if you suddenly find some kind of identification or if there is no longer any risk of damage or injury.

Arrest under specific powers

The specific statutory powers are listed in PACE and some subsequent legislation and relate mainly to the armed forces, animals, absconders, children and offences under legislation concerning immigration, emergency powers, public order, trespass and the prevention of terrorism. They are not subject to the general arrest conditions (set out above), but many of them carry other conditions (for example, that the arresting constable must be in uniform). These powers of arrest include, for example, powers under the Road Traffic Act 1988 to arrest motorists for drink-driving offences.

Arrest for the purpose of fingerprinting

This power of arrest is designed to apply to somebody who appears at court after receiving a summons and who has not been taken to a police station under arrest. A constable may make an arrest without a warrant in order to have fingerprints taken at a police station. The following conditions must apply:

- You must have been convicted of a recordable offence (i.e. most offences other than trivial or traffic offences).
- You must not have been fingerprinted in the course of the police investigation (or in connection with any matter since conviction).
- You must have failed to comply, within seven days, with the requirement made within one month of the date of conviction to attend a police station for fingerprinting.

Information to be given on arrest

An arrest is unlawful unless you are told that you are under arrest and the grounds for the arrest at the time. Such an unlawful arrest will become lawful when the police tell you the reason for the arrest. This information must be given at the time of the arrest or as soon as is practicable afterwards. The information need not be given it if was not reasonably practicable to do so because of your escape from arrest before it could be given. If you attend voluntarily at a police station (or any other place with a constable) without having been arrested you are entitled to leave at will unless placed under arrest.

Arrest other than at a police station

After arrest, a constable must take you to a police station as soon as is practicable (subject to certain exceptions and the power to release you en route). However, a constable may delay taking you to a police station if your presence elsewhere is necessary in order to carry out such investigations as it is reasonable to carry out immediately, such as a search of premises.

Search of a person on arrest (other than at a police station)

A police officer may search you to the extent reasonably required if there are reasonable grounds for believing that:

- You may present a danger to yourself or to somebody else.
- You may have concealed on you anything which might be used to assist an escape from lawful custody or which might be evidence relating to any offence.

There are similar restrictions on searching in public to those discussed above (see p. 130).

6.4 Police detention

The circumstances in which an arrested person may be kept in police detention are set out in the Police and Criminal Evidence Act 1984.

The detention is now unlawful unless the provisions of PACE are complied with. A key figure in the scheme is the 'custody officer', a police officer of at least the rank of sergeant.

Normally, the period of detention without charge should not exceed twenty-four hours, although in some cases the maximum period, with extensions, is as long as ninety-six hours. There are a number of stages at which continuation of custody must be authorised – in the early stages by police officers and in the later stages by magistrates. Provision is made for the appointment of custody officers and the performance by them (and any other constable in charge of the prisoner) of important duties. In particular, if the custody officer becomes aware at any time (perhaps after representations from a solicitor) that the grounds for the detention have ceased to apply and that there are no other grounds for continued detention, it is the duty of the custody officer to order your immediate release from custody. Conversely, you may not be released except on the authority of a custody officer at the police station where detention was last authorised. The custody officer is also responsible for keeping a 'custody record' in which all information required to be lodged by PACE and the Codes of Practice is recorded. You or your legal representative are entitled to a copy of this very important document on leaving police detention or appearing before the court. This entitlement lasts for twelve months after release.

On arrival at or after arrest at the police station
The custody officer must, as soon as is practicable after your arrival at the police station (or after arrest at the police station), determine whether there is sufficient evidence to charge you with the offence for which the arrest was made. He or she may detain you for as long as is necessary to make such a determination. If the custody officer decides that there is sufficient evidence to charge you, then you should be charged and must be released unless one of the post-charge detention conditions applies (see p. 146).

Detention without charge
If the custody officer decides that there is insufficient evidence to charge you, then you must be released, unless he or she has reasonable grounds for believing that detention without charge is necessary to secure or preserve evidence relating to an offence for which you are under arrest, or to obtain such evidence by questioning you. In such a case he or she may order further police detention, but the grounds for the detention must be recorded in writing on the custody record. You must be given these reasons.

Detention without charge cannot be authorised in your own interest, or to prevent the repetition or continuation of an offence, or to authorise police 'fishing trips' (since the evidence must relate to an offence for which you are under arrest). If the custody officer has reasonable grounds to believe that you will not answer questions (for example, because your solicitor has said so) detention cannot be necessary to obtain evidence by questioning and detention for questioning in such circumstances may well be unlawful.

There are special rules relating to those who appear to be younger than seventeen. The Code of Practice on detention, treatment and questioning prohibits the placing of any juvenile in police cells, unless no other secure accommodation or practicable supervision is available. In any event, the juvenile may not be placed in a cell with an adult. There are also rules as to the identifying of and giving information to those responsible for the juvenile's welfare. A juvenile who is not released after being charged should, if practicable, be transferred to the care of a local authority.

Review of detention

Periodic reviews of detention must be carried out for all persons in police custody pending the investigation of an offence. If you have been charged, the review is carried out by the custody officer. If you have not been charged, it is carried out by an officer of at least the rank of inspector who has not at any stage been directly involved with the investigation. The general rule is that the first review must be not later than six hours after the detention was first authorised, and subsequent reviews must take place at intervals of not more than nine hours.

Before deciding whether to authorise your detention, the review officer must give you (unless asleep) and your solicitor (or the duty solicitor) an opportunity to make oral or written representations. Representations by a solicitor may be made over the telephone. A non-solicitor (for example, a solicitor's employee or an unqualified law centre worker) does not have the same statutory right to make representations – but there is provision in the Code to hear representations from such persons unless a senior officer considers that such a visit will hinder the investigation of a crime. The representations might relate, for example, to the amount of evidence already obtained or to your refusal to answer questions, these matters being connected with the grounds on which continued detention can be authorised.

The detention clock

PACE limits the length of time for which you can remain in police detention. Such limitations are based on the passage of time from a particular point.

The general rule is that the time starts on your arrival at the first police station to which you are taken after arrest. If arrest takes place at the police station the time starts when you are arrested. There may be some delay between arrest and arrival caused by necessary investigation, but there is a general provision that an arrested person must be taken to a police station as soon as is practicable after arrest.

There are special rules if the arrest takes place outside England and Wales or in a different police area from the one in which you are questioned. Questioning in transit is prohibited by the Code but you should be very careful not to answer any questions until you have arrived at the police station and obtained legal advice.

Detention limits and police extensions

The general rule is that you may not be kept in police detention for more than twenty-four hours without being charged. This period can be extended by a maximum of twelve hours on the authority of an officer of the rank of superintendent or above after giving opportunity for representations to be made. The extension can only be authorised where:

- The officer has reasonable grounds for believing that the offence is a serious arrestable offence.
- The investigation is being conducted diligently and expeditiously.
- Detention without charge is necessary to secure or preserve evidence of an offence for which you are under arrest or to obtain evidence by questioning.

The authorisation cannot last beyond thirty-six hours from when the detention clock began.

Detention limits and magistrates' extensions

You must be released by the end of thirty-six hours from the starting point, unless an application is made to a magistrates' court sitting in private. The application is made on oath by a police officer and supported by a written 'information' which must state the nature of the offence, the general nature of the evidence for the arrest, what enquiries have been made and are proposed, and the reason for believing the continued detention is necessary.

You are entitled to a copy of the information and to be legally represented (you can have an adjournment to obtain legal representation). The police officer will be at court to be cross-examined and representations may be made to the magistrates(s). These might be directed, for example, towards any delay in the investigation or in making the application, whether there is a serious arrestable offence involved, whether detention is necessary, and whether there is sufficient evidence for you to be charged.

The court may only authorise further detention if:

- The offence is a serious arrestable offence;
- The investigation is being conducted diligently and expeditiously; *and*

- Further detention is necessary to secure or preserve evidence relating to the offence or to obtain such evidence by questioning you.

The court may authorise further detention for up to thirty-six hours from the time that the application is granted. A further extension of up to thirty-six hours may be granted if the same procedure is followed. The total maximum period of detention is ninety-six hours from the original starting point (except under the Prevention of Terrorism Act where the maximum is seven days).

Detention after charge

After you have been charged, the custody officer must order your release unless one of the following post-charge detention conditions applies:

- Your name or address is unknown or doubted.
- Detention is necessary to prevent physical injury or damage to property, your non-appearance at court, or interference with the investigation or the administration of justice.
- A juvenile needs to be detained in his or her own interest.

A person who has been detained after charge must normally be taken to court on the day after the day of charge (unless that following day is a Sunday, Christmas Day or Good Friday).

6.5 The rights of suspects in the police station

The rights of suspects after arrest are contained principally in the Police and Criminal Evidence Act 1984 and in the Code of Practice on the Detention, Treatment and Questioning of Persons and the Code of Practice on Identification of Persons by the Police.

It is in this area that the provision of the Codes are most important. Any breaches by the police may result in disciplinary action against them and, if the breaches are sufficiently serious, any confession you make may not be admitted as evidence in a trial (see p. 128). The Codes contain detailed provisions governing the conditions of detention, for instance on the right to legal advice and the right not to be held incommunicado, as well as on searches, exercise and medical treatment. The Codes also provide that if you are classed as a vulnerable person, for instance, if you are mentally handicapped or a juvenile, an appropriate adult (not a police officer) should be present to look after your interests.

Personal searches at the police station

The custody officer (see p. 143) is under a duty to list all the property you have with you on your custody record. You may be searched, using reasonable force if necessary if you refuse to cooperate, by a police officer of the same sex, and you should be told the reasons for the search. You are allowed to check the list of property and you should only sign if it is correct.

Clothes and personal effects (not including cash) may only be seized if the custody officer believes you may use them to cause physical injury to yourself or to somebody else, to damage property, to interfere with evidence, to assist an escape, or if he or she has reasonable grounds for believing that they may be evidence relating to an offence.

Strip searches

A strip search may take place if the custody officer considers it necessary, but he or she has no power to authorise an intimate body search (see below). The courts have recognised that strip searches may be deeply humiliating and that the removal of a brassiere, for instance, would require considerable justification. No person of the opposite sex who is not a medical practitioner or nurse may be present at such a search, nor anyone whose presence is unnecessary. Reasons for a strip search and the results of the search must be recorded on the custody record.

Intimate body searches

An intimate body search consists of the physical examination of any one or more of a person's bodily orifices, including the anus, vagina, mouth, ears and nose. The police can only carry out an intimate body search in limited circumstances. They can search you if a police officer of at least the rank of superintendent has reasonable grounds for believing that:

- You may have concealed on you something that you could use to cause physical injury to yourself or to others, and that you might so use it while you are in police detention or in the custody of a court.
- You have concealed Class A drugs (such as heroin and cocaine, but not cannabis or amphetamines) on yourself and that you are in possession of the drugs either with intent to supply them to somebody else or with a view to committing a customs offence.

A search for drugs (Class A drugs only) may only be carried out by a registered medical practitioner or a registered nurse. It should only be carried out at a hospital, at a registered medical practitioner's surgery or at some other place used for medical purposes. An intimate search for potentially harmful items should also be carried out by a doctor or nurse, but may be conducted by a police officer if an officer of at least the rank of superintendent believes that it is not practicable for it to be carried out by a doctor or nurse. The search may be carried out at a police station.

The right to decent conditions

The Code says that there should only be one person in each cell, but only 'so far as is practicable'. Police cells must be adequately heated, cleaned, ventilated and lit. Bedding should be clean. Access to toilet and washing facilities must be provided.

The police should check on persons in cells once an hour, or every half hour on those who are drunk. At least two light meals and one main meal should be offered in any period of twenty-four hours. Brief outdoor exercise should be offered daily 'if practicable'. For conditions for juveniles see above (p. 144).

The right to medical treatment

A detained person is entitled to a medical examination by a police surgeon on request (but not for minor ailments – although the benefit of the doubt should be given to the suspect unless the custody officer is confronted with a minor ailment). He or she may also be examined by a GP of his or her own choice at his or her own expense. He or she is entitled to have medication where appropriate.

The custody officer must also call the police surgeon if a detained person is injured, or appears to be suffering from physical illness or mental disorder, or otherwise appears to need medical attention.

All of this must be recorded on the custody record and when a doctor is called he or she must also make a record.

The right to legal advice

If you are arrested and held at a police station or other premises you have a statutory right to consult a solicitor (if you wish) in private and free of charge at any time. A duty solicitor scheme is in operation at every police station in England and Wales, so that free telephone advice or a free visit from a solicitor is available. On arrest you should be informed by the custody officer, orally and in writing, of this right, as well as the right to have someone informed of the arrest (see below) and your right to consult the Codes of Practice, and that these are continuing rights – that is if you do not take advantage of them when offered you can do so at any time you are in the police station.

Access to legal advice may be delayed by the police, however, if you are detained for a 'serious arrestable offence' (see p. 139), a drug-trafficking offence, or certain other specified offences where the police are attempting to recover property and you have not yet been charged with an offence for up to thirty-six hours from the relevant time or for up to forty-eight hours in the case of a person detained under the Prevention of Terrorism legislation. Delay may be authorised only by an officer of at least the rank of superintendent if he or she has reasonable grounds (which must be recorded in writing) for believing that the exercise of the right to legal advice would lead to:

- Interference with evidence of a 'serious arrestable offence'.
- Harm to others.
- The alerting of accomplices.
- Hindering the recovery of property.

There are further grounds where a person is detained under the Prevention of Terrorism legislation. Once the reason for authorising the delay ceases to exist there may be no further delay in permitting access. Delays are rare (1 per cent in ordinary cases and 25 per cent in Prevention of Terrorism Act cases) and even then they often will not be justified.

The Code provides that if you ask for legal advice you should not be interviewed until you have received it, unless:

- Delay is authorised (as above); *or*
- An officer of at least the rank of superintendent reasonably believes that delay caused by waiting for a solicitor involves risk or harm to persons or property; *or*
- This would unreasonably delay the investigation; *or*
- The solicitor cannot or will not attend and you do not want to use the duty solicitor scheme or the duty solicitor is not available; *or*
- You consent in writing or on tape to the interview going ahead.

If you are not allowed to see a solicitor you should not answer questions or make any statement until you are given permission to see one. In most cases you may consult either your solicitor in person, on the telephone or in writing.

The right not to be kept incommunicado
If you are detained in a police station or other premises, you are entitled to have one friend, relative or person who is known to you or likely to take an interest in your welfare notified of your whereabouts as soon as is practicable, at public expense. The right is subject to the same delay as consultation with a solicitor (see above). You may exercise this right each time you are transferred to another police station. If the person cannot be contacted you may try two others and

after that the police have a discretion as to whether you can try to contact any others.

With juveniles, the police have an additional duty to inform the person responsible for their welfare as soon as is practicable and to request their attendance at the police station. There are no provisions permitting delay.

The conduct of interviews

The conduct of interviews is covered by the Code of Practice. The overriding principle is that all persons in custody must be dealt with expeditiously and released as soon as the need for detention has ceased to apply. Except in very limited circumstances interviews should only take place in police stations. An accurate written record should be made of each interview (whether or not it takes place at a police station) unless the interview is tape-recorded. You have a right to see the interview record and you should sign it only if it records exactly what you have said.

Virtually all interviews are now tape-recorded and procedures must follow the Code of Practice for tape recording. You may find that your interview is video-recorded. But less formal interviews which are subsequently written up by police officers in their notebooks are still quite common and you usually have no chance to check the accuracy of their notes. The use of prolonged or oppressive questioning, or the denial of access to a solicitor, or other breaches of the Codes or the Act (so long as they are not merely technical) may render confessions inadmissible in evidence at court.

Questioning should cease as soon as the interrogating officer believes that there is sufficient evidence for a prosecution to be brought successfully. You should then be taken before the custody officer and charged or informed that you may be prosecuted.

The right of silence

It is a fundamental principle of English law that you need not answer any questions or provide any information which might tend to incriminate you. You should be cautioned on arrest and on arrival at the station before questioning to remind you of this right. The caution should be in the following or similar terms: 'You do not have to say anything unless you wish to do so, but what you say may be given in evidence.' No adverse inference may be drawn from this silence at any trial that takes place, but in practice both juries and magistrates may draw their own conclusions.

In 1988, the government restricted the right of silence in Northern Ireland by permitting the prosecution and the judge to invite the jury's attention to the defendant's silence at the police station or in court (if the defendant declines to give evidence) and to invite them to draw adverse inferences from that silence.

At the time of writing the government announced that it intended to abolish this right in England and Wales. Any changes are unlikely to occur before 1995.

Fingerprints

Fingerprints (the term includes palmprints) may be taken from anyone over the age of ten without consent and without a court order in any of the following circumstances:

- If an officer of the rank of superintendent or above believes that fingerprints will confirm or disprove involvement in an offence and authorises the fingerprinting.
- If you have been convicted for a recordable offence.
- If you are charged with a recordable offence or informed that you will be reported for such an offence and fingerprints have not already been taken in the course of the investigation.

Recordable offences are specified in regulations and include all but the most trivial offences.

Where fingerprints are taken without your consent reasons must be given before they are taken and those reasons must be recorded. Reasonable force may be used. If the police obtain your consent to fingerprinting it must be in writing if given at a police station. Consent in the case of a child (aged ten to fourteen) is the consent of his or her parents alone and in the case of a young adult (aged fourteen to seventeen) of the parents and him or herself.

Photographs

Your photograph may not be taken without your written consent unless you have been charged, reported for or convicted of a recordable offence and your photograph is not already on record. The police may not use force to take a photograph.

Intimate and non-intimate samples

An intimate sample is a sample of blood, semen or any other tissue fluid, urine, saliva, pubic hair or a swab taken from a bodily orifice; dental impressions are to be treated as intimate samples. In Northern Ireland, however, a mouth swab is classed as a non-intimate sample. An intimate sample (other than urine or saliva) may only be taken by a medical practitioner, and only if an officer of at least the rank of superintendent authorises it and you consent in writing (consent for juveniles is the same as for fingerprinting). The authorisation may only be given if the officer has reasonable grounds for believing the sample will confirm or disprove involvement in a serious arrestable offence.

If you refuse to consent 'without reasonable cause' the court or jury may (in committal proceedings or at a trial) draw such inferences from the refusal as appear proper, and the refusal may be treated as corroboration of any evidence against you to which the refusal is material. You must be warned of this before being asked to provide such a sample. This provision was inserted with rape suspects in mind. The provisions for breath tests and blood or urine samples in cases of drunk-drivers are quite separate.

A non-intimate sample is a sample of hair other than pubic hair, a sample taken from a nail or from under a nail, a swab taken from any part of a person's body other than an orifice, and a footprint or a similar impression of any part of a person's body other than a part of his hand (except dental impressions – see above).

Non-intimate samples may be taken with your written consent (consent for juveniles is the same as for fingerprinting) or without consent where you are in police detention or being held in custody on the authority of a court and an officer of at least the rank of superintendent authorises it. He or she may do this if there are reasonable grounds for believing the sample will confirm or disprove your involvement in a serious arrestable offence. Reasons for taking the sample must be provided to you and recorded.

DNA samples
The government has suggested that it intends to give the police extra powers to take samples for DNA identification in more circumstances and to set up a DNA database to retain the data collected. If this happens it is unlikely to be in force before 1995.

Destruction of fingerprints, photographs and samples
If you are prosecuted for an offence and acquitted, or if you are not prosecuted or cautioned, all samples, fingerprints, photographs, copies and negatives must be destroyed as soon as is practicable. You are entitled to be present to witness the destruction of your photographs and fingerprints.

Fingerprints and samples taken under the Immigration Act or the Prevention of Terrorism Act may, however, be retained.

Identification by witnesses
Procedures for identification parades or other group identifications, video identifications with others (group identifications), confrontation by witnesses and the showing of photographs to witnesses are set out in detail in a Code of Practice.

If identification is disputed an identification parade must be held if you want one and if it is practicable to hold one. You are entitled to have a solicitor or friend present. An identification parade should have at least eight persons (in addition to the suspect) who, so far as possible, resemble the suspect in age, height, general appearance and position in life. Two suspects should not be on the same parade unless they are of roughly similar appearance.

If you refuse to go on a parade or if it is impracticable to have one then there may be a group identification. Again, you may have a solicitor or friend present. It is also possible for a witness to be shown a video film of the suspect if this is considered the most satisfactory course of action. Only if it is impossible to conduct either of the above, either because you will not consent or because it is impracticable, should you be confronted directly by a witness. You have no right of veto over this last method, but the confrontation must take place in the presence of your solicitor, interpreter or friend unless this would cause unreasonable delay.

6.6 The right to make notes

If you have been involved in any incident with the police or you have witnessed an incident, it is advisable to make and keep full notes as soon as possible after the events in question.

The police are allowed to refer to notes in court. This happens not because police officers have some special status as witnesses – they do not – but because the notes are contemporaneous, that is, notes which are made at the time or as soon as reasonably practicable thereafter. Contemporaneous notes are not in themselves evidence, but they can be used to refresh the witness's memory.

You have the same right to use notes. A delay in writing the notes of several hours or even a day or so may not prevent you from using the notes. Even if you cannot use them at court they will be a helpful record of the events.

If you are detained at a police station the Codes of Conduct provide that you should be supplied on request with writing materials. When making notes:

- Write out a full and legible note of everything that happened in the correct sequence of events.
- Write down everything that was said, word for word if possible, particularly any conversation you had with police officers.
- Record the name and number, if you know them, of the police officers involved.
- Sign the notes at the bottom and put the time and date.

- If you see a solicitor, hand over the notes and make sure you get a copy to keep for yourself.
- If you are going to court take the notes with you.

If there are witnesses to the incident take the names and addresses of the witnesses if possible and ask them to make notes.

If you have been injured (for example, by the use of excessive force by the police during your arrest) you must:

- Have photographs taken if there are any visible injuries.
- See a doctor so that your injuries are recorded.

The photographs and medical evidence may be of great value to you if you are charged with a criminal offence or if you wish to make a police complaint or sue the police.

6.7 Special powers under the Prevention of Terrorism Act

The Prevention of Terrorism (Temporary Provisions) Act 1989 (PTA) covers the whole of the UK. It is based on three earlier Acts, the first of which was rushed through Parliament after the Birmingham pub bombings in November 1974. The 1974 and 1976 Acts mainly covered activities associated with affairs in Northern Ireland. The 1984 Act, however, extended the power of arrest for questioning to cover anyone suspected of being involved with International Terrorism. The 1989 Act created new offences and court powers of restraint and forfeiture relating to terrorist funds. It also created new powers of investigation into terrorist activities.

The PTA does not deal directly with acts of violence usually associated with the word 'terrorism', such as bombings and killings. These are crimes under ordinary criminal law. It is essentially a law that increases the power of the police to detain and interrogate anyone who may have information about 'terrorism', whether or not they are personally involved. 'Terrorism' is defined as 'the use of violence for political ends'. It includes 'any use of violence for the purpose of putting the public or any section of the public in fear'. The PTA is also intended to discourage support for certain Irish organisations.

This section covers the provisions of the Act as they apply to acts of political violence related to Irish or international affairs. Great Britain includes England, Scotland and Wales. The United Kingdom includes Great Britain and Northern Ireland.

If you are arrested or detained under the PTA it is essential that you obtain expert legal advice as soon as you can.

Arrest and questioning

Under the PTA a police officer can arrest you without a warrant if he or she has 'reasonable' grounds to suspect that:

- You are involved in the 'commission, preparation or instigation of acts of terrorism' connected with Northern Ireland or any foreign country. Any act connected solely with Great Britain or any part of the UK but unconnected with the conflict in Northern Ireland is not covered by the PTA; *or*
- You belong to or support any section of the Provisional or Official IRA, or the INLA (see banned organisations p. 159); *or*
- You have solicited, lent, given or received money or other property for use in connection with acts of terrorism, or you have been involved with the movement of terrorist funds.
- You wear, carry or display anything in public which gives rise to reasonable fear that you are a member or supporter of a banned organisation; *or*
- You are subject to an exclusion order and enter a territory forbidden to you, or you have helped or given accommodation to any excluded person while they were in a territory forbidden to them (see exclusion orders p. 157).

If you are unsure that you are being arrested under the PTA ask the police officer making the arrest which power is being used. Once arrested, the police can detain you for up to forty-eight hours and then for up to a further five days with the consent of a Secretary of State (in England and Wales the Home Secretary). During this time they do not have to charge you or take you before a court.

During your detention, the police (or prison officer) can take any 'reasonably necessary' steps to identify you, including photographing, fingerprinting and measuring you without your consent or a court order and with reasonable force if you refuse.

It is a criminal offence not to give the police, or the army if you are in Northern Ireland, specific information you may have about people or events concerned with acts of political violence connected with Irish affairs. You should always be careful not to pass on anything based on rumour, and you are not obliged to pass on any information at all if you have a reasonable excuse, for example, if the information incriminates you personally or if you would have reason to fear for the safety of either yourself or your family. You can be fined and/or imprisoned if convicted. Although very few have actually been charged or convicted of this offence, people have been threatened with this during interrogation. This offence does not apply to information relating to acts of international terrorism. Other than the offence of 'withholding information' the general principle of the 'right to silence' applies during detention under the PTA and you are therefore not obliged to answer any other type of question (except about your identity). For restrictions on the right of silence see p. 160.

Your rights under the PTA are, in certain other respects, more limited than those of other suspects. For example, in England and Wales, the 'safeguards' provided in the Police and Criminal Evidence Act (see p. 152) do not apply to limit the circumstances in which you can have your fingerprints taken or provide circumstances under which they will be destroyed – so records can be kept indefinitely. Also, you do not have an absolute right to legal advice until after forty-eight hours and then, under certain circumstances, a senior officer can decide that you can only consult your solicitor in the sight and hearing of a police officer unconnected with your case. You do not have an absolute right to have someone informed of your detention until after forty-eight hours. The Code of Practice under PACE provides for the physical conditions of your detention and your heating, meals, lighting, etc., should therefore be the same as for other suspects, as should those concerning medical treatment.

An arrest under the PTA does not necessarily mean that you have been suspected of a specific offence; the vast majority of people are released without being charged.

Examination or detention at ports or airports

Under the PTA, you can be stopped, questioned and detained by an examining officer while entering or leaving Great Britain or Northern Ireland to find out whether you have any connection with or information about the use of violence in relation to Irish or international affairs, or whether you have breached an exclusion order or assisted someone else to do so.

Examining officers can be police, immigration or certain Customs and Excise officers and in Northern Ireland, soldiers. They can require you to fill in a Landing or Embarkation Card which asks for your name and the details of your address, occupation, name of your employer, address where you will be staying and the purpose of your trip. They can also require you to produce a passport or other papers establishing nationality and identity, or produce any other papers establishing nationality and identity, or produce any other documents considered relevant. They can search any baggage and keep anything which they consider could be relevant in a court case or in considering an exclusion order. You can be asked any reasonable question.

If you are examined for more than an hour, you should receive a Notice of Prisoner's Rights. You can be detained for up to twelve hours in the absence of any suspicion; after this the officer must have 'reasonable suspicion' to continue your detention and you should receive a Notification of Further Examination. As with PTA arrests elsewhere, you cannot be held beyond forty-eight hours without the authority of a Secretary of State and, with the appropriate authority, you can be held for up to a total of seven days.

It is an offence to refuse to comply with directions from an examining officer and you can be fined and/or imprisoned if convicted.

Search of persons or premises

Under the PTA you can be stopped and searched without a warrant if the police suspect you of being involved in terrorism and need to establish if you are carrying anything which makes you liable for arrest. You can also be stopped and searched if you are suspected of supporting a banned organisation or of breaking an exclusion order.

The police can apply to a magistrate for a warrant to search premises in the usual way (see p. 133). However, they can also carry out a search with a note signed by a superintendent (or officer of higher rank) if he or she considers the case to be one of great public emergency.

Using these powers of search the police can seize anything considered to be evidence of an offence relating to a proscribed organisation or an exclusion order, or which would justify the Home Secretary exercising powers of proscription or exclusion.

Exclusion orders

Under the PTA, an exclusion order can be used to expel you from either Great Britain or Northern Ireland or from the whole of the UK. This process does not happen through the courts. Instead, the Secretary of State – usually the Home Secretary or the Secretary of State for Northern Ireland – signs an order when satisfied that:

- It appears expedient, in order to prevent acts of terrorism intended to influence government policy or public opinion with respect to Northern Ireland affairs;
- You are or have been concerned in the 'commission, preparation or instigation of acts of terrorism'; *or*
- You are attempting to enter Great Britain or Northern Ireland with a view to being concerned in the 'commission, preparation or instigation of acts of terrorism'.

Terrorism in this context is defined as the use of violence designed to influence public opinion or government policy with respect to affairs in Northern Ireland. This includes any use of violence intended to put the public or any section of the public in fear. You cannot, therefore, be excluded if you are believed only to be involved in international terrorism. It is possible, however, that you could be deported under the Immigration Act (see p. 239). 'Commission, preparation or instigation' covers any type of involvement.

Restrictions on exclusion

The type of exclusion order depends on whether or not you are a UK citizen. If you are a UK citizen you cannot be completely excluded from the UK. You can, however, be forbidden to enter (or be in) either Great Britain or Northern Ireland unless you are already excluded from one of these areas or you have been living in the area from which you are to be excluded for the previous three years (not including time spent in prison in the UK, Channel Islands or Isle of Man). If you are excluded you will be removed to the part of the UK you are allowed to be in.

If you are not a UK citizen you can be forbidden to enter or be in the UK or any part of it. Before excluding you the Home Secretary should consider whether you have connections which would make it appropriate to send you to another country. You can be excluded irrespective of the length of time you have been living in the UK.

Challenging exclusion

If you are excluded, you should be given a written order that says this and tells you about your right to object as soon as possible. If you want to object, you must write to the Home Secretary within seven days and try to prove your case. If you ask, you also have the right to a private interview with a government adviser appointed by the Home Secretary. You can have a solicitor with you at this interview if the adviser agrees. You will remain in custody while the Home Secretary considers your arguments against exclusion. If you do not make representations within seven days you will be removed whether you agree to this or not. If you agree to being removed before making representations you must write making your case against exclusion and asking for an interview, if you want one, within fourteen days of your removal. By making representations after you are removed you lose your absolute right to an interview since you can only have one if the Home Secretary considers it 'practicable'.

If you use either procedure the Home Secretary must consider whether or not to cancel the order, taking into account the report of any interview with the adviser, the adviser's opinion and anything else considered relevant. You can ask people to write supporting your case. However, you cannot call a witness or appeal to a court. The procedure also denies you your right to know what evidence has satisfied the Home Secretary that you should be excluded or the reasons why your representations against the order are successful or not. You cannot, therefore, be confident of being able to provide the evidence necessary to challenge the decision adequately. It is, nevertheless, worth making representations since a number of orders are cancelled as a result.

If your exclusion is not cancelled after you make representations it will last for three years. The Home Secretary can then make a new order excluding you for another three years after reviewing your case. This is done by the Home Office which writes to you at your last known address asking you to fill in a form or write if you want to take part in that review. You may also be offered an interview with the police and you can ask to take a solicitor to this. If you do not hear from the Home Office, you can write asking if you are still excluded and, if necessary, asking for a review. If you are excluded for another three years you can write making representations against this within fourteen days.

In any exclusion order case you should obtain expert legal advice to help you with the representations and to consider any possible legal remedies.

Related criminal offences

You can be arrested and charged if you disobey an exclusion order or if you help anyone else to do so. You can be fined and/or imprisoned if convicted. The consent of the Attorney General is necessary before you can be prosecuted.

Banned organisations

Any organisation in Britain can be banned ('proscribed') under the PTA if it appears to the Home Secretary to be involved in terrorism in the UK that is connected to affairs in Northern Ireland, or appears to be promoting or encouraging it. Organisations in Northern Ireland are banned under the Emergency Provisions Act. Organisations which appear to be connected with international terrorism cannot be banned. An organisation is defined as any association or combination of people. The Provisional and Official IRA were proscribed in 1974, the INLA in 1979 and the UDA in 1992.

Related criminal offences

It is a criminal offence:

- To belong or to say you belong to a proscribed organisation, except where you prove that you were a member before the organisation was banned and that you have not been a member since.
- To raise or receive money or goods on behalf of a banned organisation or to encourage any other form of support for it, except where you can prove that you did not know the money or goods were for this purpose.
- To help organise a public or private meeting of more than three people in support of a banned organisation, or where a speaker

belongs or says he belongs to one of these organisations, except where you prove that you did not know this was the case.
- To display, carry or wear in public anything which gives rise to a reasonable fear that you are a member or supporter of a banned organisation, even if you are not.

Apart from the IRA, the INLA and the UDA, it is not illegal to belong to any other group or party in Great Britain, and provided you do not call for support for a banned organisation or for political violence, you can express any views you like about the situation in Northern Ireland. The IRA, INLA and UDA are also illegal in Northern Ireland under the Emergency Provisions Act, as are certain other organisations and groups.

6.8 Stop press

The Criminal Justice and Public Order Bill being discussed by Parliament in January 1994 will, if passed, include provisions to: allow a chief constable to set up road checks and allow police officers to search without needing to have reasonable suspicion; give greater powers to pluck hairs and take mouth swabs of all those charged or convicted of recordable offences (in order to set up a DNA data base); allow courts to assume that silence under questioning and the refusal to give evidence are indications of guilt; and restrict the right to bail in some serious offences.

6.9 Further information

Useful organisations
Consult your local telephone directory for the addresses and telephone numbers of the following organisations:

- Citizens' Advice Bureaux.
- Law Centres.

Bibliography

V. Bevan and K. Lidstone, *The Investigation of Crime: A Guide to Police Powers*, Butterworth, 1991.

E. Cape, *Defending Suspects at Police Stations*, Legal Action Group, 1993.

R. Clayton and H. Tomlinson, *Civil Actions Against the Police*, Sweet and Maxwell, 1991.

J. Harrison and S. Cragg, *Police Misconduct*, Legal Action Group, 1991.

H. Levenson and F. Fairweather, *Police Powers: A Practitioner's Guide*, Legal Action Group, 1991.

N. Zander, *PACE 1984*, Second Edition, Sweet and Maxwell, 1991.

7

The rights of defendants

This chapter deals with:

- Principles and procedures.
- Representation and legal aid.
- Trial by jury or trial by magistrates.
- Committal proceedings.
- The right of appeal.
- The right to bail.
- Spent convictions and the rehabilitation of offenders.
- Further information.

7.1 Principles and procedures

If the police suspect that you have committed a crime, they can arrest you or they can stop you to request information (for example, concerning a motoring matter) or they can ask you to come to the police station voluntarily. If you are arrested and questioned at a police station, you may at the end of the police enquiries be charged there and then, and given a charge sheet which will set out the details of the offence and provide you with the date and time that you have to attend court. Alternatively, you may simply be released and in due course find that you are served, by recorded delivery post, with a summons – again a document setting out the nature of the offence you are charged with, and with the date and time that you must attend court. If you fail to turn up in court either in response to police bail following a charge at the police station or in response to a summons, a warrant may be issued for your arrest. Often the police will use the arrest and charge procedure instead of using a summons even though there is no need to do so. As well as the police, other bodies such as the DSS or Customs and Excise can bring criminal proceedings.

There are a number of fundamental principles which are at the heart of our criminal justice system:

- The accused is presumed innocent until proved guilty.
- The prosecution must show beyond reasonable doubt that you have committed the offence. This means that if there is doubt as to guilt, then there must be an acquittal.

161

- No one is under a duty to help the police with their enquiries or to make a statement to them; further, this lack of cooperation cannot be held against them at the trial.
- You can remain silent and it cannot be held against you.
- You will be tried on the evidence in the case, not as a result of your previous convictions; the court will not be told of any 'record' since that might create prejudice. You will lose the protection of this rule if you falsely tell the court that you do not have convictions (or that you are of good character) or you attack the character of the prosecution witnesses.
- The trial is based on the spoken evidence of witnesses; generally, written evidence is not allowed since there is no opportunity for the maker of the statement to be cross-examined; it is allowed however when the contents of the evidence are agreed by both sides. The evidence of a witness must be of what he or she saw or heard and not hearsay (i.e. second-hand evidence).
- There are other safeguards that protect you in your dealings with the police when you are a suspect.

Ninety per cent of prosecutions are brought by the Crown Prosecution Service but individuals themselves can also bring criminal cases. Usually these will start by summons. The Director of Public Prosecutions can take over such proceedings in order to continue them or to put a stop to them. Legal aid is not available in such cases and there may be other cost implications.

Some other institutions like local councils also prosecute, as do some individual shop owners.

7.2 Representation and legal aid

Whoever brings the proceedings and whether or not you receive a summons or are charged at a police station, it is advisable to have advice from a lawyer as soon as possible. You may think that your innocence will be obvious to the court, but you cannot be sure that you will be believed. Court procedures can be confusing and the rules of evidence which govern what you can and cannot say are complicated. Even if you do decide to plead guilty, a lawyer can tell the court about any special circumstances which might help to reduce the penalty you receive.

If you are charged by the police or receive a summons, you can go to a solicitor or a law centre for advice upon whether to plead guilty or not guilty and to obtain information as to what penalty you are likely to receive if found guilty. Advice will be free from a law centre, and will be free from a solicitor if you are in receipt of income support or on low disposable income (i.e. with less than £1,000 capital and less than £61 per week). You are entitled to receive advice in person from a solicitor in the police station if you are detained there and that assistance is always free no matter what your income is.

The police must tell you of your right to contact a solicitor. You can nominate one of your own choice, or if you do not know of one, you can request the duty solicitor. The duty solicitor is not some kind of a second-class solicitor chosen by the police – most legal aid solicitors in any geographical area are part of a duty rota and take it in turns to cover particular days and nights to give emergency help to those who need them. Duty solicitors are also provided in the court as well as the police station. They can apply for bail for you, help you with legal aid and will speak to the court for you if you decide to plead guilty. While acting as duty solicitor, they cannot represent you at a contested trial.

If your case is to progress through the courts, your solicitor will provide you with an application form for legal aid as will the court itself. The application must be granted if you cannot pay for your own defence and if it is in the interests of justice that you should be defended. Refusals of legal aid vary from court to court but are rare, except on financial grounds, if the offence is a serious one or there are complicating factors in the case. If the application is granted, the Legal Aid Order is sent to your solicitor if you have one or to a solicitor you can choose from a list kept at the court.

In any case that can be tried in the Crown Court (see below) there is a right of appeal if legal aid is refused (unless the refusal is only on financial grounds). In other cases it is possible to ask the court to review the decision to refuse legal aid by writing to the court or by making representations in person. If you are not in receipt of income support or a very low wage, you may be asked to contribute towards your legal aid up to a particular sum of money. You will be allowed to do this by way of weekly payments, and your legal aid will cover any proceedings in the Crown Court as well as in the magistrates' court.

Using a McKenzie adviser

If you are refused legal aid and cannot afford to pay a lawyer privately, or if you prefer to defend yourself, you are entitled to have a friend – known as a McKenzie adviser – with you in court. This friend cannot speak openly to the court but can sit beside you, take notes and give you advice as to what to do and what questions to ask. The reason this friend is known as a 'McKenzie' is because of the case in which this right was first established.

As soon as possible after the case begins you should say to the court, 'I would like to have a friend as a McKenzie adviser to sit beside me to help me in representing myself.' If the application is refused, you should ask for an adjournment to obtain legal advice because the

High Court can compel magistrates to accept the presence of a McKenzie adviser and you can get civil legal aid for your application to the High Court.

7.3 Trial by jury or trial by magistrates

All criminal cases start in the magistrates' court and most (93 per cent) are finally dealt with there. Others go to higher courts, the Crown Courts, where the cases are heard by a judge and jury. The question of 'venue', or where the case is to be finally disposed of, depends upon the type of offence with which you are charged:

- Some relatively trivial offences such as minor public order charges and most motoring matters can only be dealt with in the magistrates' court and are called 'summary' offences.
- Serious matters such as murder, rape and wounding with intent can be dealt with only in the Crown Court and these are called 'indictable offences'.
- Some offences can be dealt with at either court and these are called 'either way' offences.

Note that in many summary only cases there will be a time limit on bringing proceedings. Usually prosecutions have to be brought within six months of the incident. Such limits do not apply in more serious cases.

Where offences are triable either way, the magistrates will themselves express a view as to where they feel the case should proceed. If they decide the case must go to the Crown Court, you do not have any choice. If you want to be tried in the magistrates' court you should explain this to them before they decide. However, even if they say that they will deal with the matter at magistrates' level, you will have the right if you wish to choose trial by jury. Making this decision really requires legal advice and discussion with your family or friends. Amongst the things to bear in mind when making your decision are:

- The case is likely to be heard more quickly in a magistrates' court than a Crown Court.
- The chances of acquittal by a jury are usually greater than by magistrates.
- Penalties are generally lighter in a magistrates' court, although the magistrates can still send a defendant to the Crown Court for the purpose of sentencing if they think it is appropriate to do so.

- Costs will be lower in the magistrates' court which is important for those people not entitled to legal aid (although it is more likely that legal aid will be granted for Crown Court trials).
- If evidence needs to be challenged, for instance that a confession was made to the police under duress, this can only be properly handled by the Crown Court because despite any ruling on whether evidence can be used in the magistrates' court the magistrates will have heard it anyway!

7.4 Committal proceedings

If you are charged with an indictable offence or an either way offence which is going to the Crown Court, the magistrates have to decide whether there is enough evidence to send you for trial to the Crown Court. This is done at a hearing called a 'committal'. Often the written statements of the prosecution's witnesses can be accepted without any live evidence being called and the hearing will be brief and uneventful. In certain circumstances the defence may want to insist that witnesses be called to give evidence in court at the committal hearing – again you need legal advice as to whether this would be appropriate in your case. At a committal hearing, the magistrates are not deciding if you are guilty or not, but only if the prosecution evidence shows that there is at least a case for you to answer.

Trial in the magistrates' court

With a few exceptions for traffic offences where it is possible to plead guilty by post, you have to attend your trial regardless of whether you wish to plead guilty or not guilty. If you do not attend a warrant for your arrest is likely to be issued. It is often necessary for you to attend on a number of occasions before the trial itself as well.

You or your lawyers should have received a copy of all of the evidence (in the form of statements) before the trial and you should know something of what is going to be said and what prosecution witnesses are to be called. If you have decided to plead guilty you should have decided this in advance so that you can notify the prosecution to avoid them having to bring all their witnesses to court (and avoid extra costs for yourself). It is likely that your sentence will be lighter (and there may be fewer costs) if you plead guilty than if you fight the case, although you should be aware of the consequences of doing so. In particular, once the court has sentenced you it is virtually impossible to undo your conviction and subsequent record.

It is important if you are to defend yourself to be aware of the procedure in the court. Once you have said you will plead not guilty the trial will usually be adjourned to another date because the court will have to allow more time for the hearing. On the day of the trial the prosecution begins by giving a brief account of the case and then calls its witnesses. Each witness is asked questions by the prosecution and then you or your lawyer are given a chance to cross-examine them. Any matters of dispute must be put to the witnesses otherwise the court will assume that what they have said is accepted by you.

The prosecution can then re-examine the witnesses but only to 'clear-up' matters raised during the cross-examination. When all of the prosecution's witnesses have been heard you can then submit that there is 'no case to answer' if the evidence given so far does not demonstrate your guilt. If this submission is not successful you then call your witnesses, only this time of course you begin the questioning. If you intend to give evidence yourself you will be the first defence witness. After all the witnesses have been heard both the prosecution and defence make short speeches outlining why the magistrates should convict (or not!).

You do not have to call any witnesses or give evidence yourself. The prosecution has to prove its case and you can merely attack its evidence although your case is very likely to be much stronger if you give your side of the story. Because of the prosecution's duty to prove the case beyond reasonable doubt you only need to create a doubt to be acquitted.

After giving their verdict the magistrates will release you if they decide you are not guilty. You may be able to get any legal costs back if you are acquitted and you should consider whether you would be able to sue the police for assault (on arrest), false imprisonment and malicious prosecution (see Chapter 5 on p. 99).

If the court decides you are guilty they will then hear from the prosecution about your character and any convictions. You can then make a speech in mitigation pleading for a light sentence. You can call character evidence and if you are concerned that you might be imprisoned, you or your lawyer can explain and produce evidence of why it would be wrong to put you in prison (family needs, employment prospects, etc.). Before passing sentence the magistrates may wish to obtain reports from the probation service or doctors and as a result the sentence decision must be postponed.

Trial in the Crown Court

After the case is committed for trial a date will eventually be fixed (although often you will be given very little notice of this). There are some differences between trial in the Crown Court and the magistrates' court. One difference is that you must disclose any evidence of alibi or of experts that you intend to give at the trial before the trial occurs.

Otherwise the trial follows very much the same pattern as described above for the magistrates' court. Of course in Crown Court trials the jury decides on guilt or innocence and the judge decides on matters of law, whether evidence can be heard or not (in the absence of the jury) and on sentence. One other difference is that after the prosecution and defence have made their speeches to the jury, the judge then sums up the evidence and explains the law.

Although the judge will expect the jury to reach an unanimous verdict if they cannot do so after two or three hours the judge will tell them that they can reach a majority verdict (of at least ten of them).

7.5 The right of appeal

After conviction and sentence in the magistrates' court of a summary offence or an either way offence you can appeal to the Crown Court against your conviction or, if you pleaded guilty, against the sentence you received. An appeal must be made within twenty one days of the magistrates' court hearing. Appeal forms are available from the magistrates' court or the Crown Court and there are further forms to be filled in for legal aid for the appeal. If the sentence of the magistrates was one of custody, you can apply for bail to be granted until the appeal is heard, and if bail is refused at this stage it may still be possible to speed up the hearing of the appeal so that you are not detained for long before the matter is reviewed.

The hearing of the appeal against conviction does not involve a jury even though there is a complete rehearing of the case. It is heard by a judge sitting with two magistrates other than those who have already dealt with you. The Crown Court can confirm, reverse or change the decision of the magistrates' court.

Appeals on a point of law

If you think that the magistrates made a mistake in law, you can appeal to the Divisional Court of the Queen's Bench Division of the High Court, again within twenty one days of the decision, asking the magistrates to 'state a case' for the opinion of the High Court. This is a complicated procedure and again you should consult a solicitor and may well qualify for legal aid.

Appeals from the Crown Court

An appeal against conviction or sentence at the Crown Court itself is made to the Court of Appeal (Criminal Division); the necessary forms are obtained from the Crown Court that dealt with you and should be sent back there. You are entitled as of right following any Crown Court proceedings to have written advice from the lawyer who dealt with your case as to whether you have grounds for appeal. Even if your lawyer does not recommend an appeal and therefore does not put his or her name to any appeal, you can still appeal yourself. If you are in prison, the Legal Aid Office within the prison will provide you with the necessary forms.

The prosecution can only appeal against sentence (if it is unduly lenient) but not against an acquittal.

When an appeal is lodged, it is first of all considered by a single judge. If the single judge sees no merit in your appeal and says so you can still appeal against that decision to the full Court of Appeal of three judges. You may be warned that if you do this, time may be added to any custodial sentence you have been ordered to serve. In fact, in practice this scarcely ever happens. However, if leave is refused you are very unlikely to be granted legal aid and you will have to represent yourself without the help of lawyers.

Appeals to the House of Lords
An appeal from the Court of Appeal to the House of Lords is only possible if it is on a point of law which is of 'general public importance'. Permission to pursue this course must be given either by the Court of Appeal or the House of Lords itself. Very few criminal appeals reach this stage – the procedure is complicated and again legal advice is essential.

7.6 The right to bail

'Bail' means that you are released from custody either by the police or by a court, but with a duty to appear either at a police station or a magistrates' court or Crown Court as and when specified. Failure to appear without a reasonable excuse is an offence. Bail can be granted by a court subject to conditions, such as living at a particular address, reporting on particular days to a local police station, staying indoors at night between certain hours, not approaching a particular prosecution witness, surrendering your passport, or providing one or more sureties.

Sureties
A surety is somebody who undertakes to forfeit a sum of money if you do not appear in court for your trial. The exact sum is fixed by the court when granting bail and the court decides if a person is a suitable surety by considering their financial position, their character – in other words their lack of any criminal convictions themselves – and how likely the person is to be able to influence you to attend court.

Bail at a police station
After you have been charged at a police station, you must be given bail unless:

- Your name and address are unknown or doubted on reasonable grounds;

- The custody officer reasonably believes detention is necessary for your own protection or protection of others or their property: *or*
- The custody officer reasonably believes that you will fail to appear at court or that detention is necessary to avoid interference with the investigation or the administration of justice.

If you are detained by the police in this way, you must be brought before the next available magistrates' court, which, hopefully, would be no later than the following morning. If you are arrested on a Saturday, you may be held until the following Monday morning before being taken to court.

Bail at the magistrates' court

An accused person is entitled to bail unless certain exceptions apply. You are not allowed to make bail applications each and every time that you appear before the court, though if the first bail application is made in somewhat hurried circumstances and before your solicitor has had a chance to look into every aspect of the case, you will normally be allowed a further bail application one week later if bail is at first refused. If bail is refused, then you will normally not be allowed further applications unless there is a real change in your circumstances.

If the offence you are charged with does not carry a prison sentence, bail must be granted unless:

- You have previously been given bail and failed to come to court; *or*
- The court believes you should be kept in custody for your own protection; *or*
- You have been granted bail in connection with the present charge and have broken the conditions of your bail.

If the offence does carry a prison sentence, bail must still be granted unless the court believes that:

- Any of the above three factors apply; *or*
- You will probably not turn up for your trial; *or*
- You will probably commit an offence whilst on bail; *or*
- You will probably interfere with witnesses or in some other way obstruct the course of justice.

In deciding whether or not to give you bail, the court considers your own character, background, associations and connections in the community, any previous record on your part in turning up for trial after being bailed, the strength of the evidence against you, and anything else which it thinks relevant.

Bail at the Crown Court

If you are refused bail by the magistrates, you can appeal against their decision by applying for bail to a Crown Court judge. This hearing will normally be dealt with by your solicitor 'in chambers' which means that the application is heard in the judge's private room rather than in open court. You will not normally be present, but simply notified at the prison where you are held of the outcome of the application.

Bail from the High Court

If a Crown Court judge refuses you bail, you can apply to a High Court judge in chambers. Legal aid is not available for this particular step, so you would have to find out whether your solicitor would be prepared to deal with the application without charge or try to raise the necessary money through your family.

Reasons for bail decisions

Normally a court must give reasons for refusing to grant bail – and in certain cases must give reasons for granting bail, for example in cases of murder, manslaughter and rape where the prosecution have opposed the grant of bail.

Appeals by the prosecution

The prosecution now has a new right to appeal against the decision of the court to grant bail. The appeal has to be lodged quickly but you will be kept in custody pending the decision. It is very important to obtain legal advice if this happens to you. The right to appeal by the prosecution only applies where the offence charged carries a maximum penalty of five years or more and only where the defendant has previously committed an offence whilst on bail in the last ten years.

7.7 Spent convictions and the rehabilitation of offenders

The Rehabilitation of Offenders Act 1974 was an attempt to counter, at least in part, the effects of the belief that 'a leopard never changes its spots'. It was felt to be unfair that people who had at some time in the past acquired a conviction should have to carry it around their necks for the rest of their lives. The Act, therefore, provides an opportunity for offenders to wipe the slate clean.

How a sentence becomes spent

The Act applies to all types of sentence, whether it is prison, a fine, probation, absolute or conditional discharge, findings in a juvenile court that an offence has been committed, and convictions of certain offences in service disciplinary proceedings.

The rehabilitation period depends on the sentence and runs from the date of conviction. When the period has expired, the sentence becomes 'spent' and need not be revealed in the future, for example when you are applying for a job, completing an insurance proposal form, applying for credit facilities or for a tenancy of a property. Table 7.1 sets out the rehabilitation periods according to sentence.

The following sentences can never become spent:

- A sentence of imprisonment of more than two and a half years.
- A life sentence.
- Detention during Her Majesty's pleasure.

If you are convicted during the rehabilitation period of an offence which can only be tried in a magistrates' court, the new sentence will carry its own rehabilitation period and will have no effect on the earlier one. If the second offence is more serious and you receive a sentence covered by the Act, the earlier conviction will become spent only when the later one becomes spent.

Table 7.1 Spent convictions and the rehabilitation of offenders

Sentence	Rehabilitation period
Prison for more than two and a half years	never*
Prison for more than six months but less than two and a half years	10 years*
Prison for six months or less	7 years*
Fine	5 years*
Dismissal with disgrace from Her Majesty's service	10 years*
Dismissal from Her Majesty's service	7 years*
Detention in respect of conviction in service disciplinary proceedings	5 years*
Borstal	7 years
Detention for over six months but less than two and a half years	5 years
Detention for six months or less	3 years
Hospital order under Mental Health Act 1983	5 years or 2 years after order ceases to have effect, whichever is the longer
Absolute discharge	6 months
Conditional discharge, probation order, binding over, care order, supervision order	1 year after conviction of the order or 1 year after the order ends, whichever is the longer
Disqualification	The period of disqualification

* Note: These periods are reduced by half if the offender was under seventeen at the date of conviction.

It should be noted that it is the *length of the sentence imposed by the court* that is relevant and not, for example, the length of imprisonment actually served. If a person is given a sentence which can never become 'spent' this also prevents any earlier unspent conviction from becoming spent.

Under the law a sentence counts in the same way irrespective of whether you are sent to prison or the sentence is 'suspended'. The periods of rehabilitation for either are therefore the same as shown in the table above.

Where a person receives two or more prison sentences in the course of the same court case, the rehabilitation period depends on whether the sentences are ordered to take effect 'concurrently' (i.e. at the same time) or 'consecutively' (i.e. one after another). For example, if two six-month prison sentences are ordered to take effect concurrently, the sentences are treated separately, giving each conviction a rehabilitation period of seven years. However, if the two sentences are ordered to take effect consecutively, the sentences are treated as a single term of twelve months with a rehabilitation period of ten years.

Committing further offences

The aim of rehabilitation is that the person who has been convicted does not offend again. Therefore any subsequent conviction during the rehabilitation period of a previous conviction may extend the rehabilitation period of the first conviction. Whether it does depends, for example, on the seriousness of the subsequent conviction and the sentence imposed.

The effect of rehabilitation

Once the rehabilitation period has expired, not only do you not have to reveal it, but also it cannot be revealed by anyone else without your permission.

Evidence in legal proceedings

A spent conviction cannot be used in evidence in a civil court, tribunal, arbitration or disciplinary or similar hearing. You should not be asked questions about spent convictions and, if they are asked, you need not answer them unless you wish to.

This does not apply in:

- Service disciplinary proceedings.
- Applications for adoption, custody, wardship, guardianship or care proceedings.

- Where the court or tribunal is satisfied that justice cannot be done except by hearing the evidence involving the spent conviction.
- Criminal proceedings, but the Lord Chief Justice has ruled that no one should refer in open court to a spent conviction without the authority of the judge, whose authority should not be given unless the interests of justice so require.

Employment

Questions are often asked by potential employers with respect to a person's previous convictions. The general rule under the Act is that you can treat such questions as *not* relating to spent convictions. Therefore if you decide not to disclose a spent conviction you cannot be denied employment or subsequently dismissed on the grounds you failed to disclose it (although in exceptional circumstances you may be prosecuted for the criminal offence of 'obtaining a pecuniary advantage by deception'). Likewise, failing to disclose a spent conviction will not be proper grounds for excluding you from any office or profession. Nor can a spent conviction be grounds for prejudicing you in the way you are treated in any occupation or employment.

If, therefore, you are excluded or dismissed from employment on the grounds of a spent conviction, you may be able to take the matter to court for compensation or to an industrial tribunal as someone wrongfully dismissed. If you wish to pursue such action, you should first seek the assistance of a solicitor. However, many occupations and offices are specifically *excluded* from this general rule and these are dealt with below. You should read these carefully.

Some employers are adopting the practice of asking prospective or existing employees to obtain a copy of their criminal record under the provisions of the Data Protection Act 1984, which allows people the right to see their own computerised files. This record will list all your convictions including those that are spent. Although this practice is not unlawful, it is a misuse of the data protection laws and could be highly prejudicial to yourself. If you are concerned about agreeing to such a request, you should seek assistance from a union official or the Data Protection Registrar's Office at:

Springfield House
Water Lane
Wilmslow
Cheshire SK9 5AX
Tel: 0625 535777

Services

Some contracts, such as proposals for insurance, are governed by the legal principle that all relevant information will be disclosed by the person seeking insurance whether it is asked for or not – otherwise the contract could be treated as invalid. Clearly the existence of a driving offence or an offence for dishonesty may well be relevant to an insurance company. However, the Act specifically states that although the existing law requires that you disclose all relevant information in this situation, this does *not* extend to disclosing spent convictions.

Going abroad

It is important to remember that the Act applies only to the United Kingdom and has no effect so far as the laws of other countries are concerned. This means, for example, that applicants for immigration and work permits and for travel visas to the USA are still obliged to make full disclosure of their criminal record, including spent convictions. Some foreign countries have legislation similar to the Rehabilitation of Offenders Act, but to discover what safeguards apply it is necessary to consult the laws of the country concerned – you can do this by asking their embassy in this country.

Defamation proceedings

A reference to a spent conviction in a newspaper article, for example, can give rise to a claim for damages for defamation. However, in order to protect free speech, the Act states that a person who is sued in defamation proceedings for disclosing a spent conviction may rely on the defences of 'justification' (i.e. the statement is true) and/or 'fair comment' (i.e. the statement was a fair comment on a matter of public interest). In order to succeed when such a defence is raised, you would have to prove that the statement was published with *malice* – that is, it was published with some irrelevant, spiteful or improper motive.

In addition, the reporting of certain events and the making of statements in certain circumstances can give rise to the defence of 'absolute' or 'qualified privilege'. For example, fair and accurate newspaper reports of judicial proceedings are 'absolutely privileged' (i.e. protected) against a defamation action (see p. 34).

As the law relating to defamation is complex, you should seek specialist legal advice. Legal aid is not available for defamation actions.

Exceptions to the Act

The Act is frequently criticised for the many and wide exceptions made to the general principle that a person can become rehabilitated. If you fall within any of the exceptions, you will be treated as if the Act had never been passed and you are not entitled to rehabilitation for the spent conviction. These exceptions are listed in the Orders made by a relevant government minister and largely relate to matters of national security, the care of those who are considered to be vulnerable and the administration of justice.

Excepted professions, occupations and offices

A number of professions, occupations and offices have been excepted from the general rule that a person does not have to disclose a spent conviction – see above. The table below lists the professions, occupations and offices which are excepted.

If you apply, therefore, to join one of the professions, occupations or offices listed in the table below you will normally be asked (and must be told why) to disclose all previous convictions, including spent convictions, in order that your suitability for the position may be assessed. Furthermore, a spent conviction may be considered grounds for excluding or dismissing you from any profession, occupation or office listed in Table 7.2.

Table 7.2: Excepted professions, occupations and offices

Accountants	Nurses and midwives
Dealer in securities	Opticians
Dentists	Pharmaceutical chemists
Director, controller, etc. of	Police constables
insurance company or	Prison board of visitors
building society	Prison officers
Firearms dealers	Probation officers
Judicial appointments	Teachers
Lawyers	Traffic wardens
Manager or trustee of unit trust	Veterinary surgeons
Medical practitioners	

Other excepted occupations include:

- Any office or employment where the question is asked for the purpose of safeguarding national security – for example, a person employed by the UK Atomic Energy Authority, the Civil Aviation Authority or an officer of the Crown.
- Certain types of work in health and social services where the work involves access to people over sixty-five, to people suffering from serious illness or mental disorder, alcoholics or drug addicts, to the blind, deaf and dumb, or where the work is concerned with the provision of care, leisure or recreational facilities to persons under eighteen (see below for further details).

* Applications for certain certificates and licences (for example, concerning firearms, explosives and gaming) require that spent convictions be disclosed and can be taken into account by the licensing authority. Failure to disclose a spent conviction in these circumstances could result in the refusal or loss of the licence, certificate, etc., or even in prosecution for non-disclosure.

Disclosure of criminal background of those with access to children

Since 1986, procedures have been adopted to check any possible criminal background with local police forces of those applying for work (including volunteers) with substantial access to children in the statutory sector (i.e. local authorities or health authorities) – for example, staff of day nurseries, playgroups, children's homes and social workers, school teachers, community and youth workers. Since 1989, this has been extended to similar work with voluntary organisations. The check also applies to prospective foster parents, adoptive parents and childminders, including other adults in their households.

Where a police check is required in relation to such a job with a local authority or health authority, you will be requested to list any convictions (including those that are spent), bind-over orders or cautions and be asked to give your consent in writing for a police check to be carried out. It should also be drawn to your attention that by virtue of an exception to the Rehabilitation of Offenders Act, spent convictions will be disclosed by the police and taken into account in deciding whether to employ you.

Where the information provided by the police differs from that provided by yourself, this must be discussed with you before a decision is taken to employ you. If you consider that the police information is incorrect, you are entitled to make representations to the police through a nominated person. The police may also disclose 'other relevant information' concerning you. This must be restricted to factual information which the police would be prepared to present as evidence in court, or details of acquittals or decisions not to prosecute where the circumstances of the case would give cause for concern.

It is for the prospective employers to decide your suitability, taking into account only those offences which may be relevant to the particular job in question – for example, they will consider the nature of the offence, when it occurred and the frequency of offences. The fact that you have a criminal record does not automatically render you unsuitable for work with children. On the other hand, it is not only sexual offences which may render a person unsuitable.

If you are concerned that a prospective employer may take into account a conviction that you consider to be irrelevant to the job applied for, you should attach a note to your original disclosure form which explains the circumstances of the offence and why you consider it to be irrelevant. If you are denied employment on the basis of a conviction which you consider to be irrelevant, you should seek legal advice as, in limited circumstances, it may be possible to challenge the decision.

Prospective employers may also use the Department of Health's Consultancy Service and the Department of Education's 'List 99' as a further check on a person's suitability. These departments hold lists of people who, because of a previous conviction or incident, are considered to be unfit to work with children and young people. You should have been informed at the time by the department concerned that your name had come to their attention and why. You should also have been given the opportunity to make representations about the incident which they wish to record.

For further information, see Home Office Circular No. 102/88 Protection of Children: Disclosure of Criminal Background of those with Access to Children (in the statutory sector) and Home Office Circular No. 58/1989 (in the voluntary sector). Copies of these circulars are obtainable free from:

F2 Division
The Home Office
Queen Anne's Gate
London SW1H 9AT
Tel: 071 273 3000

Police reporting of convictions

The general rule is that police information (including information on convictions) should not be disclosed unless there are important considerations of public interest to justify departure from the general rule of confidentiality. Exceptions to this rule are made where there is a need:

- To protect vulnerable members of society.
- To ensure good and honest administration of law.
- To protect national security.

The effect of this means that under Home Office Circular No. 45/1986 Police Reports of Convictions and Related Information, the police may disclose when it is requested, information on a person's past convictions, cases pending and other such background information as would be admissible in court in the circumstances listed in below in respect of:

- Persons to be appointed to positions with substantial access to children (see above).
- Members of or visitors to the same household as a child subject to a case conference on non-accidental injury to children.
- Parents (and their cohabitees) to whom a local authority proposes to return a child in care.
- Applicants for compensation for criminal injury.
- Applicants to join the police.
- Applicants for certain licences; for example, gaming, lottery, sex establishments and entertainment licences.
- Applicants for and holders of licences as heavy goods vehicles and passenger service vehicle operators.
- Applicants for licences as dealers in securities.
- Applicants for consumer credit licences.
- Applicants for casual Post Office work.
- Potential jurors in cases involving national security and terrorism.
- Social enquiry reports and other reports by probation officers.
- Welfare reports for courts determining care and custody of children.
- Those subject to national security vetting.

Under the same circular, the police are asked to report convictions as they occur to the professional bodies of those groups listed in Table 7.3, particularly where the offences involve violence, dishonesty, drink or drugs, as they may reflect on a person's suitability to continue in a profession or office.

Table 7.3: Reporting convictions of those in certain professions and occupations

British Telecom staff	Post Office staff
Civil Aviation Authority staff	Probation officers
Civil servants	Social workers
Dentists	Teachers (including student
Lawyers	teachers) and ancillary staff
Magistrates	UK Atomic Energy Authority
Medical practitioners	and British Nuclear Fuels
Midwives and Nurses	Limited Staff
Pharmaceutical chemists' staff	Youth workers

Unauthorised disclosure of convictions
The Act makes it an offence if:

- An official who, in the course of their official duties, unlawfully discloses someone else's spent conviction. The penalty is a maximum fine of £2,500 (as from October 1992).

- Any person who obtains details of spent convictions from any official record by means of fraud, dishonesty or a bribe. The penalty is up to six months' imprisonment and/or a maximum fine of £5,000 (as from October 1992).

If someone wrongfully reveals that you have a past conviction, you can:

- Report the matter to the police and ask that the incident be investigated with a view to the person being prosecuted.
- Sue the person concerned for defamation (see above).
- Make a formal police complaint.

If, for example, the police reveal a conviction to an employer who is not within the categories set out in the list on p. 178, you may be able to bring a claim for damages. Although this has yet to be tested in the courts, you should consult a solicitor to see if this is possible in your circumstances.

7.8 Stop press

The Criminal Justice and Public Order Bill being discussed by Parliament in January 1994 will, if passed, include provisions to: allow courts to assume that silence under questioning and the refusal to give evidence are indications of guilt; and restrict the right to bail in some serious offences.

7.9 Further information

Useful organisations

Consult your local telephone directory for addresses and telephone numbers of the following organisations:

- Citizens' Advice Bureaux
- Law centres

Bibliography

Archbold, *Criminal Pleading, Evidence and Practice*, Sweet and Maxwell, published every year.

Smith and Hogan, *Criminal Law*, Butterworth's, 1993.

Stone's Justices' Manual, Butterworth's, published every year.

8

The rights of prisoners

This chapter sets out the rights that prisoners have. It deals with:

- Reception.
- Complaints and requests.
- The courts.
- Access to lawyers.
- Visits and letters.
- Telephones.
- Marriage and founding a family.
- Women prisoners.
- Categorisation and allocation.
- Discipline, adjudication and punishment.
- Segregation and transfer.
- Medical treatment.
- Work, exercise and education.
- Parole.
- Further information.

Prisoners retain certain basic rights which survive despite imprisonment. The rights of access to the courts and of respect for one's bodily integrity (i.e. not to be assaulted or treated medically against one's will) are such fundamental rights. Others may be recognised as the law develops. Prisoners lose only those civil rights that are taken away either expressly by an Act of Parliament or by necessary implication, for instance, prisoners detained following conviction do not have a right to vote. The test in every case is whether the right is fundamental and whether there is anything in the Prison Act, the Prison Rules or elsewhere which authorises the prison authorities to limit such a right. In law, the Prison Rules have legal force only insofar as the Prison Act gives authority for the Rule: legal challenges to the Rules have been successful because the courts have held that the Act does not authorise the scope of a particular Rule.

The Prison Rules provide a structure and framework for the regulation of prison life. Breach of the Rules by the prison authorities does not of itself give prisoners the right to sue in the courts for damages. More detailed instructions are given in the Standing Order and Circular

Instructions, the internal directives which govern the conduct of prison life issued to prison governors and prison officers. A number of the Standing Orders are now published by the Home Office. They are a vital source of information about prisoners' rights and entitlements.

8.1 Reception

On reception into prison a prisoner will be searched and may be photographed. Any property which he or she is not allowed to have with him or her in prison will be kept by the prison authorities. A list will be made on arrival of all property and the prisoner must be given the opportunity to check it is correct before signing it. All cash must be paid into an account which is under the governor's control. All prisoners should be issued on arrival with a copy of the Prisoners' Information Pack. A copy of the Prison Rules must be made available to any prisoner who requests it.

8.2 Complaints and requests

Within prison, complaints and/or requests may be made in person or in writing to a governor, or to the Board of Visitors. A governor must be available each day to hear complaints or requests. The prisoner need not give the reason for his or her application to see the governor and an application may be made direct in writing and in confidence to the governor or chair of the Board of Visitors. Prisoners will have to give the reason why they wish the complaint to be dealt with in confidence, but it may be that the person complained about will be told of the complaint – which rather discourages complaints. If a complaint is made to the governor a written reply should normally be received within seven days.

If the prisoner is not satisfied with the decision, he or she may appeal to the area manager at regional headquarters. Some issues – called 'reserved subjects' – may only be dealt with by Prison Service Headquarters. These include parole, transfer to or removal from mother and baby units, Category A status, life sentence prisoners, transfers and deportation. Complaints or requests made to the area manager should receive a response within six weeks. The booklet 'How to Make a Request or Complaint : Information for Prisoners' which gives details of the procedures should be available in prison libraries.

Prisoners may also raise complaints with any outside organisation or person, for example, their MP, the Parliamentary Commissioner for Administration (the ombudsman), the European Parliament, the European Commission on Human Rights (ECHR), the police; petitions may also be made to the Queen and Parliament. For a complaint to be admissible with the ECHR it must be made within six months of exhausting all channels of complaint in this country. Again, details of how to petition the ECHR should be available in the prison library.

8.3 The courts

Prisoners have the absolute right to commence proceedings – both criminal and civil – in the courts either directly and in person or through a solicitor. Prisoners can conduct:

* Normal civil proceedings such as divorce or breach of contract.
* Cases where the prisoner is suing the prison authorities, for example for assault or medical negligence.
* Judicial review in the High Court of an administrative or disciplinary decision which affects him or her.

The High Court will only intervene by way of judicial review when it can be shown that a decision has been taken which is wrong in law (for example, where the prison authorities had no power to do what they did) or the decision was flawed by procedural unfairness. The High Court has reviewed a wide range of decisions by the prison authorities, including parole and parole revocation, transfer, censorship, segregation and the separation of a mother from her baby. The Race Relations Act applies to prisons and discrimination (for example, in the allocation of jobs) would be actionable in the courts.

A breach of the Prison Rules does not give a prisoner grounds by itself to sue the prison authorities for their failure to comply with the Rules.

At present, a prisoner acting without a solicitor who wishes to be produced at court to present his or her case in person must apply to the Home Office by completing the relevant request form, which includes a requirement that he or she undertakes to pay the costs of his or her production. The courts have recognised that there may be an appearance of bias if the Home Office refused to produce at court a prisoner who was unable or who had refused to give an undertaking as to costs in an action when the Home Office is the defendant to the action. A prisoner faced with this difficulty should apply to the court which is to hear his or her action for guidance.

8.4 Access to lawyers

Prisoners have an absolute right to have visits from and correspond with their solicitor. They do not have to tell the prison authorities why they wish to contact a solicitor, nor make any complaint about prison treatment to the authorities before contacting a solicitor for legal advice.

8.5 Visits and letters

There are detailed regulations on communications which are set out in Standing Order 5 which is publicly available from HMSO and which should also be available in the prison library.

Visits

Convicted prisoners are entitled to a visit on reception to prison and then a minimum of two visits every four weeks. Governors should allow more visits if facilities and staffing make this possible and many prisons do so. Prisoners will be issued with visiting orders (VOs) which must be sent out, with the visitors' names on them. Visitors then present the order on arrival at prison. Up to three adults and four children are normally allowed at once.

Unconvicted prisoners may have daily visits. These should total at least one and a half hours a week, though in practice such visits are likely to be limited to short daily visits.

Visits from legal advisers, probation officers, etc., do not count against a prisoner's visits' entitlement. Nor is there a restriction on the number of visits allowed from a legal adviser.

The Assisted Prison Visits Scheme exists to help close relatives with the costs of travel. All prisoners, convicted and unconvicted, are eligible for assisted visits if the relative(s) qualify because of their low income.

The governor or Board of Visitors may grant extra visits if they are considered necessary for the welfare of the prisoner or his or her family. A prisoner who is located far from home may save up to twenty-six visits a year and then be transferred temporarily to a prison near his or her family to have these accumulated visits. The prisoner must have served at least six months since he or she was allocated to a prison to be eligible for accumulated visits.

Visitors may bring cigarettes to be smoked during visits, but this is a privilege which may be withdrawn. It is a criminal offence to pass other items to a prisoner during a visit, for which the visitor can be fined or imprisoned. The governor has power to refuse or restrict visits on the grounds of security, good order and discipline, or if he or she believes it will prevent or discourage crime, by either:

- Refusing visits from certain people.
- Ordering closed visits, i.e. in a small room with a prison officer present.

- Ordering screened visits where there is a glass partition between prisoner and visitor.

There is power to search and strip search visitors entering or leaving prisons providing that no more than reasonable force is used, that the decision to search is not perverse and that the search is conducted in a reasonable and decent manner and only by members of the same sex as the visitor.

Police officers may interview an inmate in prison, but only if the prisoner is willing to be interviewed. The provisions of the Police and Criminal Evidence Act and the Codes of Practice do not generally apply to interviews in prison but instructions to the prison authorities say that the spirit of the provisions must be observed as though the interview were at the police station. Copies of the Codes of Practice must be made available in the prison library. The prisoner of course has the right to consult a legal adviser before any interview takes place.

Letters

Convicted prisoners may send one letter a week on which the postage will be paid (the 'statutory' letter) and at least one 'privilege' letter the postage for which must be paid for out of prison earnings. The statutory letter may not be withdrawn or withheld as part of punishment for a disciplinary offence. In addition, prisoners may be granted 'special' letters which do not count against the statutory or privilege letter allowance. A special letter should be granted for example, after conviction to allow a prisoner to settle his or her business affairs, when transferred to a different prison, or to make arrangements regarding employment and accommodation on release.

In practice prisoners in many prisons may send and receive more letters than this minimum allowance. Prisoners in open prison have no restriction on the volume of their correspondence. Prisoners may also receive stamped addressed envelopes from their correspondents to help with postage costs.

Unconvicted prisoners may send as many letters as they wish at their own expense and will be allowed two second-class letters per week on which the postage will be paid by the prison authorities.

Censorship

Mail is censored in dispersal prisons (those designed to accommodate high-risk prisoners) and for all category A prisoners, but otherwise letters will not be read. There is power for the governor to return an 'excessive' number of letters from a correspondent, and if they are 'overlong' the governor may request letters be limited to four sides of A5 paper. Letters may be returned to the sender if these requests are ignored.

Complaints about prison treatment are no longer prohibited and letters – whether to family or to MPs, the ECHR, etc. – may not be stopped on this ground.

Letters between a prisoner and his or her legal adviser are protected from interference and may not be read nor stopped, whether or not legal proceedings have been issued. There may be examination of such correspondence only to the minimum extent necessary to check that it is bona fide legal correspondence. If a letter is to be inspected it must be done in the presence of the prisoner.

8.6 Telephones

Card-operated telephones for the use of prisoners are being installed in all prisons so that closer links with family and friends can be maintained by those in prison. Prisoners who are category A or who are on the escape list (a list of those prisoners most likely to escape) will not be allowed use of cardphones. For security reasons all calls will be recorded and all calls may be monitored, except those to legal advisers, the Samaritans and other 'reputable organisations'. Use of the telephone may be limited by the governor, but should not be restricted as part of a disciplinary punishment unless the offence was directly related to the misuse of the cardphone or phone card.

8.7 Marriage and founding a family

High-risk prisoners who wish to get married will have to make arrangements with the prison authorities for a service to take place within the prison. Low-risk prisoners may be given escorted leave to marry outside prison.

Prisoners, especially those serving long sentences, may wish to start a family with their partner by artificial insemination. Prison Department policy is that this should only be allowed where there are 'exceptionally strong reasons', and where the applicant couple are legally married. Article 12 of the European Convention on Human Rights guarantees the right to marry and found a family: a refusal by the Prison Department to allow artificial insemination could be challenged in the ECHR proceedings.

8.8 Women prisoners

Male and female prisoners will be held completely separately from each other, though this may be in the same prison. As a matter of practice, women prisoners are allowed to wear their own clothes and do not have to wear prison uniform.

There are a limited number of mother and baby units within the prison system. A baby may be kept up to the age of nine months in Holloway, eighteen months at Styal (both closed prisons) and eighteen months at Askham Grange. If the baby has reached these age limits before the mother has served her sentence, the mother may be forced to give up looking after her baby either then or at an earlier stage.

8.9 Categorisation and allocation

There are broadly two categories of prison: local prison for short-term prisoners, and training (or dispersal) prisons for longer-term prisoners. Immediately after conviction a male prisoner will be held at a local prison while his security categorisation and allocation is decided. Because there are fewer women prisoners and prisons, the arrangements are not exactly the same.

Categorisation
There are four security categories:

- Category A: prisoners whose escape would be highly dangerous to the public, police or security of the state.
- Category B: prisoners who do not need the highest conditions of security but for whom escape must be made very difficult.
- Category C: prisoners who cannot be trusted in open conditions but who do not have the ability or resources to make a determined escape attempt.
- Category D: prisoners who can reasonably be trusted to serve their sentences in open conditions.

There is no internal appeal against a categorisation decision, though a review could be requested through the complaints or requests procedure. However, a prisoner could apply to the High Court for judicial review of his or her categorisation if there were evidence that it had been arrived at unfairly, for example by taking account of irrelevant information.

Category A prisoners have greater restrictions upon them for security reasons, and their visitors will be vetted by the police on behalf of the prison authorities.

Allocation
Prisoners may be allocated to any prison in England and Wales according to the offence, sentence, security category and individual circumstances of the prisoner. There is no right to be located close to home, but the prisoner can apply for transfer (as can his or her family,

who might wish to put in evidence, for example from a GP about the difficulties illness causes in travelling long distances).

Again, the High Court could intervene in an allocation decision if it could be shown to be, for example, wrongly motivated, and especially if it deprived an unconvicted prisoner of access to his or her lawyers and family.

8.10 Discipline, adjudication and punishment

The Prison Rules create a number of offences against discipline which can be punished by the governor. The Board of Visitors no longer has any powers in relation to disciplinary matters. If the alleged offence is too serious for the governor to deal with, it will be referred to the police for prosecution in the criminal courts. If there is to be a referral to the police a disciplinary charge should still be laid against the prisoner and, if the governor is satisfied that there is a case to answer, he or she should adjourn the hearing pending the outcome of the police investigation. If the police decide not to proceed in the outside courts the governor may continue the proceedings. However, a prisoner cannot be tried for the same offence in both the criminal courts and before the governor.

There is a new offence of prison mutiny which can be punished with imprisonment up to ten years, a fine or both. It is committed if two or more prisoners engage in conduct intended to 'further a common purpose of overthrowing lawful authority' in a prison. Prisoners may be regarded as taking part in a mutiny if they fail to leave when there is a reasonable opportunity to do so.

Offences under the Prison Rules range from the more serious, for example, assault, which are also criminal offences to more minor offences, for example, refusing to work or the catch-all 'in any way offending against good order and discipline'. If the governor is to deal with the alleged offence then the procedure as set out in the 'Manual on the Conduct of Adjudications' should be followed (a copy of this should be available on request). The essential points are:

- A charge must be laid as soon possible and, 'save in exceptional circumstances', within forty-eight hours of the discovery of the offence.
- Pending enquiry by the governor a prisoner who is to be charged *may* be segregated. After the governor's first enquiry, segregation is only permissible under Rule 43 (see below).
- The charge must be in sufficient detail for the prisoner to know exactly what is alleged against him or her.

- The governor must ask if the prisoner understands the procedure and if he or she wishes to be legally represented or assisted, but is not obliged to grant a request for legal representation; as an alternative, the prisoner can ask for the assistance of a 'McKenzie friend' (see p. 163).
- If legal *representation* is refused, the prisoner may still request an adjournment in order to get legal *advice* from a solicitor.
- The prisoner may request copies of statements or other written material which is to be used in evidence and the governor should usually allow this.
- At the hearing the prisoner must be allowed to put questions to witnesses who give evidence against him or her and to call witnesses who are relevant to his or her defence.
- The case must be proved to the criminal standard of proof, i.e. beyond a reasonable doubt.

The maximum number of additional days which a governor may order to be served as punishment for an offence is fifty-six. If found guilty of more than one offence arising from the same incident punishment may be ordered to run consecutively, but the total period may not exceed fifty-six days. Other punishments include loss of privileges (maximum twenty-eight days), stoppage of earnings (maximum twenty-eight days), cellular confinement (maximum fourteen days).

A prisoner may appeal against the finding of guilt and/or against the sentence from the governor to the area manager. Governor's disciplinary hearings can now be reviewed by the High Court, but only if the governor made a mistake in law or adopted a procedure which was unfair.

Prisoners may apply to the governor for cancellation of additional day awards. Neither the seriousness of the original disciplinary offence, nor the criminal offence for which the prisoner is serving his or her sentence are relevant to the question of whether an award of additional days should be reduced in whole or part. The question is whether the prisoner's behaviour and attitude have shown a improvement which should properly be rewarded by a reduction either in whole or in part of an award of additional days.

8.11 Segregation and transfer

Prisoners can be segregated either as punishment following adjudication (maximum fourteen days), or 'for the maintenance of good order and discipline', or at the prisoner's request for his or her own protection. Prisoners segregated as a punishment must first be certified fit for such punishment by the medical officer, who should also see the prisoner daily during segregation and may order a return to normal location on medical grounds.

Prisoners segregated in the interests of good order and discipline (GOAD) may not be segregated for more than fourteen days without the authorisation of either a member of the Board of Visitors or the Home Secretary. This authorisation may be for a maximum of one month, but may be renewed from month to month up to a maximum of six months. Reasons for the segregation must be given as soon as possible and 'as far as practicable' in writing if the prisoner so requests.

Additionally, prisoners considered to be seriously disruptive or subversive may be transferred on a temporary basis to another prison for a period of up to one month for a 'cooling off' period. Again, inmates must be told of the reason for transfer as far as is practicable and as soon as is possible, and in writing if so requested. In a change from previous practice, a prisoner transferred under this provision must not be automatically segregated at the new prison, but only if the governor of the new prison considers it necessary. As above, the governor may only authorise segregation for up to fourteen days; a longer period must be authorised by the Board of Visitors or the Home Secretary. Prisoners segregated are still entitled to exercise as on normal location.

Temporary confinement and restraints

Prison officers are instructed not to use force 'unless absolutely necessary' and when necessary to use no more force than is 'absolutely necessary' to achieve the required objective.

A violent or unmanageable prisoner may be placed temporarily in a special cell, but not as punishment, nor may he or she be held in a special cell after he or she has ceased to be violent. The cell will be stripped of furniture except for a mattress or have cardboard furniture which cannot cause injury. Furthermore, the governor may order a prisoner be put in physical restraints where necessary to prevent injury to him or herself, others, damaging property or creating a disturbance. Body belts, which are made of a leather belt around the waist with handcuffs attached to restrain movement, may be used for this purpose. The use of physical restraints should only be in rare and extreme cases. If so restrained, the medical officer and a member of the Board of Visitors must be informed without delay. If the medical officer disagrees with the order to put the prisoner under restraint the governor must comply with his or her recommendation.

Prisoners put into a special cell or mechanical restraint must be observed every fifteen minutes and be visited by the governor and medical officer twice every twenty-four hours. A prisoner may not be held for longer than twenty-four hours in mechanical restraints without the written authorisation of a member of the Board of Visitors or an officer of the Home Office (who is not an officer of the prison). If a prisoner is held wrongly – either unnecessarily or for too long – in a body belt or other restraint he or she will be entitled to claim damages in the court for assault.

8.12 Medical treatment

Convicted prisoners are in the care of the Prison Medical Service, which is not part of the National Health Service; they therefore have no right to consult the doctor or dentist of their choice for treatment. Unconvicted prisoners, if willing to pay any expenses involved, may be visited and treated by the doctor or dentist of their choice. However, a prisoner who is party to legal proceedings may be visited by an independent doctor where examination is relevant to those proceedings.

The Access to Health Records Act 1990 gives the prisoner the right to see (and have copies made on request) their medical records since 1 November 1991 (though disclosure can be refused on the basis that it would cause serious harm to the physical or mental health of the patient or any other individual).

All medical information on a prisoner should be treated in confidence and is not to be disclosed except for 'specifically defined purposes'. The same confidentiality applies to prisoners who are HIV positive. The prison guidelines say 'If it seems desirable in the inmate's interest to inform a third party [that he or she is HIV positive] a member of staff must consult the prisoner and must obtain the prisoner's consent before disclosing the information'. The prison authorities may be liable in damages if they negligently reveal confidential information (for example, that a prisoner has committed sexual offences) as result of which he is assaulted.

8.13 Work, exercise and education

Work

All convicted prisoners may be required to work unless the medical officer has certified the prisoner unfit for all or a specific type of work. It is a disciplinary offence to refuse to work or intentionally to fail to work properly. Account should be taken of a prisoner's religion so that he or she is not required to work on recognised days of religious observance.

The Prison Rules give the maximum working day as ten hours, but do not give a minimum working day. Prison workshops are exempt from the provisions of the Factories Act: if injured at work prisoners must rely upon a civil claim of negligence in order to claim damages for their injury. In practice, governors are required to observe the requirements of the Factories Act and the Health and Safety at Work Act 1974; governors are also instructed to give Health and Safety Executive inspectors access to all areas of the prison.

If found guilty of a disciplinary offence a prisoner may be excluded from working with other prisoners as part of his punishment for a maximum of fourteen days and/or have his earnings stopped or reduced for a maximum period of fifty-six days, the total amount stopped or deducted not to exceed twenty-eight days' earnings.

Exercise

Convicted prisoners have a right to daily exercise which should be for one hour unless they are already engaged in outdoor work. This can be reduced to half an hour, and in practice it often is where there is evening association with other prisoners. Unconvicted prisoners are allowed an hour a day of outdoor exercise, weather permitting.

Education

The prison department is under a general duty to provide evening classes at every prison and to encourage prisoners to 'profit' from the educational facilities provided. This does not mean that every prisoner has a right to the educational course of his or her choice, and the prison authorities have a wide discretion as to what educational facilities they provide and who is to benefit from them.

Local education authorities provide a programme of evening classes in all prisons but classroom space is often limited. Facilities for daytime study and remedial teaching vary. The governor is responsible for assessing a prisoner's needs and suitability for further study. He or she can release individuals from work duty for study. Permission from the prison authorities can be obtained to take a correspondence course and long-term prisoners often study Open University courses leading to a degree. All prisons have at least one library.

Governors are instructed that prisoners of compulsory school age should have educational and vocational training for at least fifteen hours per week and should be denied education only as a last resort.

The governor may suspend or end attendance at educational classes if he or she believes it necessary to prevent disruption or for security reasons, or if a disciplinary punishment, for example segregation, prevents it, but removal from education may not in itself be ordered as a punishment.

Reading and writing materials

Prisoners are entitled to have supplied to them at their own expense 'books, newspapers, writing materials and other means of occupation' except those which appear objectionable. Generally material should only be denied if it includes matters which incites or involves criminal or disciplinary offences. While it may be permissible to withhold a particular issue of a publication, a blanket ban may be challengeable in the courts.

8.14 Parole

The rules regarding release from custody changed in October 1992 and a different scheme applies to all those *sentenced* on or after 1 October 1992.

Sentence prior to 1 October 1992

Prisoners serving more than twelve months will be eligible for release on parole one third of the way through the sentence. Release will be automatic at the two-thirds stage (subject to any loss of remission for disciplinary offences). Consideration for parole happens automatically but after October 1994 all prisoners will be considered under the new system described below.

Sentence on or after 1 October 1992

Remission has been abolished. Those serving less than four years will automatically be released halfway through their sentence. For those serving twelve months or less release is unconditional. Those serving over twelve months will be released on licence until the three quarters point of their sentence and will be subject to compulsory supervison by the probation service. Conditions may be attached to the licence, for example to attend medical or psychiatric treatment, not to undertake certain types of work, not to communicate with named persons. For short-term offenders only, failure to comply with licence conditions is an offence which can be tried and punished at the magistrates' court.

If the released prisoner commits any offence punishable by imprisonment between the time of his or her release and the date when his or her original sentence runs out, then he or she will be liable to serve the balance of the original sentence which is outstanding at the time of the fresh offence.

For those serving four years or more the system of parole remains and is as follows: prisoners will be eligible for release on parole once half of the sentence has been served; at the two-thirds stage of the sentence the prisoner will be released automatically. Between the two-thirds automatic release point and the three-quarters point in the overall sentence, the 'at risk' provisions with regard to further offences which are imprisonable apply as they do for short-term prisoners. Long-term prisoners who are in breach of parole licence conditions may be recalled to prison and if recalled may remain in prison until the three-quarters point of the original sentence. If recalled, the prisoner must be told of the reasons for recall and can appeal against the decision in writing to the Parole Board.

The parole process will begin six months before the prisoner is first eligible for release on parole. Following interview by a member of the Parole Board a dossier will be compiled of all the material to go before the Board. The prisoner will be shown all such reports (unless it is considered some material should not be shown: any proposal to withhold material must be referred to the chair of the Parole Board) and his or her comments and representations will go before the Board when the case is considered. The prisoner should be told whether parole has been granted three weeks before he or she is eligible for release and reasons for the decision will be given. The release dates of long- and short-term prisoners will be subject to postponement if 'additional day awards' have been made as punishment for disciplinary offences.

The Home Secretary has power to release any prisoner on compassionate grounds 'in exceptional circumstances'. A prisoner so released will be subject to supervision up to the three-quarters point in the sentence (or, for those serving less than twelve months, the halfway point).

Life sentence prisoners

There are two categories of life sentence: a life sentence is *mandatory* if convicted of murder. For other offences (for example, rape, grievous bodily harm) the court *may* impose a life sentence. This is referred to as a discretionary life sentence.

Discretionary lifers

The trial judge will usually, when sentencing, fix the punishment period – the tariff – to be served before release can be considered. Towards the end of this period there will be a hearing before a panel of the Parole Board to decide whether the prisoner should be released. The Discretionary Lifer Panel will meet at the prison where the prisoner is located to consider the case. The prisoner is entitled to legal representation (and legal aid is available for this) to prepare and conduct his or her case. The prisoner is entitled to see all reports which go before the Panel except those which would 'adversely affect the health or welfare of the prisoner or others'; in such a case the reports must still be shown to the legal representative.

If the Panel is satisfied that it is no longer necessary for the protection of the public that the prisoner be detained, then he or she will be released. If the Panel does not direct release, the prisoner is entitled to have his or her case considered again by the Panel at two-year intervals.

Mandatory lifers

Those serving a sentence for murder may be released if the Parole Board recommends release to the Home Secretary and the Home Secretary, after consultation with the Lord Chief Justice and the trial judge (if available), accepts that recommendation. The decision is that of the Home Secretary, but the prisoner must be given:

- Information as to the period the judges have recommended should be served for the purpose of deterrence and retribution.
- The opportunity to make written representations to the Home Secretary as to how long he or she should serve before he or she can be considered for release.
- Reasons for any decision of the Home Secretary not to follow the recommendation of the judges as to how long should be served for the purposes of retribution and deterrence.

Pre-release
Prisoners may be granted home leave in the weeks or months prior to release so that they can visit their families and take steps to find work. Some long-term prisoners may be placed in pre-release hostels in order to help work towards release.

Discharge
On release, personal clothing and belongings are returned. Suitable clothing will be provided if the prisoner's clothing is inadequate. Money received on reception will be returned and most prisoners will be eligible for a discharge grant. Those serving under fourteen days are not entitled to the discharge grant, though the prison authorities may give a subsistence allowance to enable the prisoner to get to the local DSS office.

8.15 Further information

Useful organisations

Inquest
Ground Floor Alexander National House
330 Seven Sisters Road
London N4 2JP
Tel: 081 802 7430

Justice
11–12 Bouverie Street
London EC4Y 8BS
Tel: 071 353 5100

NACRO (National Association for Care and Resettlement of Offenders)
169 Clapham Road
London SW9 OP0
Tel: 071 582 6500

Prison Reform Trust
59 Caledonian Road
London N1 9BU
Tel: 071 278 9815

Prisoners' Advice Service
57 Chalton Street
London NW1
Tel: 071 388 8586

Rastafarian Advisory Centre
17a Netherwood Road
London W14
Tel: 071 602 3767

Women in Prison
Unit 3b
Aberdeen Studios
22 Highbury Grove
London N5
Tel: 071 226 5879

Women Prisoners' Resource Centre
Room 1 Thorpe Close
Ladbroke Grove
London W10 5XL
Tel: 081 968 3121

Bibliography

Shirley Cooklin, *From Arrest to Release*, Bedford Square Press, 1989.
Stephen Livingstone and Tim Owen, *Prison Law*, Oxford University Press, 1993.
Nancy Loucks, *The Prison Rules: A Working Guide*, Prison Reform Trust, 1993.

9

The right not to be discriminated against

This chapter deals with:

* Race discrimination.
* Sex discrimination.
* Sexual orientation.
* Disability discrimination.
* Further information.

9.1 Race discrimination

The Race Relations Act 1976 deals with race discrimination in employment and training; education; housing; the provision of goods, facilities and services; and advertising. It also set up the Commission for Racial Equality (CRE). The Act applies to England, Wales and Scotland, but not to Northern Ireland. Complaints by individuals who believe they have been discriminated against must be made either to the industrial tribunal (for employment-related matters) or to the County Court (in Scotland, the Sheriff Courts).

The Act refers to 'racial grounds' or 'racial group' which are defined to relate to colour, race, nationality or ethnic or national origin.

What is discrimination?

The Act sets out the circumstances in which discrimination on the grounds of race is unlawful. It defines three types of discrimination: direct discrimination, indirect discrimination and victimisation. Where the type of discrimination experienced by an individual cannot be described in one of these terms then the discrimination is not unlawful.

Direct discrimination occurs when a person treats another less favourably on racial grounds than he or she would treat, or treats, some other person. Sometimes direct discrimination is very obvious (for example, 'no blacks here'), but it may be more subtle. For example, quotas are sometimes operated by some clubs or pubs to prevent their black members or customers from exceeding a specific number or proportion. Or a person might be refused a job or promotion on the grounds that customers would not like it. Both of these situations are examples of direct discrimination. Intention and motive are irrelevant to the question of whether a person has been subject to unlawful direct discrimination on the grounds of race.

Segregation on racial grounds is defined by the Act as direct discrimination. Providing separate washing facilities for white and Asian employees, even if the facilities are of the same standard, might be an example of segregation on racial grounds.

Indirect discrimination occurs when a racial group is unjustifiably at a disadvantage in its ability to comply with a specific requirement or condition. For example, a job that requires the employee to be clean-shaven would put Sikhs in general at a disadvantage. Excluding job applicants who live in a certain area of a city, where that area is occupied by a higher proportion of ethnic minority people would put ethnic minority candidates at a disadvantage. If the requirement cannot be objectively justified with reference to criteria other than race, a claim for indirect discrimination would lie. Only people who themselves suffer this disadvantage can bring a complaint.

The concept of indirect discrimination is not user-friendly. The legal definition and the case law it has generated are complex and abstruse. Perhaps as a result, this provision of the Act is greatly underused. If you consider you unjustifiably suffer a disadvantage because you cannot comply with a requirement or condition you should consider seeking specialist help (see p. 226).

Intention is a relevant question in a claim based on indirect discrimination. The motive of the alleged discrimination is not considered when the tribunal or court is deciding whether, in fact, you have been discriminated against. However, once a finding of indirect discrimination has been made, a tribunal or court can decide not to make an award of compensation to you because it is satisfied that the discrimination was unintentional.

Victimisation occurs when one person treats another less favourably then he or she treats, or would treat, someone else in those particular circumstances because the person victimised has done any of the following:

- Brought proceedings against the discriminator or any other person under the Act; *or*
- Given evidence or information in connection with proceedings brought by any person against the discriminator or any other person under the Act; *or*
- Otherwise done anything under or by reference to the Act in relation to the discriminator or any other person; *or*

- Alleged that the discriminator or any other person has committed an act which (whether or not the allegation so states) would amount to a contravention of the Act; *or*
- The discriminator knows that the person victimised intends to do any of those things or suspects that the person victimised has done, or intends to do, any of them.

A person making allegations of discrimination must make those allegations in good faith in order to be protected by the victimisation provisions of the Act. An example of a situation in which a claim of victimisation might arise is where another employee accuses his or her boss of discriminating against him or her on the grounds of race and as a result of the complaint is demoted or disciplined.

Responsibility for acts of discrimination

The Act makes unlawful certain types of discrimination which are considered below. It also makes it unlawful to instruct someone to carry out an unlawful act of discrimination or to induce or attempt to induce, directly or indirectly, such an act; but only the CRE may bring proceedings in respect of such discrimination. Employers are made responsible for the unlawful acts of their employees, unless they can show that they took such steps as were reasonably practicable to prevent their employees from doing such unlawful discriminatory acts.

It is also unlawful for a person, including an employee, to aid another to do an unlawful act of discrimination. Thus where an employee devises a plan to send a racially offensive card to an employee who is a member of a racial group and enlists the help of a colleague to carry out that plan, both the originator of the plan and the colleague may be guilty of unlawful discrimination on the grounds of race.

Employment and training

This is dealt with in Part II of the Act. It is unlawful for an employer to discriminate against you on grounds of race in any of the following ways:

- Refusing to hire you or consider you for a job.
- Offering you a job on less favourable terms than other people.
- Refusing to promote you or transfer you to another job.
- Refusing to make provision for you to be trained.
- Giving you less favourable fringe benefits.
- Putting you on short-time work, dismissing you or making you redundant.

In order to succeed in a case brought in the industrial tribunal (see p. 292 for more information about making a complaint of race discrimination) you must show that you were being treated less favourably than someone of different racial or national origins would be treated and that the treatment you received was because of or on the grounds of your race. It is also necessary to show that you suffered some detriment or disadvantage as a result of this differential treatment. Injury to feelings is a detriment or disadvantage recognised by industrial tribunals and the courts. It is important to remember that the burden of proof is on you. This means that you must provide the industrial tribunal or court with enough evidence to prove your claim.

The Act covers both permanent and temporary jobs, whatever the size of the firm. It covers apprentices and trainees as well as other employees; partners in a firm of six or more partners (such as a solicitors' firm); the police (who are not technically employees); sub-contracted workers (such as the 'lump' building workers or night cleaners); and employment agencies.

It is unlawful for the government to discriminate on race grounds in appointing people to serve on public bodies. It is also unlawful for trade unions and professional associations to discriminate in any of the following ways:

- Deciding who to admit to membership.
- Refusing to let you join.
- Only allowing you to join on less favourable terms.
- By giving you fewer benefits, facilities or services or refusing to let you have any of these benefits (for example, legal services, representation in a dispute).
- Expelling you or subjecting you to any other disadvantage.

Similarly, it is unlawful for any licensing body (for example, the Law Society, which licenses solicitors; the Director General of Fair Trading, who licenses credit and hire businesses or the police, who license taxi-drivers) to discriminate on race grounds in deciding who can have a licence. Furthermore, whenever one of these bodies has to consider an applicant's 'good character' before giving a licence, they will be able to take into account any evidence about previous unlawful race discrimination. So, for instance, magistrates who are renewing a publican's licence should also take account of any evidence that the publican or his or her employees had previously refused to serve black people.

The Courts and Legal Services Act 1990 extended the non-discrimination provisions of the Act to the legal profession.

Racial abuse and harassment at work
If you are subjected to racial abuse and/or racial harassment at work you may be able to bring a claim under the Act. However, you will have to prove on a balance of probabilities that the insult, abuse or harassment

is aimed at you so that it will (or is likely to) come to your notice and that you are thereby disadvantaged at work, in order to succeed in your complaint. A complaint about race discrimination in the field of employment must be brought to an industrial tribunal (see p. 292) within three months.

Exceptions

It has already been noted that not all race discrimination is made unlawful by the Act. Racial discrimination is still lawful in any of the following situations:

- Employment in a private household.
- If an employer wants to employ someone who is not ordinarily resident in Great Britain, but who will be trained here before going to work abroad.
- Employment of workers on ships who were recruited outside Great Britain.
- Employment outside Great Britain.
- Employment in dramatic performances, or for artists' or photographic modelling, where someone of a particular racial group is needed for reasons of 'authenticity'.
- Employment in restaurants, etc., with a particular setting where someone of a particular racial group is needed for reasons of authenticity (for example, Chinese waiters or waitresses in a Chinese restaurant).
- Employment of someone to provide personal services to a particular racial group, where someone of the same racial group can do the job most effectively.

The last three exceptions are known as genuine occupational qualification exceptions. If race is genuinely an occupational qualification, then the employer may legitimately discriminate in the last three ways described above. In any of these cases, the employer must try to fill a vacancy from existing workers before discriminating on racial grounds. The CRE has published a Code of Practice for the elimination of racial discrimination and the promotion of equality of opportunity in employment which is obtainable from the CRE (see p. 226). The Code sets out guidelines of good race relations practice although it is not enforceable in law.

Training

It is unlawful for any of the following training organisations to discriminate on race grounds:

- Industrial training boards.

- Employment Services Agency.
- Training Services Agency.
- Employers' organisations which provide training.
- Any other organisation designated by the Home Secretary.

These organisations are, however, allowed to practise positive discrimination where there have been no people of a particular racial group, or very few, doing a particular kind of work, either in the whole of Great Britain or in a region, in the previous twelve months. In this case they will be allowed to run training courses or provide facilities for that racial group only, or to encourage people from that group to take up a particular kind of work.

Employers will also be allowed to run training courses for a particular racial group only, or to encourage them to take up a particular kind of work, where there have been no people of that racial group, or very few, doing that kind of work in the firm during the previous twelve months.

Trade unions and professional organisations are also allowed to organise special training courses to encourage people from a particular racial group to hold posts within the organisation (for example, as shop stewards or officials) where there have been very few or no people from that group holding such posts in the previous twelve months.

Education

Part III of the Act deals with discrimination in the field of education. The Race Relations Act applies to schools or colleges maintained by a local education authority (LEA), independent ('public' or fee-paying) schools, or colleges, special schools, grant-maintained 'opted-out' schools and universities. The Home Secretary can also designate other establishments to be covered by the law.

It is unlawful for any educational body (including the governors of a school or college and an LEA) to discriminate on race grounds in any of the following ways:

- The terms on which they admit you.
- Refusing to admit you.
- Providing more facilities or better facilities for particular racial groups.
- Expelling you or in any other way putting you at a disadvantage.
- Acting in any other way which involves race discrimination.

If you or your child has been discriminated against, you will have to make a complaint to the Secretary of State for Education (this does not apply to complaints against independent schools or universities where you apply to the institution directly). The Minister will have two months in which to do something about your complaint. If the Minister rejects your complaint, or the two months run out, you can make a complaint to the County Court. A County Court action must be brought within six months (or eight months if the complaint has first gone to the Minister).

The Act also puts a general duty on LEAs to ensure that educational facilities are provided without race discrimination. This duty is a general duty and cannot be enforced by you directly. You can, of course, draw the attention of local councillors and school governors to it. The general duty can only be enforced by the Secretary of State for Education ordering the LEA to carry out its duties reasonably.

It is lawful for LEAs and other bodies to provide special facilities to meet the particular needs of a racial group (for example, for language classes).

Overseas students

There is only one exception to the education sections of the Act and this concerns overseas students. It is lawful for any organisation or individual providing education or training to discriminate on racial grounds against people who are not ordinarily resident in Great Britain and who do not intend to remain in Great Britain after their period of education or training. This means, for instance, that it is lawful for colleges or halls of residence to charge higher fees to overseas students.

Housing

Housing and premises, such as business premises, are also covered by Part III of the Act. In general, it is unlawful for someone to discriminate on race grounds, when selling, letting, subletting or managing property, in any of the following ways:

- In the terms on which you are offered the premises.
- By refusing to let you buy or rent the premises.
- By treating you differently from other people on a list of people wanting to buy or rent the premises.
- By refusing to agree to the transfer of a lease to you.
- By refusing you access to any benefits or facilities in the premises you occupy.
- By evicting you or subjecting you to any other disadvantage.

The law covers private landlords and owner-occupiers as well as local authorities.

Exceptions

There are three main exceptions. First, owner-occupiers selling or letting their property are excluded, provided that they do not advertise or use an estate agent.

Second, small residential premises (for example, small boarding houses or shared flats) are excluded. To qualify as 'small residential premises', the owner or occupier (or a near relative) has to live permanently in the house or flat; at least part of the house or flat, other than stairs or storage space, has to be shared with other people; and there must be only two households (other than the owner's or occupier's household) or not more than six people (other than the owner's or occupier's household) in the house or flat. A boarding house containing more than six lodgers, in addition to the landlord/lady's family, would not be allowed to discriminate, but a boarding house with fewer lodgers would be allowed to.

Third, charities and membership bodies whose main purpose is to provide benefits for a particular racial group are allowed to provide housing for that group only. But these organisations will not be allowed to discriminate on grounds of colour, only on grounds of race, nationality or national or ethnic origin.

Goods, facilities and services
Part III of the Act also covers any 'goods, facilities or services' which are offered to the public or a section of the public. This means, for instance, the services and facilities offered by hotels, boarding houses, pubs and restaurants, banks, insurance companies, credit houses and hire purchase firms, transport authorities and local authorities. Direct or indirect discrimination (see p. 196) by any such organisation will be unlawful.

If you have been discriminated against on race grounds by someone offering goods or services to the public, you must bring your action in the County Court. An action must be brought within six months.

Any contract (for example, to buy goods or supply services) which includes a term which discriminates on race grounds is void and can be amended by applying to the County Court to strike out that term formally.

Exceptions
There are a number of situations where race discrimination remains lawful:

- Any arrangement where someone takes a child, elderly person or someone needing special care and attention into his or her home to be looked after (for example, fostering children).
- Goods, facilities or services provided outside Great Britain, or insurance arrangements to cover a situation outside Great Britain. (But the services of, for instance, a travel agent in this country, even though it arranges foreign travel, will still be covered.)

- Charities and voluntary organisations whose main purpose is to provide benefits for a particular racial group (but these organisations will not be allowed to discriminate on grounds of colour, only on grounds of race, nationality or national or ethnic origin).
- Special arrangements can be made for members of a particular racial group who have particular needs for education, training, welfare, etc. (for example, language classes).
- Discrimination on grounds of nationality, place of birth or length of residence is permitted in:
  (1) selecting people to represent a particular place or country in a sport or game; *or*
  (2) deciding who is eligible to compete in any sport or game, according to the rules of the competition.

Prisons

The provisions prohibiting unlawful discrimination in housing and in relation to goods, facilities and services have been held to prevent the unlawful discrimination by prison officers in the allocation of work to prisoners. They also probably make unlawful other discrimination occurring in the prison regime (for example, more unfavourable withdrawal of privileges from, and more frequent strip searches of black prisoners).

Clubs

Under the previous race relations laws, private clubs, such as political and working-men's clubs, were allowed to discriminate on race grounds. It is now unlawful for any club or society with twenty-five or more members to discriminate on race grounds in any of the following ways:

- Refusing to allow you to join.
- Offering you less favourable terms of membership.
- Giving you fewer benefits, facilities or services or refusing to let you use or have any of these benefits (for example, social facilities).
- Expelling you from the club or changing the terms of your membership.
- Putting you at a disadvantage in any other way.

But a club or society whose main purpose is to provide benefits for people of a particular racial group, whatever its size, will continue to be allowed to discriminate on race grounds (although not on grounds of colour).

Advertisements

It is unlawful to insert, publish or cause to be published an advertisement which indicates that an employer, a company or anyone else intends to discriminate unlawfully. The absence of an intention to discriminate is no defence.

Only the CRE (see p. 226) will be able to take legal action against discriminatory advertisements. If you see an advertisement which you believe breaks the law you should bring it to the Commission's attention. You can also make a complaint about the advertisement to the person displaying it yourself.

Discrimination is allowed where exceptions in the law exist, for example, advertisements for jobs to which the genuine occupational qualification applies; for employment outside the United Kingdom and for posts and training where positive action is permitted. But an advertisement for employment in a private household must not be racially discriminating.

Commission for Racial Equality

The Commission for Racial Equality (CRE) was set up by the Race Relations Act 1976 with the duties of:

- Working towards the elimination of discrimination.
- Promoting equality of opportunity and good relations between persons of different racial groups generally.
- Keeping under review the working of the Act and, when required by the Home Secretary or when it otherwise thinks it necessary, to draw up and submit to the Home Secretary proposals for amending it.

In carrying out its duties, the CRE has the following powers:

- To undertake formal investigations into discriminatory practices which are unsuitable to be dealt with on an individual basis.
- To support, including financially, individuals taking up complaints of discrimination.
- To issue Codes of Practice on employment. The first Code was approved by Parliament in 1984. It is not legally binding but can be used in evidence at an industrial tribunal.
- To examine areas of policy outside the scope of the Act.
- To issue non-discrimination notices. This happens if the CRE decides, as a result of a formal investigation, that the law has been broken.
- To fund research and other projects.
- To apply for an injunction if it believes someone has broken the law and is likely to go on doing so. In the following circumstances, it is the CRE alone which can take action, such as applying for an injunction, if discrimination has taken place:

(1) if an advertisement demonstrates an intention to discriminate unlawfully;

(2) if someone instructs an employee or agent to discriminate unlawfully;

(3) if someone puts pressure on anyone else to discriminate unlawfully.

Investigations

The CRE can conduct 'formal investigations' into any subject it chooses – for instance, employment patterns in a region; the recruitment policies of a firm; housing allocation policies in local authorities, and so on.

The CRE must give notice of its intention to hold a formal investigation and draw up terms of reference. If it is investigating a particular organisation or person and states in the terms of reference that it believes they are discriminating unlawfully, then it will be able to require them to give evidence or produce information. The power to take evidence and summon witnesses will also apply in other investigations with the consent of the Home Secretary, or if the aim of the investigation is to see whether a non-discrimination notice is being obeyed (see below).

Either during or at the end of an investigation, the CRE can make recommendations for changes which would promote equality of opportunity. These recommendations will not be legally binding, but could be used to bring pressure on the organisation or person, or as evidence in an individual case against them.

Non-discrimination notices

The CRE will be able to issue a non-discrimination notice if it decides, during a formal investigation, that an organisation or individual has discriminated unlawfully.

The non-discrimination notice requires the organisation or person named in it to stop discriminating unlawfully and, if necessary, to let the people concerned know what changes have been made in their procedures or arrangements in order to obey the non-discrimination notice. Before issuing the notice, the CRE must warn the organisation or person concerned that it is thinking of doing so, and give it or them twenty-eight days to make representations. Once the notice is issued, the organisation or person named can appeal to the industrial tribunal (in an employment case) or the County Court. The appeal must be made within six weeks of when the CRE issued the notice.

If the appeal fails, or no appeal is made, the non-discrimination notice becomes final – in other words, it can be enforced. The CRE keep a register of notices which have become final and anyone is entitled to inspect this register and take a copy of any notice in it.

Injunctions

A non-discrimination notice can only be enforced if the CRE goes to court and gets an injunction. It can do this at any time within five years of when the notice becomes final if it thinks that the organisation or person named in the notice will continue to discriminate unlawfully. An injunction is an order by a County Court or the High Court ordering someone to stop acting in a particular way. If the organisation or person does not obey the injunction, they will be in contempt of court and the CRE can apply to the court to have the people involved fined or imprisoned.

The CRE may also apply to the County Court for an injunction without issuing a non-discrimination notice in the following circumstances:

- If someone has successfully brought a complaint against an individual or organisation and the CRE considers that the individual or organisation will go on discriminating unlawfully.
- If the CRE considers that someone has discriminated unlawfully and is likely to go on doing so; in this case, the CRE must itself apply to the industrial tribunal or county court to get a finding that the person concerned has in fact discriminated unlawfully.
- If the CRE considers that someone has published an unlawful advertisement (see p. 204); instructed an employee or agent to discriminate unlawfully; or put pressure on anybody else to discriminate unlawfully. Only the CRE can take action on these kinds of unlawful acts.

Local authorities and race equality

The Act imposes a duty on every local authority to make appropriate arrangements with a view to seeing that their various functions are carried out with due regard to the following needs:

- To eliminate unlawful racial discrimination.
- To promote equality of opportunity and good relations between persons of different racial groups.

This duty affects every power and duty of a local authority.

Criminal acts to stir up racial hatred

The Public Order Act 1986 prohibits certain acts intended or likely to stir up racial hatred (see p. 42). No prosecution for these offences may be brought without the Attorney General's permission. The Act covers:

- The use of words or behaviour or displays of written material which are threatening, abusive or insulting and intended to stir up racial hatred. The acts do not have to be committed in public; however, such acts, if committed in a private dwelling, are outside the Act.
- Publishing or distributing to the public written material which is threatening, abusive or insulting and intended to stir up racial hatred or which, in the circumstances, is likely to stir up racial hatred. This will include racist graffiti as well as newspaper articles and other similarly offensive racist material which is threatening, abusive or insulting.
- The public performance of a play which involves the use of threatening, abusive or insulting words or behaviour intended to stir up racial hatred or which, in the circumstances, are likely to stir up racial hatred. There are defences to this offence which apply in very limited circumstances. The offence is primarily aimed at the presenter and director, but actors who alter their lines will be within the prohibition.
- Distributing, showing or playing a recording of visual images (including video recordings) or sound which is threatening, abusive or insulting and which is intended to stir up racial hatred or which, in the circumstances, is likely to stir up racial hatred.
- Broadcasting (including a programme in a cable programme service) which is threatening, abusive or insulting and which is intended to stir up racial hatred or which, in the circumstances, is likely to stir up racial hatred. (For further controls on broadcasting see chapter 2).

Inflammatory material

The Public Order Act 1986 also makes it an offence to have possession of written material which is threatening, abusive or insulting, or a recording of visual images or sound which is threatening, abusive or insulting with a view to use it, and with the intention that racial hatred will be stirred up or in circumstances in which it is likely to be stirred up. Powers of entry, search and forfeiture are given in respect of such material. Again, prosecutions may only be brought with the Attorney General's consent.

In the Public Order Act 1986, 'racial hatred' is defined as hatred against a group of persons in Great Britain defined by reference to colour, race, nationality (including citizenship) or ethnic or national origins. This definition does not include religion. It may also exclude travellers (see also p. 305).

9.2. Sex discrimination

This section deals with sex discrimination in education; housing; the provision of goods, facilities and services; advertising; and social security. The duties and powers of the Equal Opportunities Commission are also explained here.

Sex discrimination in pay and terms and conditions of work is dealt with in Chapter 13, as is information on maternity rights for working women. Sex discrimination as it relates to immigration and nationality is dealt with in Chapter 10.

What does the law cover?

The Sex Discrimination Act 1975, as amended by the Sex Discrimination Act 1986 (SDA), covers discrimination in the following areas:

- Employment.
- Education.
- Goods, facilities and services.
- Housing.

The Act covers discrimination against men and women. The Act also makes it unlawful to discriminate against married people in the fields of employment and training. But this does not apply to the other areas of the Act listed above. Discrimination against single people because of their marital status is lawful.

The SDA does not cover:

- Tax.
- Social security.
- Immigration.
- Nationality.

There are other exceptions within the areas that are covered by the law. These are mentioned below, under the relevant headings.

What is discrimination?

The Sex Discrimination Act 1975 defines discrimination in two ways: direct and indirect.

Direct discrimination is when you are or would be treated less favourably in the same circumstances than someone of the opposite sex, just because of your sex. For example, admitting only boys to a GCSE course in electronics at a mixed school would be direct discrimination. So would offering hire purchase facilities only to men, or half-price entry to a disco only to women.

Indirect discrimination occurs when a requirement or condition is applied to both sexes in any area covered by the Act with which, in practice, far fewer members of one sex than the other can comply. Indirect discrimination is unlawful if it cannot be shown to be justifiable irrespective of sex and if the aggrieved person can show that the discrimination causes them detriment. For example, an after-school computer club open only to pupils taking an exam course in computer science could be against the law if hardly any girls took the exam course. Similarly, a housing association which excluded single parents from membership would be indirectly discriminating because the vast majority of single parents are women.

Victimisation

The Act also protects you against victimisation for taking action under either the Sex Discrimination Act or the Equal Pay Act. This provision makes it unlawful to treat you less favourably than anyone else because you have done any of the following:

* Made a complaint under either of the Acts.
* Helped someone else to make a complaint.
* Given evidence in a court or tribunal in a case under either of the Acts.
* Accused someone of breaking either of the Acts.
* Taken any other action in connection with either of the Acts.

Sexual harassment

The SDA does not contain any express provisions in relation to sexual harassment. However, sexual harassment is a serious issue and the source of much misery and distress for victims and their families. Unwanted sexual attention – including touching, suggestive and offensive language – has been interpreted by the tribunals and the courts as direct discrimination on the grounds of sex and as therefore falling within the scope of the Act. Non-verbal conduct may also constitute sexual harassment. Sexual harassment may take many forms including ridicule, unwelcome comments about appearance, demands or requests for sexual favours and even actual physical assault. Men may also be subject to sexual harassment as some recent industrial tribunal decisions have acknowledged.

In order to succeed in a claim founded on sexual harassment the complainant must show that the behaviour complained of is less favourable treatment on the grounds of sex and that she or he has suffered a detriment as a result.

The fact that industrial tribunal hearings, in particular, are public hearings and are often attended by the press has on occasion deterred individuals who have been subjected to harassment from pursuing their case to tribunal. From the end of November 1993, where cases involve allegations of sexual misconduct or conduct related to sex, gender or sexual orientation, an industrial tribunal has been able to make an order prohibiting publication of any matter likely to enable members of the public to identify an individual affected by or making the complaint. The tribunal will be able to make such an order either on the application of the parties or of its own motion.

Education

The SDA makes it unlawful to discriminate on grounds of sex, directly or indirectly, in any of the following areas:

- Admissions policies.
- Access to classes, courses or other benefits, facilities or services provided by the school or college.
- Any other unfavourable treatment.

The Act permits the continuation of single-sex schools, but also places a general duty on local education authorities to provide education without sex discrimination. This might mean, for example, that although a single-sex girls' school may not offer a design and technology course through its own curriculum, the LEA has to ensure that if boys in the same area have the opportunity to study this subject, arrangements are made to enable girls to take it, perhaps by attending a nearby mixed school for those lessons.

The following bodies can be held responsible for discrimination under the SDA:

- All schools, colleges and other educational establishments maintained by LEAs. Depending on the circumstances of the case, the LEA itself and/or the governors of the institution can be held responsible. Governors can be held responsible individually or collectively.
- Independent or private schools. The proprietors would be responsible.
- Universities. The governing body would be responsible.
- Other establishments designated by the Secretary of State for Education. These include other establishments in receipt of grants (such as grant-maintained schools) from the DES or the local authority. The governing body in each case is responsible for any discrimination.

Educational trusts

The SDA allows educational trusts to change their terms, with consent from the Secretary of State for Education, in order to apply their benefits to both sexes.

Exceptions

- Single-sex schools and colleges. A single-sex institution planning to turn co-educational can apply for permission to discriminate by admitting more members of one sex for a limited period.
- Co-educational schools which provide boarding accommodation for one sex only may continue to do so. If provided for both sexes, accommodation must be equal though it may be separate.
- Education provided by charities set up to benefit one sex only.
- Further education courses in physical training.
- In sport, single-sex competitive sport is allowed 'where the physical strength, stamina or physique of the average woman puts her at a disadvantage to the average man'. In practice, this has often been used to exclude girls from certain sports at school, although in primary schools as least, boys and girls often do all physical education together. The Equal Opportunities Commission is seeking an amendment to the Act to exclude primary school age children from this part of the Act.

Housing

The SDA makes it unlawful to discriminate in renting, managing, subletting or selling accommodation. Owner-occupied properties, small boarding houses and flat-sharing, however, are excluded from the Act. Single-sex housing associations are also exempt.

Mortgages

Building societies, local authorities or any other body which grants mortgages are breaking the law if they treat women applicants any less favourably than they would treat a man in the same circumstances. For example, they may not apply different rules regarding earnings levels, age, dependents, and so on.

Goods, facilities and services

This covers a wide range of public and private services, including pubs, cafes, restaurants, hotels, transport, banking, insurance, hire purchase, recreation and entertainment.

The list of exceptions to this part of the Act, however, is just about as long as the list of situations it does cover, some of them understandable, others more dubious. The exceptions are:

- Private clubs, such as working-men's clubs and sports clubs. (*Note*: these *are* covered by the equivalent section in the Race Relations Act 1976.)
- Political parties. Women's sections and conferences are still lawful.

- Religious bodies may continue to discriminate if necessary because of their doctrine or because not to do so would offend 'a significant number' of its members.
- Hospitals, prisons, hostels, old people's homes and any other places for people needing 'special care'.
- Competitive sport, if an average woman would be at a disadvantage because of her physical capacity compared to the average man.
- Charities and non-profit-making organisations set up to provide facilities or services for one sex only. This doesn't mean such organisations may discriminate across the board – for example, by restricting their office workers to one sex only – but they may discriminate in the provision of services, including who is employed in actually providing those services.
- Insurance companies and similar bodies. These may discriminate if it is on the basis of 'reasonable actuarial information'. For example, women can be offered cheaper car insurance than men because statistics show they are safer drivers.
- Facilities and services which need to be restricted to one sex only in order to preserve 'decency and privacy'. This covers toilets, saunas, changing rooms, and so on.
- Certain provisions in relation to death or retirement are also excluded. Occupational pension schemes and redundancy payment schemes are outside of the Act.

Discriminatory contractual terms
Contractual terms which conflict with the Act are void. This applies to any term of a collective agreement, rule made by employers, organisations of workers, professional organisations or regulatory bodies. From the end of November 1993, individuals affected by such terms or rules have the right to apply to the industrial tribunal to have the term or rule declared invalid.

Advertisements
If an advertisement for a job covered by the SDA states or implies an intention to discriminate against men or women applicants, a complaint could be made to an industrial tribunal under the employment sections of the Act, as the advertisement would count as part of the arrangements made by the employer to fill a vacancy.

Advertising in other areas, for example, for accommodation, entertainment or services, is also covered by the SDA but complaints about discriminatory advertising may only be taken up by the Equal Opportunities Commission (EOC). If you see a discriminatory advertisement, you can report it to the EOC (the address is at the end of this chapter).

Sexism in advertising, through offensive images of women used to sell products for example, is not outlawed by the SDA. But complaints of sexism or anything else you consider to be illegal, indecent, dishonest or untruthful can be made to:

Advertising Standards Authority
15–17 Ridgmount Street
London WC1E 7AW
Tel: 071 580 5555

How to complain about sex discrimination

A complaint under the SDA must be taken to an industrial tribunal if it concerns employment, including cases of victimisation concerned with employment. Your complaint of discrimination must be lodged within three months of the discrimination complained of. Complaints of discrimination in education, housing, and the provision of goods, facilities or services must be made to the County Court. Complaints concerning education must first be made to the Secretary of State for Education. If the matter has not been resolved to your satisfaction within two months, you may then proceed with action in the County Court. Complaints about housing, goods, facilities and services must be made within six months of the discrimination taking place.

The Equal Opportunities Commission (EOC)

The EOC was set up under the Sex Discrimination Act 1975 (SDA) with the following duties:

* To work towards the elimination of sex discrimination.
* To promote equality of opportunity between men and women generally.
* To keep the SDA and the Equal Pay Act under review and propose amendments to the Home Secretary.

In carrying out its duties, the EOC has the following powers:

* To undertake formal investigations into discriminatory practices which are unsuitable to be dealt with on an individual basis.
* To support, including financially, individuals taking up complaints of discrimination.
* To issue Codes of Practice on employment. The first Code was approved by Parliament in April 1985. It is not legally binding but can be used in evidence at an industrial tribunal.
* To examine areas of policy outside the scope of the Act, for example, social security, taxation, maternity rights.
* To issue non-discrimination notices. This happens if the EOC decides as a result of a formal investigation that the law has been broken.

- To fund research and other projects.
- To apply for an injunction if it believes someone has broken the law and is likely to go on doing so. In the following circumstances, it is the EOC alone which can take action, such as applying for an injunction, if discrimination has taken place:
  (1) if an advertisement demonstrates an intention to discriminate unlawfully;
  (2) if someone instructs an employee or agent to discriminate unlawfully; *or*
  (3) if someone puts pressure on anyone else to discriminate unlawfully.

Local authorities
Unlike the Race Relations Act, the Sex Discrimination Act does *not* impose a statutory duty on every local authority to carry out its functions with regard to eliminating unlawful discrimination and to promoting equal opportunity.

Social security
An EEC directive on equal treatment in social security has led to some changes in Britain's social security benefits in recent years. For example, men and women now have equal treatment in short-term, contributory benefits, such as unemployment benefit. Women may also claim income support (formerly supplementary benefit) on behalf of their partners and dependents, although in practice this is rare. Discrimination against married women claiming the invalid care allowance (ICA) has now been outlawed following a successful test case under the European directive. Married and co-habiting women claiming ICA may also put in for back payments to December 1984, if applicable to their case.

9.3 Sexual orientation

There are no laws specifically criminalising sex between lesbians. As a general rule consensual sexual activity between men over twenty-one in private is legal. However, a recent decision of the House of Lords ruled that certain sado-masochistic sex which involves the infliction of injury which is more than merely 'transient and trifling' and even where there is express consent to the act or acts constitutes a criminal offence. Although the defendants in that case were gay men it applies both to the activities of heterosexuals and lesbians. This decision is being challenged in the European Commission of Human Rights.

There is no statutory protection against discrimination on grounds of sexual orientation, such as the Sex Discrimination and Race Relations

Acts (see p. 196 and p. 208). This means that, broadly speaking, there is little legal sanction against such discrimination in the fields of employment, housing, immigration, the provision of services and parental rights.

Criminal law

Women

There are no laws specially restricting lesbian behaviour, except in the armed forces where women can be charged with committing 'disgraceful conduct of an indecent or unnatural kind'.

Technically, lesbians can be prosecuted for the following acts, but they rarely are:

- Insulting behaviour (see p. 219).
- Indecent assault on another woman who did not consent or who is under sixteen.
- Although there is no age of consent for lesbians, the Indecency with Children Act 1960 provides that a woman committing an act of gross indecency, i.e. having sex (see p. 219) with a girl under fourteen, would be breaking the law.

Men

It is legal for two men over twenty-one to have sex together, provided they are in private and both consent (this is now the law throughout the whole of the UK). In this context, sex means any form of sexual activity (subject to the potential restriction mentioned above) including intercourse (buggery). The following restrictions apply to sex between men:

- The age of consent is twenty-one – five years older than the age at which heterosexuals can have lawful intercourse.
- 'In private' does not include places such as public lavatories (even if no one can see), nor when more than two people are present (even if they all consent). It is up to the prosecution to prove that the activity did not take place in private, and many courts have decided that particular places were 'in private', even if the public theoretically had access to them (for example, a dark lane; behind a clump of bushes; in an enclosed yard after normal working hours, etc).
- Meeting another man with a view to having lawful sex may itself be illegal. Because of the law of importuning or soliciting, it may be an offence for a man to chat up another man if done in a public place. Even just smiling at someone can be classified as importuning and if a man 'persistently' importunes for an 'immoral purpose'

that is an offence. It is up to the court to decide if lawful sexual activity amounts to an 'immoral purpose' in any particular case, but they can (and sometimes do) find men guilty of this offence even though the sexual activity would have been lawful, i.e. between two consenting men over twenty-one and in private.

- Members of all branches of the armed forces are still denied the right to a homosexual sex life. All forms of lesbian or gay sex are illegal and can lead to a court martial and a dishonourable discharge, plus up to two years' imprisonment.
- It is illegal for merchant seamen to engage in gay sex on board a ship on which either of them is serving, though this does not apply to deep-sea oil rigs.
- Displays of affection in public by lesbians or gay men might be illegal on the ground of 'insulting behaviour' (see p. 219).

Offences

Cruising/picking up men

A man making an approach to another man with a view to having sex may itself be a crime, even though it was intended to have sex in circumstances which would be legal. Under the Sexual Offences Act 1956, it is an offence persistently to importune in a public place for an immoral purpose. This law was enacted originally at the end of the nineteenth century to outlaw pimping for female prostitutes in the Leicester Square music halls. Now it is used almost exclusively to stop men approaching other men with a view to sex – known as cruising, or more commonly, picking someone up.

Usually the police arrest men for importuning (also called 'soliciting') outside or near gay pubs or clubs, or in parks, public lavatories or other places where it is likely that one man can pick up another. This law is not used primarily against men who are prostitutes, though male prostitution is covered by it.

Importuning is any kind of approach to another person – a smile is enough – and either words or gestures will do. 'Persistently' means more than once to the same person, or to two or more people. If a man speaks to or gestures towards another man just once it is not an offence under this section, but it may still be caught by the offence of 'attempting to procure an act of gross indecency' (see below). Whether a purpose is an 'immoral purpose' depends entirely on the view of the court applying its own standards. Magistrates are known to convict of this offence much more frequently than juries. The higher courts have made it clear that a man can be convicted of this offence even though he was chatting someone up with a view to having perfectly lawful sex – i.e. both consenting, twenty-one or older and in private. Many juries have taken the view that picking up another man, even a stranger, for sex is not an 'immoral purpose' caught by this Act, and the majority of such cases result in acquittals if fought in the Crown Court.

Sentences vary widely from place to place. For most men convicted of this kind of offence it is the publicity, the social costs, exposure and humiliation that are far greater penalties than those imposed by the courts which are frequently in the form of a fine.

Sexual activity

Any kind of sexual activity involving a man *under* twenty-one or taking place 'in public' is illegal. The law uses the term 'gross indecency' to describe all sexual activity between males other than buggery (anal intercourse). By a curious anomaly, the 1967 Sexual Offences Act made buggery (in private, etc.) between men legal but it remains illegal between a man and a woman, though this is almost never enforced.

'Gross indecency' includes sexual activity short of physical contact as well as touching. For example, two men masturbating in sight of each other, although separated by a wall, have been found guilty of gross indecency even though they were in adjacent locked cubicles of a public lavatory and no one else could see them (except police officers peering down from a hole in the ceiling). It is not 'gross indecency' to engage in sexual activity merely directed towards another man unless he too is a willing participant in the sense that he is aware of what is going on and cooperates in an 'indecent exhibition'. This offence was once used to prosecute the director of a play in which the actors simulated gay sex.

The term 'gross indecency' is not defined anywhere in the law. It is a question for the court to decide as to whether the activity that was taking place amounts to 'gross indecency'. If either or both of the parties are under twenty-one they can both be prosecuted, though in practice this is rarely done if both are under twenty-one. The Director of Public Prosecutions must give his or her consent to a prosecution for an offence involving someone under twenty-one.

In many cases sexual activity will only be illegal because it takes place in public. It is for the prosecution to prove that an act of gross indecency took place otherwise than in private. Whether a place is public or private is a question for the court. In the case of Reakes (1974), the Court of Appeal approved the following definition of 'in private': 'Look at all the surrounding circumstances, the time of night, the nature of the place including such matters as lighting and you consider further the likelihood of a third person coming upon the scene.'

As with cases of importuning, a majority of juries acquit on charges of gross indecency. There is a better chance of acquittal in the Crown Court than in the magistrates' court, which has no jury.

It can also be an offence to approach another man with a view to having sex, either by 'importuning' (see p. 217) or by 'attempting to procure an act of gross indecency'. This means no more than making an approach to another man. It differs from importuning in two ways: there does not need to be any 'persistency' or repetition of the approach; but also, for it to be an offence, the prosecution must prove that the sexual activity sought would have been illegal, i.e. in public usually.

Buggery between men is legal or illegal in the same circumstances as gross indecency, i.e. it depends on the ages of the parties and the place where it happens.

Displaying affection in public

Lesbians or gays who hold hands or kiss or fondle each other in public in the same way as heterosexuals may be committing an offence of 'insulting behaviour' under the Public Order Act 1986. Much will depend on the particular facts of the case and, as it is an offence which can only be tried in the magistrates' court, it will usually depend on the moral and political views of the magistrates as to whether the behaviour is regarded as insulting. The term 'insulting' is not defined by the law; it has to be given its ordinary meaning, but the higher courts have upheld a conviction under similar (though not identical) legislation where two men were fondling each other's genitals and buttocks over their clothes in the course of saying goodnight in a public place.

Policing and agents provocateurs

The police have a very wide discretion in the way they enforce the offences referred to above. In some areas of the country they are far more rigorous about seeking out gay offences than in others, and the attitudes of the same police force may change from time to time depending on the views of the senior officers responsible for operational decisions.

In some instances the police themselves try to lure men into committing offences, especially importuning. They do this by standing around, often dressed to attract an advance, usually outside gay pubs or in public lavatories, making it obvious that they are looking for a pick-up. A man who approaches a policeman who is acting as an agent provocateur will not thereby automatically have a defence to a charge of importuning or attempting to procure an act of gross indecency, despite the fact that police and Home Office regulations specifically prohibit this activity. However, a jury in such a case may well be more disposed to acquit the man on other grounds as an indication of their disapproval of the police behaviour.

Conspiracy to corrupt public morals

This is a rarely used but powerful criminal offence, invented by the judiciary rather than passed by Parliament. It has been used in particular to prohibit gay men advertising in the 'contact' pages of magazines.

Essentially, it is an offence to conspire or agree to do some act which, in the opinion of a jury, is calculated to corrupt or debauch public morals. In 1973, the House of Lords upheld, by a majority, the conviction of a magazine containing explicit gay contact ads on the ground that encouraging homosexuality is the sort of thing a jury might properly consider to be a 'corrupt practice'. However, the people placing the advertisements were not prosecuted. Since 1973, there have been no further prosecutions of this kind and explicit advertisements are now commonplace. The law, however, has not been repealed so there is always the possibility of a prosecution in the future.

Young people
While the criminal law prohibits any kind of gay sex life for men under twenty-one, lesbian and gay teenagers who assert their independence once they become sixteen could find themselves taken into care by the local authority on the grounds that they are in 'moral danger'.

If they are under seventeen they can be detained by the police or other agencies. This is quite rare, however there are a number of cases of young lesbians and gays who have been dealt with in this way simply because they wanted to live with other lesbians or gay men, even at an age when they were old enough to marry and live with another person of the opposite sex.

However, these possibilities are unlikely.

Civil law
There is no difference in the way in which the civil law affects lesbians and gay men. Both groups are treated in the same way in principle, though in practice there may be a difference if a man's civil rights are threatened as a result of a conviction for one of the consensual sexual offences referred to above which do not affect lesbians. There are no specific statutes protecting lesbians and gay men from discrimination on the grounds of their sexual orientation.

Employment

Recruitment
Broadly speaking, there is no way a lesbian or gay man can challenge an employer who refuses to give her or him a job on the grounds of their sexual orientation. The Sex Discrimination Act 1975 prohibits discrimination on grounds of sex or marital status (see 9.2, p. 208) but not sexual orientation. However, in rare cases it might be possible to use this legislation when the real reason for the discrimination is sexual orientation.

An example is the Dan Air case. The airline company had a policy of only employing women cabin staff and not even considering for interview men who applied for posts on the grounds that, if any of them were gay, passengers might be exposed to the risk of becoming HIV positive.

The Equal Opportunities Commission investigated Dan Air's policy and found that there were no medical grounds for implementing it, with the result that the company was in breach of the Sex Discrimination Act. They issued a non-discrimination notice (see 9.1, p. 214) and subsequently Dan Air changed their policy.

The case illustrates the point that the company was discriminating against *all* men in their desire to exclude gay men, and so was breaking the law.

Existing workforce

Many employees suffer discriminatory treatment at work because they are known or believed to be lesbian or gay. There are even some cases of discriminatory treatment of gay men by colleagues and employers on the grounds that they may be HIV positive solely because they are gay.

The difficulty in challenging such treatment is that there is no specific law prohibiting it, and lesbian and gay workers have to depend on general employment laws which have not always proved of much use in these circumstances.

If an employer discriminates against a lesbian or gay worker (for example, by denying them promotion) or responds to hostile pressure by colleagues (for example, by moving the worker concerned to different duties or a different location), the only way that the worker can challenge the decision in law is by resigning and claiming 'constructive dismissal' (see Chapter 13) on the ground that the employer has acted in breach of contract. This is obviously a high-risk strategy.

Dismissal on grounds of sexual orientation

The response of the industrial tribunals and the Employment Appeal Tribunal (EAT) to dismissals on grounds of sexual orientation has varied from case to case and is difficult to predict, except that it is more often unfavourable to the employee than the employer. In one notorious decision in 1980, the EAT in Scotland upheld as fair the dismissal of a maintenance worker at a children's camp solely on the ground that he was gay. It was held reasonable for the employer to dismiss him on the basis of prejudice by parents whose children attended the camp, even though that prejudice was without any basis. Most of these cases come to the tribunals following a man's conviction for a gay offence.

In another of the few sexual orientation cases to be heard by the EAT, it was held fair to dismiss a teacher following his conviction for gross indecency outside working hours. The EAT went to some pains to emphasise that each case must be decided on its merits and it was neither automatically fair nor automatically unfair to dismiss in such cases.

The overall impression is that, with a few exceptions, industrial tribunals are more likely to uphold the dismissal of a gay employee who is convicted of a consensual offence if he works with, or in proximity to, children and young people than other kinds of employees. Even in cases when dismissal has been found unfair, the tribunals often make remarks to the effect that no danger is posed because the worker concerned does not have contact in their job with young people, the public, etc. This fails to recognise the nature of the offences for which gay men are usually convicted – i.e. consenting acts with other adults.

Few cases involving lesbians have reached the tribunals, partly because of the different criminal laws. However, one of the best-known cases, Boychuk (1977), demonstrates the hazards of showing one's sexual orientation openly at work. Ms Boychuk wore a badge with the words 'Lesbians Ignite' in her job as a receptionist at an insurance company's office. She was dismissed for refusing to take it off and her dismissal was upheld as fair by the EAT. Although the decision was based on general principles of what an employer might reasonably require by way of standards of dress and political messages on badges, it is very unlikely that the dismissal would have occurred or been upheld had the badge borne a heterosexual message.

There are a number of trade unions which have specific lesbian and gay sections or groups which have campaigned effectively within the workplace to prevent discrimination. They can be contacted through the lists of lesbian/gay organisations (see pp. 228–9).

Housing

A lesbian or gay relationship is not treated as being equivalent to a heterosexual marriage in the eyes of the law. The result in housing law is that lesbians or gay men have no right to succeed to a tenancy if their partner dies, regardless of how long-established their relationship was, and even though the surviving partner in a heterosexual couple living together 'as husband and wife' would be entitled to succeed to the tenancy under the Housing Act 1985. However, some local authorities accept succession for lesbians and gays and accept applications for housing from same sex couples.

Immigration

The same approach has been taken by the courts to lesbian or gay relationships in immigration law as in housing law, i.e. they cannot be compared to a heterosexual marriage. Lesbian and gay relationships are not recognised for immigration purposes though the Home Office has suggested that applications could be considered if there were exceptional circumstances such as the grave illness of the British partner. Also a foreign national would be entitled to apply for asylum (see p. 241) if they could demonstrate that they would likely to be persecuted, for instance on the grounds of their sexuality, in the country that they would be returned to.

Transvestites

There is nothing in the law to stop anyone dressing in clothes traditionally worn by members of the opposite sex. Sometimes, however, transvestites have been arrested for 'insulting behaviour' (see p. 219) and in theory they could in some circumstances be convicted of this offence, but such situations are very rare.

Transsexuals

It is lawful to undergo gender reassignment (sex change) surgery but there is no consequent right in law to be regarded as a member of the opposite sex from that into which you were born. In practice, however, transsexuals are able to obtain most official documents except a birth certificate in their new name and sexual identity. Medical cards, driving licences, income tax forms, passports, etc., will be issued by the relevant authorities in the new identity.

There is no right to be married as a member of the opposite sex and for the purposes of the law any such marriage is void in this country. The European Court of Human Rights has ruled that refusal of an amended birth certificate and the right to marry is not a breach of the right to a private life contained in the European Convention on Human Rights, although a more recent case against France suggests that the Court may be reconsidering its position.

Parental rights

There is no law against lesbians or gays being parents and many lesbians and gays marry or live in heterosexual relationships before coming out and thus already have children. Lesbians sometimes have children using artificial insemination by donor or by other means.

Lesbians or gays who seek custody of or access to their children following a break up may discover that the law treats them less favourably than heterosexuals in the same circumstances. Although there is a right to apply to the courts for a residence order (custody) or for access this right is entirely at the discretion of the judges who have often been biased against lesbian or gay parents. For example, mothers are usually given a residence order in disputes between parents but if the court knows she is a lesbian her chances are then much less than that of the father. However, courts have granted custody to both lesbians and gays. Local authorities allow applications to foster from both single lesbians and gays and from those in couples and obviously the special needs of young people who are lesbian or gay should be considered.

Ban on promoting homosexuality

The most significant piece of legislation affecting homosexuals since the reforming 1967 Act is section 28 of the Local Government Act 1988, which bars the 'intentional promotion of homosexuality' by local authorities. The section prohibits the intentional promotion of homosexuality, the publishing of material with the intention of promoting homosexuality or the promotion of teaching in any maintained school of 'the acceptability of homosexuality as a pretended family relationship'.

The section does not prohibit such activities if done for the purpose of treating or preventing the spread of disease. The section came into force on 24 May 1988, yet there have been no court decisions interpreting its precise breadth and meaning at the time of writing this book.

Legal opinion generally expects that the section will be interpreted narrowly by the courts to prohibit only things done or publications which actively advocate a homosexual lifestyle or sexual experimentation to whose not otherwise so inclined. Nevertheless, many local authorities throughout Britain have reacted to its enactment by adopting policies of self-censorship and extreme caution, in most cases probably unnecessarily. There have been examples of local authorities banning:

- The publication of a list of advice agencies for young people because a couple of the hundreds of entries were lesbian and/or gay organisations.
- The performance of a play by a 'theatre in education' group because it contained a scene involving a gay man.
- The publication of a cartoon in a Women's Unit newsletter because it was a lesbian parody of heterosexual attitudes.
- The confirmation by a gay teacher of his sexuality when asked about it by children in his class.

Expert legal opinion is of the view that none of those examples fell within the terms of section 28 and all these local authorities misinterpreted the section by imposing such bans. These cases do, however, illustrate the real impact of the section, which is to inhibit, censor and undermine the legitimate functions of local government and schools.

The ban on promoting the teaching of the 'acceptability of homosexuality as a pretended family relationship' in maintained schools is, in strict legal terms, greatly weakened by two factors. First, it is school governors and not local authorities who are legally responsible for sex education in schools. School governors are not affected by section 28. Second, it is highly unlikely on any interpretation of the section that discussion of and counselling about homosexuality would be prohibited or restricted by this law. However, as we noted, some local authorities have already acted as though they are prevented from discussing or offering advice and counselling about homosexuality, despite the fact that the law will not prohibit it.

Note that it is local authorities not individuals who are liable under this section.

9.4 Disability discrimination

There is no real protection against discrimination based on disability and unfortunately discrimination in employment, the provision of services or in any other way is not against the law. The European Convention on Human Rights provides that discrimination in respect to the other rights in the Convention (see p. 112) is unlawful in respect of 'sex, race, colour, language, religion, political or other opinion, national or social origin, association with a national minority, property, birth or other status'. It does not mention disability but it is arguable that 'other status' would give people a right if another right of the Convention was violated in a discriminatory way.

There are some specific rights that disabled people have but they are usually directed at public bodies and enforcement is in the hands of officials with a wide discretion rather than being a right that the invidual has him or herself.

Employment

There are, however, some inadequate provisions in the employment area. Certain jobs like car park and lift attendants are reserved for people registered as disabled. Also employers who employ more twenty employees should ensure that 3 per cent of their posts are also similarly reserved for people with disabilities. It is a criminal offence for employers who are below their quota to employ someone other than a registered disabled person. Prosecutions are rare (the last one was in 1975). Exemptions are available if no suitable disabled people are available for the post.

Employers subject to the quota system are obliged to keep monitoring records. Companies who employ more than 250 staff have to give a statement in the directors' annual report setting out their policy in the previous year on recruitment, training, career development and promotion of people with disabilities, including the retention of employees who develop a disability after being employed.

In July 1986, the EEC made a recommendation to member states that they should take all appropriate measures to promote fair opportunities for disabled people in the field of employment. It sets out a programme of positive action and encourages member states to deal positively with disabled people. It is not yet law!

9.5. Further information

Race discrimination

Useful organisations

Anti-Racist Alliance
PO Box 150
London WC1X 9AT
Tel: 071 278 6869

Commission for Racial Equality
10–12 Allington Street
London SW1E 5EH
Tel: 071 828 7022

Community Race Equality Councils exist throughout the country. You can get the address of your nearest CREC from a Citizens' Advice Bureau, the town hall or the telephone directory.

Law Centres' Federation
Duchess House
18–19 Warren Street
London W1P 5DB
Tel: 071 387 8540
Contact them to find out the address of your nearest law centre.

Race Discrimination Legal Defence Fund
Brixton Small Business Centre
444 Brixton Road
London SW9 8EJ
Tel: 071 274 4000

Runnymede Trust
62 Chandos Place
London WC2N 4HG
Tel: 071 836 3266

Society of Black Lawyers
Unit 325
Brixton Small Business Centre
444 Brixton Road
London SW9 8EJ
Tel: 071 274 4000 ext. 290/291

Trade Unions will often be able to help you if you suffer discrimination at work.

Bibliography

The CRE publish a number of useful pamphlets on the workings of the Race Relations Act 1976, including a code of practice.
Paul Nichols, *Tolley's Handbook on Discrimination*, Tolley, 1990.

Sex discrimination

Useful organisations

Citizens' Rights Office
Child Poverty Action Group
1 Bath Street
London EC1V 9PY
Tel: 071 253 3406

Equal Opportunities Commission
Overseas House
Quay Street
Manchester M3 3HN
Tel: 061 833 9244

Liberty
21 Tabard Street
London SE1 4LA
Tel: 071 403 3888

Rights of Women (ROW)
52–54 Featherstone Street
London EC1Y 8ET
Tel: 071 251 6577

The addresses of your local Citizens' Advice Bureau or Rape Crisis Centre can be found in the telephone directory.

Bibliography
M. Benn, etc., *The Rape Controversy*, NCCL Rights for Women Unit, 1986.
Equal Opportunities Review, IRS, 18–20 Highbury Place, London N1
   1QP. Tel: 071 354 5858
R. Evans and I. Durward, *Maternity Rights at Work*, NCCL, 1986.
C. Palmer, *Discrimination at Work: the law on sex and race discrimina-
tion*, LAG, 1992.

Sexual orientation

Useful organisations

Beaumont Society (for Transvestites and Transsexuals)
BM 3084
London WC1N 3XX
Information tel: 0582 412220
Advice tel: 071 730 7453

Campaign for Homosexual Equality (CHE)
PO Box 342
London WC1X ODU
Tel: 071 833 3912

GALOP (Gay policing project)
36 Old Queen Street
London SW1H 9JF
Tel: 071 233 0854

Gay Rights at Work
c/o Pickwick Court
London SE9 4SA

GLAD (Gay and Lesbian Legal Advice)
BM/GLLAD
London WC1N 3XX
Tel: 071 976 0840

LAGER (Lesbian and Gay Employment Rights)
21 St Margaret's House
Old Ford Road
London E2 9BL
Tel: 081 983 0694 (lesbians), 081 983 0696 (gays)

Lesbian and Gay Youth Movement
BM GYM
London WC1N 3XX
Tel: 081 317 9690

London Friend (Counselling and advice organisations for lesbians and gays)
86 Caledonian Road
London N1
Tel: 071 837 3337

London Lesbian and Gay Switchboard
BM Switchboard
London WC1X 3XX
Tel: 071 837 7324 (twenty-four hours)

Organisation for Lesbian and Gay Action
PO Box 147
London WC2H OBB
Tel: 071 833 3860

OutRage!
5 Peter Street
London WC1V 3RR
Tel: 071 439 2381

Stonewall Group
2 Greycoat Place
London SW1P 1SB
Tel: 071 222 9007

Terrence Higgins Trust
BM/AIDS
London WC1N 3XX
Tel: 071 242 1010
For advice and support on HIV and AIDS issues.

Bibliography

C. Beer, etc., *Gay Workers, Trade Unions and the Law*, NCCL, 1982.
Madeleine Colvin, et al., *Section 28 – A practical Guide to the Law*, Liberty, 1989 (£4.50).
Caroline Gooding, *Trouble with the Law*, Gay Men's Press, 1992 (£8.95).
Liberty, *Lesbians and Gay Men and the Criminal Law*, 1990 (£1).
April Martin, *Lesbian and Gay Parenting Handbook*, Harper Perennial, 1993 (£11.95).

Disability discrimination

Useful organisations

The British Council of Organisations for Disabled People (BCODP)
De Bradelei House
Chapel Street
Belper
Derby DE56 1AR
Tel: 0773 8288182

The Disability Alliance
First Floor East Universal House
88–94 Wentworth Street
London E1 7SA
Tel: 071 247 8776

Bibliography

Colin Barnes and BCODP, *Disabled People and Discrimination*, Hurst and Co, 1991.

Ian Bynoe, *Equal Rights for Disabled People*, Institute of Public Policy Research, 1991.

Disability and Work, Labour Research Department, 1993.

The Disability Rights Handbook, The Disability Alliance (published each year)

Jan Luba, *The Disabled Person's Handbook*, Sphere Rights Guides, 1989.

10

The rights of immigrants

This chapter deals with:

- Immigration control.
- Coming to settle.
- Coming to work.
- Coming for temporary purposes.
- Enforcement of immigration controls.
- Refugees.
- Rights to British nationality.
- Further information.

10.1 Immigration control

The present laws on immigration are governed mainly by the Immigration Acts of 1971 and 1988 which came into force on 1 January 1973 and 1 August 1988 respectively. These Acts lay down general principles about who is subject to immigration control and who is not. In addition, the Asylum and Immigration Appeals Act came into effect on 26 July 1993. This new Act places restrictions on asylum seekers and their dependents and gives a new right of appeal to asylum seekers refused at a United Kingdom port of entry. The Act also takes away the right of appeal from visitors and others here for temporary purposes, and those wishing to come here for those purposes.

The Immigration Acts are the statutory basis for the control of immigration. However, the powers granted under the Immigration Acts are very general. How that power is exercised is contained in the Immigration Rules, which, although wide ranging and fairly precise, are not exhaustive. The Rules are both numerous and change frequently, often without close parliamentary scrutiny. The main Rules currently in force are called House of Commons Paper No. 251 of 1990 (HC 251). Most of its provisions came into force on 1 May 1990. These have been amended or added to several times since that date, the latest addition being HC 725, most of which took effect from 26 July 1993. At the time of writing, the Home Office were in the process of further revising and consolidating the Rules. The Home Office's current proposals appear much stricter and allow for less discretion. These Rules were expected to take effect in early 1994 and if passed will significantly affect the rights described in this chapter.

There are also detailed instructions to immigration officers as to how they should operate the Rules; these instructions are not published and are secret. To understand immigration law, therefore, it is also necessary to know about the practice of the Home Office, and it is advisable to contact one of the organisations listed at the end of this chapter for advice before approaching the Home Office.

There are other statutes which have a bearing on immigration control: they range from nationality laws which extend or restrict rights of abode (to the Falkland Islands and Hong Kong respectively), to the Carriers' Liability Act which gives the power to impose fines on carriers who bring passengers without the required documents to the UK.

The European Community has a growing influence on domestic immigration law, firstly because of the direct effect of Community law relating to the free movement of persons and secondly from increasing harmonisation on matters of immigration and asylum within the Community. The latter is too often secretive and outside of democratic or judicial control. Finally, the European Convention on Human Rights offers, in this context, minimum standards for the protection of the rights of migrants, their families, refugees and asylum seekers.

Who is subject to control?

Persons *not* subject to control
These are British citizens, Commonwealth citizens with the right of abode and Irish citizens travelling from Ireland are not subject to immigration control. If you fall into one of these categories, you can come and go as you like, you do not require permission from an immigration officer to enter and your passport will not be stamped when you travel in and out. Commonwealth citizens have the right of abode if either:

- One of their parents was born in the UK.
- They are women who were married before 1983 to a man who was a British citizen or a Commonwealth citizen with the right of abode.

Persons subject to limited control
The position of nationals of the European Community is, at the time of writing, not yet resolved. Under the Single European Act (1987) an internal market without frontiers was to have been established by 31 December 1992. The current United Kingdom practice is for an Immigration Officer at the port to examine the passport or other identity

document of an EC national in order to establish identity and to confirm nationality. An exception is Irish citizens travelling from Ireland, who as mentioned above are not subject to control.

As an EC citizen you can come here to take up a job or to look for work, to do business or to become self-employed. There are also provisions for those who are economically inactive, such as students and pensioners. If you establish yourself in one of these activities you can get a residence permit, usually valid for five years. Although this is not an absolute requirement, it has practical advantages. You can be joined by your spouse, children up to the age of twenty-one, other dependent children, grandchildren, parents, grandparents and great-grandparents. Once you have been established here for four years, you and your dependents will be considered 'settled'.

Full control
Everybody else is subject to full immigration control and will be allowed to enter only with permission of an immigration officer if you qualify under the Immigration Rules to enter for a specific purpose. If you are coming to stay permanently or to work you have to get permission from a British Embassy or High Commission abroad before travelling; this is called entry clearance and could be either a visa, an entry certificate or a letter of consent.

Citizens of many countries are 'visa nationals'. A list of these countries appears in the Immigration Rules. Being a 'visa national' means that you must always get permission before travelling, whatever you are coming for. Almost without exception, visas are required of nationals from the poorer countries of the south and most of the former ex-Warsaw Pact countries and the former Yugoslavia. Visa nationals have to apply for permission to come here for a specific purpose and are in the main not allowed to obtain an extension for a different purpose. Thus a visa national who is here as a visitor and applies to remain here longer as a student will be refused.

10.2 Coming to settle

Normally only the close relatives of people already settled here (allowed to stay permanently) will be allowed to settle with them. You must get entry clearance and satisfy other conditions before travelling. There are still long delays in processing these applications, particularly in the Indian subcontinent. Most people will only be allowed to come if their relatives can show that the person joining them can be supported and accommodated 'without recourse to public funds'. Public funds for immigration purposes are only income support, housing benefit, family credit and rehousing under Part III of the 1985 Housing Act; claiming any other benefit should not have any effect.

Husbands and wives
You have to prove to an entry clearance officer that:

- You are the husband or wife of the person you are coming to join and he or she is settled in the UK.
- You did not get married mainly in order to come to Britain.
- You intend to live together permanently as husband and wife.
- You have met each other.
- You have adequate accommodation for yourselves and any dependents in the UK.
- You will be able to support yourselves without relying on public funds.

There are particular difficulties for people from the Indian subcontinent. The officers who issue entry certificates expect applicants to prove that he or she qualifies under the complex and unfamiliar immigration rules. There is little regard for social and cultural differences in the way questions are asked or the way answers are interpreted. An applicant is rarely given the benefit of the doubt. Details of family and social relationships are gone into in order to bring out 'discrepancies' which could lead to refusal. The questioning by officers is often hostile and this too leads to unjustified refusals.

If the application is successful, you will be allowed in for a year when you arrive. Before the end of that year, you must apply to the Home Office for permission to stay permanently. The Home Office must be satisfied that you and your spouse still intend to stay together and can support and accommodate yourselves without relying on public funds before this is granted.

Fiances and fiancees
To come here to get married you have to prove the same things as husbands and wives and show in addition that you intend to get married soon after your arrival in Britain. If you are granted entry clearance, you will be allowed in for six months during which time you are expected to get married. You will not be allowed to work until you get permission from the Home Office to stay. If successful you will be granted permission to stay for an initial year, after which you will be granted settlement if you continue to satisfy the requirements.

Children
Children under eighteen may be allowed to join parents here (or to join one parent if the other parent is dead) if:

- You get entry clearance.
- Both your parents are settled here.
- Your parents have adequate accommodation for you here.
- Your parents can support you here without having to claim public funds.

If children are coming to join one parent and the other parent is still alive but not coming to live here, or coming to join a relative other than a parent, you also have to prove either:

- The parent living here has had the sole responsibility for your upbringing.
- There are serious and compelling family or other considerations making your exclusion from the UK undesirable.

These rules are very difficult to satisfy. In practice, they are not interpreted so strictly for children under twelve coming to join their mothers but this has never been written into the rules. Special consideration can also be given to unmarried daughters (but not sons) between the ages of eighteen and twenty-one.

Adopted children will only be allowed to come if it can be shown that there has been a genuine transfer of parental responsibility and adoption was necessary because the natural parents were unable to care for the child, and not if the reason for the adoption was to bring a child here. Legal adoptions abroad are recognised if the adoption has taken place in a country on a designated list, but the other requirements will still have to be met.

Parents and grandparents
You may be able to join your children or grandchildren settled here if:

- You get entry clearance.
- If a couple, that one of you is over sixty-five; if a widower, you are over sixty-five or a widowed mother of any age.
- You can be supported and accommodated by your children here without needing to rely on public funds.
- You were financially or in some other way dependent on your children here while living in your country of origin.
- You have no other close relatives in your country of origin who could look after you there.

In practice it is very difficult to prove all this.

Other relatives

Other relatives wanting to join family in the UK have to get entry clearance, and have to show that they were financially dependent abroad, that they can be supported and accommodated here without recourse to public funds, and that they were living alone in the most exceptional compassionate circumstances without other close relatives to turn to. This applies only to sons, daughters, sisters, brothers, uncles and aunts of people settled here, normally only when they are over sixty-five. It is very rare for anyone to qualify to come here under this rule.

The United Kingdom has a narrow definition of family for the purposes of immigration control. Many of the other countries in the European Community have a broader definition based on extended families and shared households. However, in the process of harmonisation of immigration laws within the European Community, the United Kingdom's position regarding non-EC nationals appears to be gaining favour.

10.3 Coming to work

If you want to come to work here you need to get a work permit before you travel. The employer here needs to apply to the Department of Employment for permission to employ a foreign worker, and has to satisfy restrictive conditions about your skills and experience and show there is nobody already allowed to work here who could do the job instead.

If you get a work permit you will be allowed in for four years and will only be allowed to do the job for which you were given your permit. If you change jobs, the new employer must first get a new permit for you and all the original conditions must be satisfied again. Because work permit holders are not freely 'available for work' you do not qualify for income support if you have lost a job. After four years, you can qualify to settle.

The spouse and the children under eighteen of a work permit holder may be allowed to come here to join him or her as long as both parents are living or coming to live in the United Kingdom and they can be supported and accommodated without recourse to public funds. They must get entry clearance before coming and will be allowed to stay for the same length of time as the work permit holder.

Some work can be possible without a work permit. If you are coming to do one of a specific list of jobs (which includes ministers of religion, missionaries, journalists working for overseas newspapers, servants of diplomats, people working for overseas governments and international organisations), you do not need a work permit but still have to get permission before you come. You may be allowed to come here as a writer or artist if you can show that you can support and accommodate yourself from the proceeds of your art or writing and any savings without having to take any other work or to claim benefits. Employees of high commissions and embassies are not subject to immigration control. If you have capital of at least £200,000 and satisfy other requirements, you may be allowed to come here to set up in business or be self-employed, or to live off your capital.

General

Once you have been allowed to settle there are no further immigration restrictions on what you can do here. You are able to work without needing any extra permission, you can claim any benefits without this having any effect on your right to remain. If you leave Britain, you will be allowed in again for settlement provided you have not been away for more than two years and that you confirm you are returning to stay. People who were settled and have been away for more than two years may still be allowed to settle again in certain circumstances, for example, if you have lived here for the majority of your life.

10.4 Coming for temporary purposes

If you want to visit Britain you need to satisfy an immigration officer that you are coming just for a visit, for a definite length of time and intend to leave at the end of it and that you have enough money to support and accommodate yourself for the length of your visit without needing to work or to claim benefits. You can be supported and accommodated by someone who lives here, but you may be asked detailed questions about your relationship with them, what they do here and how they can support and accommodate you. Immigration officers may also look at your personal circumstances, such as your education, employment and family ties and form a view about your 'incentive to return' to your country at the end of your stay. If you are a visa national, you need to get a visa in advance; if not, you can arrive at a port or airport and seek admission there. Six months is the longest time allowed to a visitor. Applications for extensions as a visitor will be refused and may jeopardise future visits.

Study

If you want to study, you may be allowed to come here if you can show that you have been accepted for a full-time course of study at a recognised college or independent (fee-paying) school, that you have the money to pay the fees and to live here without needing to work or to claim benefits and that you intend to leave Britain at the end of your studies. 'Full-time' normally means at least fifteen hours of daytime classes per week, studying one subject or related subjects. Overseas students have to pay fees which cover the full cost of their courses and are not usually eligible for local authority grants.

A student will normally be allowed in for a year or the duration of the course, whichever is shorter, and can apply to the Home Office to extend this time to continue a course. If you have not yet been accepted by a college you may be allowed in for a short time in order to enrol and can then apply to the Home Office for an extension.

A student wanting a short period of post-qualification training or on-the-job experience may be allowed to stay on as a trainee on the understanding that this is temporary and that a transfer to ordinary employment will not be allowed. If a student has spent more than four years on short courses of under two years, or appears to be chopping and changing courses with no end in sight, or has not been attending studies regularly, an extension will be refused. The wife of a student and children under eighteen may be permitted to live here with him while he is studying as long as they can be supported and accommodated, but will have no right to stay on after he has finished his studies. The husband of a student may be permitted to join her exceptionally.

Students may be permitted to take part-time or holiday jobs provided the college does not object and provided the employer obtains a permit from the Department of Employment. Students' wives are normally allowed to work – husbands very rarely.

Registration with the police
If you are not a Commonwealth or EEC citizen and not allowed to stay permanently but are permitted to stay in Britain for more than six months, you have to register with the local police. The police have to be informed of your name, date of birth, nationality, marital status, address and occupation and of any change in any of these in future. This requirement will only be lifted if you are later allowed to stay permanently.

10.5 Enforcement of immigration controls

There are three stages to immigration control: before entry, at the port of entry and after entry.

Before entry
All visa nationals have to obtain entry clearances from British diplomatic posts designated by the Foreign Secretary. The rules have recently been changed so that applicants requiring visas must apply to the designated post in the country where they are living and not all posts

grant a full range of visas. If you are refused an entry clearance, you do not have the right of appeal if your application was to come here as a visitor, to study for not more than six months or with an intention to study without a definite place.

At the port of entry
If you had obtained entry clearance before travelling, but are refused entry here you have a right of appeal in this country and can remain here while the appeal is pending. Immigration officers have the right to detain you while this is going on; after seven days you can apply to the immigration authorities for bail.

If you are refused entry and did not have entry clearance you can be sent straight back. There is no longer a right of appeal against this. You can be detained at the port until there is a flight back, or while any representations made on your behalf are under consideration, and you have no right to apply for bail. However, in some circumstances, you may be allowed temporary admission requiring you to reside at a particular address and to report back at a given date and time.

After entry
If you have been allowed in for a temporary period and you are refused permission to stay longer you can appeal against this *only* if your application was made to the Home Office before your permission to stay here ran out. If the application was made late there is no right of appeal and as an overstayer you are in Britain illegally.

All immigration appeals are heard in Britain, even when the appellant is abroad. An appeal is made first to a single adjudicator and then, if leave is granted, usually on a point of law only, to a three-person tribunal. Adjudicators used to be appointed by the Home Office but now both they and tribunal members are appointed by the Lord Chancellor's department. You may be represented, but legal aid is not available; few appeals succeed.

Police constables and immigration officers have the power to arrest, without warrant, anyone who has or who they suspect has committed an immigration offence. It is a criminal offence not to give information to an immigration officer, or to give false information or documents. There is effectively no right of silence as the responsibility is on you to show that you qualify for the status you claim under the law. The very wide power under the immigration laws allows for the investigation and detention of suspects under these administrative provisions who do not benefit from the same level of rights as others. This leads to frequent questioning of black people about their immigration status when they come into contact with the police for any other reason, often when there is no rational cause for suspicion. The Police and Criminal Evidence Act provides for Codes of Practice for the police in connection with the detention and questioning of people and searches of premises, but in law these do not apply to immigration officers, though they have agreed to follow them voluntarily. Breaches of these Codes of Practice have little consequence to the outcome of a case.

If you knowingly remain longer than you have been allowed by the immigration officers or the Home Office without asking permission you have become an overstayer and are committing a criminal offence. It makes no difference whether you have overstayed for many years or for a few days. You can be arrested and appear before a magistrates' court charged with this. You can be fined, imprisoned and recommended for deportation.

If you are not a British citizen, or a Commonwealth citizen with the right of abode, or a Commonwealth or Irish citizen who settled here before 1 January 1973 and who has lived here ever since, you can be recommended for deportation by a court if you are convicted of any crime for which the penalty could be imprisonment, even if you have been allowed to stay in Britain permanently. You can appeal against this as part of the sentence and it is then up to the Home Office whether to carry out the recommendation. Unless the court specifically directs your release, you will be detained while the Home Office decides what to do, which could be several weeks.

The Home Office can also make its own decision to deport people for overstaying or for breaking other conditions of stay, for example, working without permission. If it makes a decision to deport you, there is a right of appeal to the immigration appeal authorities. If you have lived here for more than seven years, compassionate aspects, as well as the law, can then be considered. If you have been here less than seven years, the appeal is only based on the facts, that is whether or not you are an overstayer. The Home Office has the power to detain people it has decided to deport, even while an appeal is pending.

If a man is being deported a decision to deport his wife and his children under eighteen (assuming that they do not have a right of abode of their own) can also be made solely on the grounds of their relationship. This will not apply if the family live in separate independent households. The children may be deported when their mother is deported, but a husband is not subject to the same risk.

The Home Office can also decide to deport you on the grounds that your presence is 'not conducive to the public good', a very vague term which can include people who have been convicted of a criminal offence but whom the court did not recommend for deportation, or people who are alleged to have made a marriage of convenience. You do have a right to an immigration appeal, but if the Home Secretary decides that your presence is non-conducive on the grounds of national security there is no appeal, nor do you have the right to representation or even to know the grounds of the Home Office's decision. You can only put your case to three 'advisers', chosen by the Home Office, who may make a secret recommendation to the Home Secretary, but this recommendation does not have to be followed.

Once all appeals have been exhausted, the Home Secretary can sign a deportation order against you and you can be sent out of the country. While the order is in force, you cannot return here. You can apply for the order to be revoked, either to the British post in your own country or to the Home Office, but this is not normally done until the order has been in force for at least three years. If the order is revoked that does not entitle you to return, but only to apply to return if you can satisfy the immigration rules.

If the Home Office claims that you entered the country illegally, you have no right of appeal until after you have been sent out of the country. You can be treated as an illegal entrant either because you entered the country without being questioned by immigration officers at all or because it is alleged that you misled immigration officers or did not tell them information that was relevant and, therefore, should not have been allowed in. People alleged to be illegal entrants have no rights; they can be arrested and detained solely on the decision of an immigration official and can be held for an indefinite length of time. The Bail Act does not apply to them and they have no right of appeal until after they have been removed from the country. They may also be removed very quickly, without being given the chance to seek advice. Judicial review of the decision may be sought but it is rare for the court to reverse the Home Office's decision.

There are also provisions in the law for fares to be paid for people settled here who want to return to their countries of origin if it is 'in that person's interest to leave the UK'. People receiving in-patient treatment in mental hospitals may be sent back, under the provisions of section 90 of the Mental Health Act, to receive treatment in their country of origin, again if it is 'in the interests of the patient to remove him'; no definition of this is given and there are no legal safeguards against these powers.

10.6 Refugees

A refugee is defined by the 1951 Convention Relating to the Status of Refugees as someone who has a 'well-founded fear of being persecuted for reasons of race, religion, nationality, membership of a particular social group or political opinion'. The Convention has for the first time been brought within domestic law by the Asylum and Immigration Appeals Act (1993), which in addition states that nothing in the immigration rules and practice should contravene the Convention. However, the United Nations High Commissioners for Refugees have expressed their reservations about many parts of the new Act.

The 1993 Act allows for the fingerprinting of asylum seekers, a practice which was confined to those suspected of a criminal offence. It also restricts the right of appeal in certain cases where an asylum seeker is said to have an unfounded claim, or where the asylum seeker has not come directly to the United Kingdom. Further, once a person has sought asylum, the Home Office has the power to take away any previous permission granted to remain in some other capacity. In all cases, the new Act gives asylum seekers the right of appeal against being required to leave the United Kingdom, although the time limits for appeal in certain cases are so short that it may be practically impossible to get legal advice and to prepare a case thoroughly.

The rules which relate to the practice governing asylum seekers place additional hurdles. Asylum seekers are required to apply for asylum on arrival, to tell their story in a consistent way, not to damage or destroy any relevant document and not to undertake activities which are inconsistent with previous beliefs or calculated to enhance his or her claim. The asylum seeker can also be penalised for the actions of anyone acting on his or her behalf.

However, most refugees never have the opportunity of claiming asylum here. The visa requirement of nationals of countries which are considered to be 'refugee producing', effectively prevents most asylum seekers from coming here. The threat of sanctions against the carrier bringing improperly documented passengers, currently a fine of £2,000, is another measure that effectively denies asylum. The introduction of this new law governing asylum seekers is set against a background of increasing hostility towards refugees. Popularly held misconceptions are reinforced by politicians and others who demand tough action against 'bogus refugees and economic migrants'. In practice, this means that the Home Office is less likely to accept as refugees people fleeing from poorer countries or people who are fleeing from civil war or other circumstances not strictly within the narrow definition of the Convention.

If you are recognised as a refugee, you will normally be allowed to stay for four years and can then apply for settlement. If the Home Office does not believe that asylum is justified, but thinks that in the circumstances you should not have to return at present, 'exceptional leave to remain' may be granted. After seven years' exceptional leave to remain you may apply for settlement. However, you have no right to do so and this will be entirely up to the Home Office. Refugees are allowed to be joined by their families once they are recognised, but those who are granted exceptional leave to remain must wait four years before they can apply for their families to join them and must satisfy the other requirements of the Immigration Rules.

If you are applying for asylum here, you are entitled to claim the 'urgent cases' rate of income support to live on while waiting for a decision. The Home Office has stated that they will give permission to work if no decision has been made on your application within six months. Your ability to receive help with housing is restricted by the Asylum and Immigration Appeals Act (1993).

If you are recognised as a refugee, you are then free to work and will be treated as a home student for the purposes of fees and eligibility for grants. Those with exceptional leave to remain can work but must fulfil other criteria to be entitled to educational grants. Refugees are entitled to a Convention Travel Document, but those with exceptional leave are generally required to travel on their national passports unless they can show that this facility has been denied them.

10.7 Rights to British nationality

The British Nationality Act 1981 came into force on 1 January 1983. It defines who is British by birth and how people may become British through naturalisation or registration. Some limited rights under the previous 1948 British Nationality Act remain; if you are a Commonwealth or Irish citizen who was settled in Britain before 1973 and who has continued to live here since then and you were under eighteen on 1 January 1983, you have an automatic right to become British if you apply for it within five years after your eighteenth birthday. This right will extinguish at the end of 1995. The fee for this in October 1993 was £85.

Other people who are settled here may be eligible to apply for British citizenship by naturalisation. If you are married to a British citizen it is easier to be granted citizenship. In this case, you must show:

- That you are settled here.
- That you have lived here legally for at least three years and have not been out of the UK for more than 270 days in that period, nor more than ninety days in the year before the application.
- That you are of good character.

There is a fee of £135 and acceptance of the application is at the discretion of the Home Office.

If you are not married to a British citizen you have to show:

- That you have been settled here for at least a year.
- That you have lived here legally for at least five years and not been out of the UK for more than 450 days in those years, nor more than ninety days in the year before you apply.

- That you are of good character.
- That you have a sufficient knowledge of the English, Welsh or Scottish Gaelic language.
- That you intend to continue to live in Britain.

There is a fee of £170 and acceptance is at the discretion of the Home Office, which also decides the standard of your knowledge of language and what being 'of good character' means; these have not been publicly defined.

In all cases of naturalisation, the Home Office does not have to give any reasons for refusing an application and there is no right of appeal against refusal, although if the reason is technical such as you being abroad longer than allowed, they generally tell you. Applications for naturalisation are, in October 1993, taking between twelve to eighteen months to process.

People who were born in Britain before 1983 were automatically British citizens by birth. The only exception to this was children whose parents were working here as diplomats at the time they were born. If you were born here after 1 January 1983 you are only automatically British if at the time of your birth:

- Either of your parents was a British citizen: *or*
- Either of your parents was allowed to stay here permanently.

If your parents were not married, only your mother's status counts. There are no plans to remove this discrimination against non-marital children.

If your parent later becomes settled, he or she can then apply for you to become British. If you are not able to inherit a nationality from either of your parents and are born stateless, and if you live here for the first ten years of your life without gaining any nationality, your parents can apply for you to become British.

10.8 Further information

Useful organisations

British Refugee Council
Bondway House
3–9 Bondway
London SW8 1SJ
Tel: 071 582 6922

Immigration Appeals Advisory Service
County House
190 Great Dover Street
London SE1 4YB
Tel: 071 357 6917

Joint Council for the Welfare of Immigrants
115 Old Street
London EC1V 9JR
Tel: 071 251 8706

Law Centres' Federation
Duchess House
18–19 Warren Street
London W1P 5DB
Tel: 071 387 8570
For information about your nearest law centre.

National Union of Students
461 Holloway Road
London N7 6LJ
Tel: 071 272 8900

Refugee Legal Centre
Sussex House
39–45 Bermondsey Street
London SE1 3XF
Tel: 071 827 9090 (advice: 071 378 6242, emergencies: 0831 598057)

UK Council for Overseas Students' Affairs
60 Westbourne Grove
London W2 5FG
Tel: 071 229 9268

United Nations High Commission for Refugees
36 Westminster Palace Gardens
Artillery Row
London SW1P 1RR
Tel: 071 222 3065

For Citizens' Advice Bureaux and other advice centres, consult your local telephone directory. The Immigration Law Practitioners' Association (115 Old Street, London EC1V 9JR, tel: 071 250 1671) can provide a directory of practitioners.

Bibliography

A. Dummett and A. Nichol, *Subjects, Citizens, Aliens and Others*, Weidenfeld & Nicholson, 1990.

JCWI, *Ethnic Minority and Migrant Organisations, European Directory*, 1991.

JCWI, *Immigration and Nationality Law Handbook*, 1992.

F. Klug and P. Gordon, *British Immigration Control: A Brief Guide*, Runnymede Trust, 1985.

I. Macdonald and N. Blake, *Immigration Law and Practice*, Butterworths, 1991.

Vincenzi and Marrington, *Immigration Law : The Rules Explained*, Sweet and Maxwell, 1992.

See also publications from the Joint Council for the Welfare of Immigrants, Manchester Immigration Aid Unit, Divided Families campaign and individual law centres.

11

The rights of mental patients

This chapter covers:

*   Applications for compulsory detention.
*   Detention of offenders.
*   Mental health review tribunals.
*   Rights in mental hospitals.
*   Further information.

Nearly half of all hospital patients are there because of some mental disorder. Anyone can apply voluntarily for treatment and may be admitted to hospital informally. Most patients are admitted to hospital in this way and they are entitled to leave at any time although, as an informal patient, they may be faced with the possibility of being compulsorily detained by one of the methods set out below if they do try to leave. Some patients, however, are compulsorily detained. This chapter is mainly concerned with the position of compulsorily detained patients and the rights of their relatives, as covered by the Mental Health Act 1983.

There are four categories of mental disorder which may result in detention in hospital or under special care. These are legal and not medical categories.

*   Mental illness: this means any mental disorder not included in the three categories below. It includes illnesses such as schizophrenia or paranoia which may last a relatively short time, or permanent brain damage resulting from an accident.
*   Severe mental impairment: this means arrested or incomplete development of mind, which includes severe impairment of intelligence and social functioning and is associated with abnormally aggressive or seriously irresponsible conduct on the part of the person concerned.
*   Mental impairment: this means arrested or incomplete development of mind, which includes significant impairment of intelligence and social functioning and is associated with abnormally aggressive or seriously irresponsible conduct, but which does not amount to severe mental impairment.

247

- Psychopathic disorder: this means a persistent disorder or disability of mind, which may or may not include significant impairment of intelligence, and which results in abnormally aggressive or seriously irresponsible conduct.

Before the 1959 Mental Health Act, it was quite common for people to be detained in mental institutions because of promiscuity or other 'immoral' conduct. Such behaviour by itself may not now be considered a form of mental disorder; nor may sexual deviancy or dependence on alcohol or drugs. Such people should be detained in hospital only if they appear to be suffering from a disorder so severe that it warrants assessment or treatment and it would be necessary for their health or safety or for the protection of others that they should receive assessment or treatment and that it cannot be provided unless they are detained.

11.1 Applications for compulsory detention

An application for someone to be compulsorily detained in hospital may be made by that person's nearest relative or by an approved social worker. Except in an emergency (see below), the application must be supported by the recommendation of two doctors one of whom must be acquainted with the patient. The two doctors must not have family or business connections with the patient or with each other and one of them must be approved by the local authority as having experience in dealing with mental disorder. If the application is successful, the applicant may authorise anyone to take the patient to hospital, by force if necessary.

There are three kinds of applications: assessment, treatment and emergency.

Admission for assessment
An admission for assessment may be made in cases where the disorder justifies detention to enable the doctor to decide what treatment is needed, if any, and that detention is necessary for the patient's health or safety or for the protection of others.

The patient may not be detained for assessment for more than twenty-eight days and the application cannot be immediately repeated. A patient may appeal within fourteen days of the admission to a mental health review tribunal (see below).

Admission for treatment
An application may be made for admission for treatment of a person outside hospital or of a patient already admitted for assessment. An approved social worker may not apply for admission for treatment until

the nearest relative has been consulted, if that relative is readily available. The approved social worker cannot make the application if the nearest relative objects. Although it is not essential, it is advisable for the nearest relative to make any objection in writing to the local health authority or the approved social worker. In an extreme case, the approved social worker can challenge the decision of the nearest relative in court.

The grounds for such admissions are that the person is suffering from a disorder so severe that it warrants treatment and it is necessary for that person's health or safety or for the protection of others that such treatment should be given and that it cannot be provided unless they are detained. If they are suffering from psychopathic disorder or mental impairment it is also necessary for the disorder to be susceptible to treatment.

An admission for treatment is valid for a maximum of six months. The responsible medical officer (i.e. the psychiatrist in charge of the patient) may then renew it for another six months and after that for periods of a year at a time.

Emergency admission

In an emergency, the nearest relative or an approved social worker may apply for admission for assessment with only one medical recommendation. A patient cannot be detained in this way for more than seventy-two hours unless within that time a second doctor recommends it, in which case the admission becomes an admission for assessment.

Anyone who is voluntarily in hospital can be detained for seventy-two hours on a recommendation by the doctor in charge of the patient. A nurse can also detain such a patient for a period not exceeding six hours if a doctor is not immediately available and the patient is suffering from mental disorder to such a degree that it is necessary for his or her health or safety or for the protection of others for him or her to be stopped immediately from leaving the hospital.

A police officer who finds a person in a public place who appears to be suffering from mental disorder and to be in need of care or control can take him or her to a safe place such as a police station or hospital. Such detention must not be for more than seventy-two hours and during that time an application may be made for admission for assessment or treatment.

A magistrate may issue a warrant authorising a police officer to enter any premises, by force where necessary, in which it is believed someone suffering from mental disorder is living alone and is unable to care for him or herself or who is being neglected or ill-treated. The police officer may then remove such a person to a safe place for not more than seventy-two hours.

Discharge from hospital

The responsible medical officer or the nearest relative may discharge a patient at any time, but the medical officer may forbid discharge by the relative on the grounds that the patient is detained for treatment and is potentially dangerous to him or herself or others. If that happens, the relative can appeal, within twenty-eight days, to a mental health review tribunal.

Leave of absence from a mental hospital may be granted indefinitely or for a specific period. A patient is automatically discharged if leave has been continuous for six months and at the end of that time he or she is not absent without leave and has not been transferred to guardianship (see p. 251).

Patients who are absent without leave may be detained and forcibly returned to hospital, unless they have been absent for twenty-eight days in which case they are automatically discharged.

The nearest relative

The nearest relative is the first of the following who is over eighteen and resident in the UK, the Channel Islands or the Isle of Man: a legally appointed guardian, a relative the patient ordinarily resides with, husband or wife, child, father or mother, brother or sister, grandparent, grandchild, uncle or aunt, nephew or niece, anyone other than the relative with whom the patient has been ordinarily residing for five years if the patient is separated from his or her spouse.

Note that:

- A husband, wife or parent need not be over eighteen.
- A person who has been living with the patient for six months as a spouse will be regarded as such if the patient's real spouse is permanently living apart from him or her.
- If the rights and powers of a parent have been taken away under the Children Act 1989, the local authority or guardian will act as the nearest relative, unless the patient is married in which case the spouse will be the nearest relative.
- An adopted child is treated as the child of the adopters.
- An illegitimate child is treated as the legitimate child of its mother.

Anyone who is a relative or spouse of the patient, or an approved social worker, may apply to a County Court for an order depriving the nearest relative of all rights concerning the patient and appointing someone else. This can be done on a number of grounds, the most important of which is that the nearest relative objects unreasonably to the patient being admitted to hospital or misuses the power to discharge.

If an order has been made displacing the nearest relative and somebody else wishes to take over the responsibilities of nearest relative, he or she may apply to the court to vary the order. This might happen if, for instance, a relative reached the age of eighteen or returned from abroad and therefore became eligible to act as the nearest relative.

Appeals

A patient can appeal to a mental health review tribunal:

- Within fourteen days of admission, if admitted for assessment.
- If admitted for treatment:
  (1) at any time within six months of admission for treatment;
  (2) within twenty-eight days when reclassified from one form of mental disorder to another;
  (3) at any time when the order for detention has been officially renewed;
  (4) within twenty-eight days if not released at the age of twenty-five and the patient is classified as suffering from psychopathic disorder or mental impairment.

A patient's nearest relative can appeal:

- Within twenty-eight days when the doctor has overruled the relative's order for discharge.
- Within twenty-eight days if the patient's disorder is reclassified.
- Within twenty-eight days when a patient suffering from psycho-pathic disorder or mental impairment is not released at the age of twenty-five.

The managers of a hospital must refer a patient's case to a tribunal if:

- The patient does not apply within six months of admission for treatment.
- The patient does not apply within six months of being transferred for guardianship to hospital.
- A tribunal has not considered the case during the previous three years.

Guardianship

A person over sixteen who is suffering from mental disorder may be put into the care of a guardian instead of being detained in hospital. The guardian may be the local health authority or anyone else. An application for guardianship should be made to the local health authority or anybody accepted by them. Patients can be transferred from hospital to guardianship and vice versa. But a transfer from guardianship to hospital needs two medical recommendations and the patient can appeal to a tribunal within six months of the transfer. The nearest relative has an absolute right of discharge from guardianship unless the patient has been transferred to hospital.

A patient suffering from psychopathic disorder or mental impairment must always be discharged from guardianship at the age of twenty-five.

11.2 Detention of offenders

Detention by court order

When a person is convicted of an offence punishable by imprisonment, the court may make a hospital order on the evidence of two doctors that the person suffers from mental disorder needing treatment. In that event, the court may not impose any sentence of imprisonment or fine nor make a probation order.

A patient may appeal to a tribunal within six months of the hospital order and then has the same rights of appeal as someone detained without a court order. The nearest relative can appeal after six months and then every twelve months.

Restriction orders

When a Crown Court makes a hospital order, it may also make a restriction order if it considers it is necessary to do so to protect the public from serious harm. In this case, the person is still sent to hospital but is subject to greater restrictions. A magistrates' court may not make a restriction order but may refer a case to the Crown Court for that purpose.

If a restriction order is made, the Home Secretary can release the patient at any time either absolutely or subject to conditions. The patient has the right to apply to a tribunal once in each year while detained or once in each two-year period while conditionally discharged. If a person is conditionally discharged and then recalled to hospital, the Home Secretary must refer the case to a tribunal within one month of the recall.

Detention by direction of the Home Secretary

A person serving a prison sentence may, on the recommendation of two doctors, be transferred to a hospital by direction of the Home Secretary. When making a transfer direction, with or without a time limit, the Home Secretary may also make a restriction direction. This has the same effect as a restriction order made by a court, with one exception: it lapses at the end of the prison sentence. After that occurs, the patient is in the same position as if he or she had been admitted for treatment (see above).

11.3. Mental health review tribunals

Mental health review tribunals hear appeals by mental patients or their nearest relative for the discharge of patients from hospitals and institutions and from guardianship. Application forms can be obtained from the patient's hospital, from the tribunal's office or from the local health authority if the patient is in the care of a guardian (see above).

The tribunal consists of three members chosen from three panels consisting of lawyers, doctors and lay members with administrative or social work experience. All three must be independent of the hospital and the local health authority concerned in the case.

Powers of the tribunal

Detentions for assessment
The tribunal must discharge a patient detained for assessment (see above) unless it is satisfied that he or she is suffering from a mental disorder severe enough to justify detention for assessment, or that detention is necessary for the patient's health or safety or the protection of other persons.

Other detentions
In all other cases (except restricted patients) the tribunal must discharge a patient if satisfied he or she is not suffering from mental illness severe enough to justify detention for treatment, or that it is not necessary for the health or safety of the patient or the protection of other persons that such treatment should be given.

In a restricted case, if the tribunal agrees that the person should be released using the provisions referred to above, but believes that the person would benefit by remaining liable to be recalled to the hospital for further treatment in future, it should order a conditional discharge.

The only appeal against a decision of a tribunal is on a point of law.

Procedure of the tribunal
The hearings are normally held in private at the patient's hospital. The applicant may ask for a public hearing but this may be refused if it would be harmful to the patient's interests. The applicant and the hospital representative (usually the consultant responsible for the patient) are both present and give evidence. They can question each other and any other witnesses. The applicant can also address the tribunal but otherwise the tribunal conducts the proceedings as it thinks best.

The tribunal has power to take evidence on oath, to order witnesses to appear and to produce any documents. The medical member of the tribunal examines the patient before the hearing date and enquires into all relevant aspects of his or her health and treatment.

Advice and representation

It is most important that a patient should receive advice and representation when appealing to a tribunal. This can be given by a solicitor under the Legal Aid Act by using the scheme known as 'advice by way of representation'.

Expenses may be paid to the applicant, witnesses and their representatives unless the representatives are lawyers. Expenses consist of rail fares, subsistence and any loss of earnings agreed by the tribunal. It is often very useful to obtain the expert evidence of another doctor. The costs of doing so can be paid using the legal aid system.

11.4. Rights in mental hospitals

Consent to treatment

A patient in any hospital cannot be treated without specific consent, except in cases of necessity. There are exceptions for mental patients, whose treatment is divided into three types:

• Psychosurgery or the implantation of hormones to reduce male sexual drive may be given only with both the consent of the patient and opinions from two doctors.
• The administration of medicine for three months or longer or electro-convulsive therapy may be given only either with the consent of the patient or opinions from two doctors.
• Any other treatment can be given if the doctor thinks fit.

It should also be noted that:

• These rules apply to treatment for the patient's mental disorder, not to any physical illness he or she may have. The restrictions on treatment do not apply to treatment which is immediately necessary to save the patient's life, to prevent a serious deterioration of his or her condition, to alleviate serious suffering or, if it is needed, to prevent a danger to self or others. However, treatment which is irreversible or hazardous cannot be given in any of these cases except the first (i.e. if it is necessary to save the patient's life).

- These rules do not apply to mental patients detained under the various short-term powers in the Mental Health Act 1983. Only the first rule applies to voluntary patients.

The right to visits
Patients have no legal right to visits, except to give them assistance in connection with a decision to release them, when they make a complaint, or to see their lawyer.

Letters
A postal packet sent by a detained patient may be withheld if a request to do so has been made by the addressee. If the patient is detained in a special hospital (Broadmoor, Ashworth or Rampton) it may also be withheld if it is likely to cause distress or danger to anyone.

Post sent to a patient in a special hospital may be withheld if it is necessary for the patient's safety or the protection of others.

No letters to or from the following people can be withheld under any circumstances: an MP, and officer of the Court of Protection, the various ombudsmen, a mental health review tribunal, the managers of the hospital, a lawyer instructed by the patient or the European Commission or European Court.

Independent medical examination
A patient can be examined by an independent psychiatrist. The patient's medical notes must be shown if the psychiatrist wishes to see them. Any fee charged may be covered by the Legal Advice scheme.

Property
A patient's property cannot be interfered with unless he or she consents or someone is authorised to do so by the Court of Protection. The Court of Protection manages the property of people who, through mental disorder, are incapable of managing their own affairs whether or not they are in hospital.

Voting
A detained patient cannot be entered on the electoral register. A voluntary patient in hospital can register to vote at his or her former address.

Suing the doctor or the hospital
A doctor is not liable in any civil or criminal proceedings in respect of anything done under the Mental Health Act unless it was done in bad faith or without reasonable care. Civil proceedings need the permission of the High Court and criminal proceedings must be by or with the consent of the Director of Public Prosecutions.

This protection does not apply to the Secretary of State for Health or a health authority.

Jury service

Mentally disordered people resident in a psychiatric hospital or who regularly receive treatment cannot serve on juries.

11.5 Further information

Useful Organisations

Law Centres – consult your telephone directory for local addresses and telephone numbers.

Mencap
123 Golden Lane
London EC1Y ORT
Tel: 071 454 0454

MIND
22 Harley Street
London W1N 2ED
Tel: 071 637 0741

Bibliography

Richard Jones, *Mental Health Act Manual*, Sweet and Maxwell, 1991 (£30).
Liberty, *Your Rights Under the Mental Health Act*, 1993 (£1).
MIND Rights Guides: *Civil Admission and Discharge; Patients Involved in Criminal Proceedings; Your Rights in Hospital and Mental Health Review Tribunal*, (45p each or £2 for set).

12

The rights of children and young people

This chapter deals with:

- Parental responsibility.
- Decision making.
- Money and financial support.
- Citizenship and nationality.
- Education and schooling.
- Children, young people and the courts.
- Further information.

Because of both their inherent vulnerability and society's attitudes towards their independence, children and young people have considerably fewer rights than adults. Children do not acquire full legal independence until they are eighteen (or later in relation to the age of consent to homosexual sex or becoming an MP). However, before then, the law states that children can do things or can be treated in particular ways at certain ages – for example, the right to drink alcohol in private at five, to buy a pet at twelve, to work part time at thirteen and a number of different things at sixteen. For more information about this, see the bibliography on p. 267.

The past few years have seen a number of important changes for children's rights. There is now a far greater recognition that children and young people should be seen as people in their own right and not as possessions of their parents nor objects of investigation. The Gillick judgement (see below) recognised the rights of older mature children to make decisions concerning their lives in certain circumstances. The discrimination against non-marital children has all but disappeared. The 1989 Children Act has given children and young people greater rights to participate in decision making where social services or the family courts are involved. And the United Nations Convention on the Rights of the Child sets out a broad range of basic standards and principles relating to children's civil, political, economic, social and cultural rights. The Convention has been ratified by the government which means that it should introduce its principles into English law.

But there are backward steps too such as the introduction of the 1991 Child Support Act.

The law is complex and the following inevitably simplifies to a great degree. Where in doubt, legal advice should always be obtained.

12.1 Parental responsibility

Parental responsibility is the new term for parental rights and duties in relation to children and young people. The law does not actually say what this means but it has been understood to mean the rights and responsibilities to make decisions involved in all aspects of the child's upbringing, including the duty to look after the child and pay for his or her keep. Parental responsibility lasts until the child is eighteen although the way in which it is exercised should reflect the age and maturity of the child (see below).

Parents and others

Mothers and married fathers automatically have parental responsibility for their children. This lasts even if they get divorced. Unmarried fathers do not have parental responsibility but they can obtain this by going to court for a parental responsibility order or by a special written agreement with the mother. Other people may get parental responsibility in certain circumstances, for example, where a residence order is made (see below) or where social services obtain a care order.

Sharing parental responsibility

Each person with parental responsibility can do what he or she thinks is best for the child. They do not have to consult with the other parent to do this but they must not do anything which infringes the law or what a court order says. If there are disagreements about how parental responsibility is being carried out the court can make a prohibited steps order (stopping a parent from doing something) or a specific issues order (telling the parent(s) to do something in a certain way).

Separation and divorce

The law now tries to encourage parents to agree about their children's future when they separate or divorce so that it is not necessary to make a court order unless it is better to do so for the child. However, it may make a residence order (saying with whom the child should live) and/or a contact order (stating arrangements for the child to see the other parent). Unless the court says otherwise the non-resident parent has the right to be involved in major decisions concerning the child such as medical treatment, religion, education, etc.

Delegating parental responsibility

Unless there is a court order to say so, other people in charge of children, such as childminders, teachers, or foster carers do not have parental responsibility. But they do have a general duty to the children they are looking after to do what is reasonable to make sure that the child is well cared for.

If parents are experiencing difficulties in caring for their children they can ask social services to look after them for them. This used to be called voluntary care. It is now called provision of accommodation. Social services do not get parental responsibility and should agree in writing with the parents about how the child is looked after. Parents can ask for the return of their children at any time (although it should of course be done in the best way for the child). Over sixteens cannot be forced to return home if they do not wish to do so.

12.2 Decision making

The Children Act does not require parents to consult with their children or take their views into account in making decisions about their upbringing. However, in an important court case decided in 1985 the court looked at this issue. It said that parental powers to control their children dwindle as the child matures. The rights of parents should give way to the child's right to make decisions when 'he or she is of sufficient understanding and intelligence' to be able to make up his or her own mind. This is known as the Gillick principle.

Names

Mothers, married fathers and others with parental responsibility have the right to choose the name of their child. They also have a duty to register the child's name with the Registrar General of Births, Marriages and Deaths within forty-two days of the child's birth.

Either parent may change the child's name unless there is a residence order which automatically stops this or a prohibited steps order which prevents the parent from doing so. With parental consent, young people may use a different name to that on their birth certificate. Applying the Gillick principle, parents should allow children of sufficient understanding to change their name even if they do not agree with this. Where there is a dispute, parents or the young person him or herself (with the court's permission) can apply to the court for a prohibited steps or specific issues order.

Religion

Following on from the Gillick decision, young people can choose their own religion if they have the maturity to understand the implications of that decision. Again, if there is a dispute the court can be involved. If the parents thought that the religion was harmful they could ask the court to intervene by making the child a ward of court. Only parents have the right to withdraw children from religious assembly and instruction at school or to send the young person for religious instruction elsewhere provided it does not interfere with attendance.

Medical treatment

At sixteen, young people have the right to give consent to medical, dental and surgical treatment as if they were adults. This includes contraceptive advice and treatment.

Young people under the age of sixteen can give consent provided that the doctor thinks the young person is mature enough to understand what is involved in the treatment and the consequences of this. Although the law says that doctors should encourage young people to inform their parents, they may give treatment without parental knowledge or consent if the young person does not wish to involve them. These principles also apply to termination of pregnancy but in practice doctors very rarely perform abortions on under sixteens without parental consent because of the possible risks associated with general anaesthesia.

Although the law is unclear it appears that young people's rights to refuse consent to medical treatment are more limited. Young people (over sixteens and mature under sixteens) may not have the right to refuse consent to medical treatment if their parents (or if they are in care, social services) disagree with them. This usually arises in relation to serious mental health matters, and the courts have said that the young person's refusal to give consent should be an important matter for parents, doctors and the courts in deciding whether to override the young person's views.

Leaving home

Under sixteens cannot leave home without parental consent unless there is agreement or a court order to this effect. Where social services are not involved and there is another adult who can take over the care of the child, then the court can be asked to make a residence order on the application of the adult or the child (provided that he or she has first obtained the court's permission) or the adult.

The law relating to sixteen to seventeen year olds is not clear but they can probably leave home without parental consent. The police will not intervene unless they believe that the young person is at risk in which case they can hold them in police protection for up to seventy-two hours. Likewise, social services will not become involved unless they believe that the young person is at risk. They may apply for an emergency protection order (as may any other person concerned for the young person's welfare) or they may start court proceedings for a care order (in relation to sixteen year olds only). While the child's welfare is the court's paramount consideration, it must also take into account the wishes and feelings of the young person. Where the family relationship has clearly broken down it is most unlikely to allow the return of the child to the parents.

The parents themselves may take legal action for the return of their child by making him or her a ward of court. Again, the court is most unlikely to order the return of the young person where there is a clear breakdown of the family relationship or where the young person is safe and does not wish to return home.

12.3 Money and financial support

Parents should support their children financially until they are eighteen and the 1991 Child Support Act reinforces this principle. On separation or divorce, the absent parent is responsible for paying maintenance in support of the child. This is administered, collected and enforced through the Child Support Agency (CSA), a branch of the Department of Social Security (DSS). The amount of maintenance is worked out by reference to a standard formula. In operating the system, the CSA should take into account the welfare of the child but the rules are very complex and the outcome may not always appear to do so. Young people have no right to make their own applications for maintenance assessment against their parents. However, over eighteens may apply to court for maintenance where they are at school, in full- or part-time further or higher education or training.

Sixteen and seventeen year olds can only claim income support in certain limited circumstances, such as the inability to work or when caring for dependents. They may be able to claim a discretionary payment of income support to avoid 'severe hardship'. Matters such as the health and vulnerability of the young person and whether there are friends or relatives to support them should be taken into account by the DSS in making this decision but many young people estranged from their parents do not receive any income support.

12.4 Citizenship and nationality

Children born in the United Kingdom before 1 January 1983 are automatically British citizens irrespective of the nationality or immigration status of their parents. Children born in the UK after that date are only British citizens if one parent (or the mother only of a non-marital child) is a British citizen or is settled in the UK at the time of the birth (see

p. 243). Children and young people may apply for British citizenship by application to the Home Office for registration.

Travel and passports

Children may travel on their parents' passports until the age of sixteen. The child must be with the parent at the time of travel and his or her name must be on the parent's passport. Children and young people may have their own passport but this must be on the application of the parent if he or she is under eighteen.

Parents must not take their children out of the UK without the consent of the other parent or the permission of the court. However, a child can leave the country for up to four weeks with a parents (or anyone else) with a residence order. Removal of a child without the consent of the parent(s) is known as child abduction. This is very complex area about which legal advice should always be obtained.

12.5 Education and schooling

The law relating to education is very complex and there are now a number of different kinds of state school with different forms of school government and organisation. The following is a very brief summary of essential rights relating to state schools only. Independent schools fall outside the remit of the law unless they are boarding schools, in which case social services must inspect them to check the children's welfare.

Compulsory education

The law makes education compulsory for all children from the age of five to sixteen. Parents must ensure that their children go to school or otherwise receive 'efficient full-time education suitable to his or her age, ability, aptitude and any special educational needs'. This means that children may be educated at home but the local education authority (LEA) must be satisfied that the education is suitable. Criminal proceedings may be brought against parents where their child is not attending school or being suitably educated. The LEA may also start court proceedings for an education supervision order. This places the child under the supervision of the LEA which has the power to make arrangements (where possible in consultation with the child and parents) to ensure that the child is properly educated.

Admissions

Schools and LEAs must allow parents their choice of state school unless that school is oversubscribed and it can be shown that admitting the child would prejudice the provision of efficient education or use of resources in that school. Children have no independent right of choice. Parents may appeal to an LEA appeals committee against a refusal. LEAs must ensure that a child has a school place.

Curriculum

Schools must ensure that there is a broadly balanced curriculum which 'promotes the spiritual, moral, cultural, mental and physical development of pupils at the school and of society and prepares pupils for the opportunities, responsibilities and experiences of adult life'. Within this, schools must teach the National Curriculum (NC), religious education (RE) and sex education (in secondary schools only). The NC consists of the three core subjects of English, maths and science plus foundation subjects of history, geography, technology, physical education, art, music and a foreign language (at secondary level). These subjects are evaluated by means of teacher assessment and Standard Assessment Tasks (SATs) which have been introduced for seven and fourteen year olds and are due to be introduced for eleven year olds in 1995.

Parents may withdraw their children from RE at school and arrange for alternative RE during school hours. The law about sex education has recently changed. It is now part of the broad curriculum for secondary schools but parents have now been given the right to withdraw their children from it. It also forms part of the National Curriculum for science for eleven to fourteen year olds from which parents may not withdraw their children. Primary schools may decide whether to offer sex education and parents must be informed of the school's policy about this.

Parents, but not children, have a right to complain about the curriculum.

Special educational needs

The law gives parents the right to ask the LEA for their children with special needs to be formally assessed so that appropriate educational provision can be offered by the LEA. This is called statementing. There are detailed rights about parental consultation during this process. If the parents are not satisfied with the eventual provision contained in the statement of special educational needs they may appeal to a Special Educational Needs Tribunal.

Behaviour and discipline

Schools have the right to make rules about what pupils can do both inside and outside school. There are no procedures for parents or pupils to make complaints about these issues. Some schools have behaviour policies which have been drawn up in consultation with the pupils. Corporal punishment (which includes things like throwing missiles and hair pulling as well as smacking and caning) is banned in all state schools.

Pupils may be excluded from school permanently (expelled) or for a fixed period (suspended). Although a decision to exclude should only be made as a last resort, it is entirely up to the headteacher. Parents must be informed about the exclusion and the reasons for it and they have the right to make representations to the governing body. Parents, but not children, may appeal against a permanent exclusion to an LEA appeals committee but the vast majority of appeals are unsuccessful.

12.6 Children, young people and the courts

Criminal cases

Child as defendant

Children under the age of ten are below the age of criminal responsibility and cannot be arrested by the police or charged with any criminal offence. Younger children who persistently offend may be dealt with by social services which can offer help to the family or may start court proceedings for a care order (see below).

The rules for police questioning, search and detention of juveniles (people under seventeen) are the same as for adults but juveniles have additional rights. The parents must be informed of the young person's arrest and detention. Except in certain circumstances, interviews should take place only in the presence of an appropriate adult. This is usually the parent but may be another adult such as a social worker or youth worker if the young person is estranged from the parent(s).

The police may decide not to prosecute by taking the matter to court. Instead they can issue a caution. This can only be done where the crime is not a very serious one, if the young person admits the offence and if he or she has been in relatively little trouble before. A caution is a severe reprimand by a senior police officer. It does not form part of the young person's criminal record although it may be brought up if there are court proceedings in the future.

If the case goes to court, it will usually be to the youth court which is part of the magistrates' court. The court may impose a range of punishments such as a fine, an attendance centre order or a supervision order which may contain a requirement that the young person lives in social services' accommodation for up to six months. Young people cannot be sent to prison but fifteen to twenty-one year olds can be sentenced to detention in young offender institutions. However, ten to thirteen year olds who have been found guilty of murder or manslaughter can be locked up indefinitely in social services' secure accommodation and fourteen years olds can also be detained in secure accommodation if they have been found guilty of a grave offence (i.e. offences with a maximum of fourteen years' imprisonment if an adult).

Child witnesses

A child of any age can give evidence as a witness in a criminal trial unless the court thinks that he or she is not able to understand what is involved. There are special rules about how young people can give evidence in relation to sexual or violent offences. The evidence of young people under the age of seventeen (in relation to sexual offences) or fourteen (in relation to violent offences) may be recorded in advance of the trial by means of a video-recording. This evidence is transmitted by live television link at the trial so that the child does not have to appear in court. He or she may, however, have to attend court personally to answer questions put by the defendant or lawyer.

Family cases

Section 8 proceedings

Parents may apply for a residence order, contact order, prohibited steps order or specific issues order (see above). Other people, such as relatives, can ask for the court's permission to do so. Children and young people may also ask the court for permission to take a case to court but this will only be granted if the court thinks that he or she has sufficient understanding to make that application. In these circumstances, children will be represented by their own lawyer.

In any court proceedings, the court must decide what is in the best interests of the child. It must also listen to and take into account the wishes and feelings of the child in light of his or her age and understanding. The court will usually be helped by a report prepared by a court official called a court welfare officer. In some cases, children are separately represented by a guardian ad litem or a solicitor.

Care and supervision proceedings

Social services may apply to the court for a care order where they consider that a child or young person is at risk. A child cannot apply to be taken into care by social services. The court can only make a care order where it is satisfied that the child is suffering, or is at risk of suffering, significant harm as a result of the way the parents are caring for the child, or because the child is beyond parental control and that it is in the best interests of the child to do so. The court must always weigh up the different kinds of orders that could be made instead, for example a supervision order or a residence order to relatives or friends. It must also decide whether it is better for the child to make an order at all since the family could be helped on a voluntary basis by social services. The law now recognises the importance for children of keeping in touch with their families. Before making a care order the court must look at the arrangements for contact that social services have made.

Again, the court must take into account the wishes and feelings of the child. Children and young people are represented by a guardian ad litem and a solicitor. A guardian is a social worker appointed by the court whose job it is to write a report making recommendations about what is in the best interests of the child. Where an older child disagrees with the guardian, the solicitor must represent the child as if he or she were an adult.

A care order means that social services have parental responsibility for the child. They share this with the parents but they can cut back the extent of the parents' responsibility in the interests of the child. A care order lasts until the child is eighteen unless it is set aside earlier. Children will usually be placed with foster carers but young people may be placed in a children's home. Sometimes, young people are locked up if they have run away from care a lot and are thought to be at risk. This can only happen if a court has made a secure accommodation order (unless it is for less than three days).

Social services must make plans for the child's future which are reviewed every six months. They must consult with children, parents and others concerned for the child and take into account issues of the child's religion, race, language and culture in decision making. They must also encourage contact with parents, extended family and friends where this is in the interests of the child. They must also have a complaints procedure for use by both parents and children.

A supervision order means that the child will continue to live at home with the parents but with formal visits from social services. It lasts for a year but can be extended for up to three years. If the parents don't let social services see the child the police can come to check his or her safety.

Adoption

An adoption order means that parental responsibility for the child is transferred from the birth parents to the adoptive parents and the child is regarded as having been part of the adoptive family since birth. A child can only be adopted with the consent of the birth parent(s) but this may be set aside if the court is satisfied that consent has been withheld unreasonably and because the child's welfare is the court's first consideration. Children are not usually represented in adoption proceedings but the court should take into account their wishes and feelings.

Children usually have no contact with their birth family and although the courts can now make contact orders in adoption proceedings they are reluctant to do so. At eighteen and over, young people can apply to the Registrar General for a copy of their original birth certificate.

Adult adoptees and birth family members may also apply to the Registrar General for entry of their names on the Adoption Contact Register. Details of birth family members will be given to adoptees so that contact can be established if the adopted person wishes to pursue this.

Civil (non-criminal) cases

Children and young people can start their own court cases or have one brought against them. This must be done through an adult (usually the parent) called a next friend or guardian ad litem, and they must act in the child's best interests.

12.7 Further information

Useful organisations

ChildLine Freepost 1111
London N1 0BR
Tel: freephone helpline 0800 1111

Children's Legal Centre
20 Compton Terrace
London N1 2UN
Tel: advice service Monday to Friday 2–5 p.m. 071 359 6251

Citizens' Advice Bureaux – consult your Yellow Pages telephone directories, or your local library to find your local office.

National Association for Young People in Care
8A Stucley Place
London NW1
Tel: 071 284 4793

NSPCC Child Protection Line
67 Saffron Hill
London EC1N 8RS
Tel: freephone 0800 800500

Bibliography

At What Age Can I? Children's Legal Centre, 1993 (£2).
Working with Young People, Children's Legal Centre, 1992 (£6).
Children Law and Practice, Family Law, loose leaf encyclopedia.
The Law of Education, Butterworths, loose leaf encyclopedia.

13

The rights of workers

This chapter deals with:

- Unions.
- Contracts of employment.
- Drug taking, drinking and workers' rights.
- Women.
- Health, safety, sickness and disability.
- Dismissal.
- Redundancy.
- Industrial action.
- Claims.
- Further information.

Central to any system of civil liberties is a recognition of the importance of workers' rights. In the UK, there was grudging acceptance of workers' rights in the form of the Trade Union Act 1871, which allowed trade unions to exist when hitherto they had been illegal. The expression of trade union rights in the form of calls for industrial action was made lawful by the Trade Disputes Act 1906. The foundation of modern workers' rights lies in those two statutes, now repealed, and it was not until the 1960s that attention was given to the rights of workers as individuals with the passing of legislation on minimum periods of notice and redundancy pay. Ironically, the first comprehensive statute dealing with individual and collective workers' rights – the Industrial Relations Act 1971 – lasted only three years before it was defeated by trade union opposition and the passing of the Trade Union and Labour Relations Act 1974, the starting point for the basic freedoms of people at work. Since then, a general expansion of individual rights – as contained in the Employment Protection (Consolidation) Act 1978 (EPCA), the Sex Discrimination Act 1975 – the Race Relations Act 1976 and the Equal Pay Act 1970 (which became effective at the end of 1975), has been trimmed back both by the decisions of tribunals and courts, and by a series of administrative measures and statutes imposed since 1979. These include the Employment Act 1980, the Trade Union Act 1984, the Trade Union and Labour Relations (Consolidation) Act 1992, the Trade Union Reform and Employment Rights Act

1993, the Wages Act 1986, the Social Security Act 1986 and several codes of practice issued by the Department of Employment.

On the other hand, European Community law has had a noticeable impact in the fight for women to achieve equal pay for doing work which is the same as, or of equal value to, a man's, and in challenging other forms of discrimination on the grounds of sex. It is also the source of the protection of workers' rights on business transfers.

European law applies throughout the UK. Employment legislation applies in England, Wales and Scotland, and most of it applies (in the form of parallel Orders) in Northern Ireland. The Scottish and English laws of contract have different terminology but similar substance.

This chapter deals principally with the rights contained in the Acts, codes and cases arising since 1974. From the outset it is important to recall that the courts have been hostile to the concept and practice of workers' rights, particularly when these rights are advanced by way of industrial action by trade union members. Because union membership is the key to enforcing workers' rights at workplace level through collective bargaining and industrial action, union rights are dealt with first.

13.1 Unions

Why join?
Employment law has traditionally viewed workers' problems as definable in individual contracts of employment. In reality, your rights as an individual worker are largely determined by the negotiating position you have with your employer and individuals have little opportunity to influence the specific terms and conditions of employment, whereas collectively workers can and do. Furthermore, although just over one in three of the twenty-one million or so people in employment are members of trade unions, two-thirds have their terms and conditions affected by collective bargaining between their employer, or a group of employers, and trade unions.

Rights against employers
You are protected by the EPCA against refusal of employment, dismissal and victimisation short of dismissal on the grounds that you are or are not a trade union member. This includes seeking to become a member and taking part, at an appropriate time outside working hours but on your employer's premises, in the activities of the union. You are also protected if the grounds of your dismissal or victimisation are your trade union activities in the past, for example, when you were working for another employer, when the basis of the employer's action is fear that you will repeat those actions in your current employment.

The rights entitle you to recruit members, hand out literature, collect subscriptions and hold meetings during the times when you are not working. If management allows you to talk while you are at work, you are also allowed to talk about trade union membership and to encourage people to join.

Anything which prevents or deters you from being a member, or from taking part in the union's activities, or which penalises you for so doing, is unlawful. This includes the refusal to allow representation by a union official in accordance with agreed procedures. Generally any form of disadvantage is unlawful so long as the target of the management action is genuinely 'trade union activity'. That includes the presentation of, for example, a complaint or grievance relating to health and safety, and does not include simply the activities of a group of individuals who happen to be union members. The union content of the issue must be clear, and the management action must be taken against you as an individual and not as a form of retaliation against the union which may be seeking to organise. However, it is not unlawful for an employer who wants to change terms and conditions of employment, for example, by introducing personal contracts and when this is opposed by the trade union to give bigger pay increases to those employees who accept the change, even when the aim is to deter or penalise trade union membership.

You can make a claim to an industrial tribunal (see p. 292). Compensation is available for dismissal and victimisation of up to £43,950 (1993) with unlimited further compensation available if management refuses to comply in full with an order for reinstatement or re-engagement made by the tribunal.

The most important remedy for dismissal is an order for reinstatement. In order to make a claim, you should use the 'interim relief' procedure available while you are under notice or during the first seven days afterwards, which requires a certificate from a union official confirming that in their opinion you were dismissed because of your trade union activities and are likely to win a claim for unfair dismissal on those grounds. A very quick hearing will then be arranged by the tribunal which has power to order management to continue your contract until the full hearing of the case.

With the exception of the requirement of a union official's certificate, all of the above rights and procedures apply to someone who has been victimised or dismissed on the grounds that they refused to join or take part in the activities of a trade union.

Union recognition

Recognition means that management is prepared to negotiate with an independent trade union or unions over terms and conditions of employment. Negotiation is stronger than consultation, which is essentially a one-way process, and the mere right to represent individuals in, say, grievance or disciplinary hearings. Recognition has the advantage that the union has negotiated a procedure for the settlement of disputes and also some legal advantages flow from it. These are:

- The duty to deal with and give facilities to safety representatives appointed by the union under the Health and Safety at Work, etc. Act (see p. 284).
- Consultation on occupational pensions.
- Consultation on redundancies, on take-overs and mergers and the automatic transfer of collective agreements (see p. 291).
- Disclosure of information, for instance financial information, for the purposes of collective bargaining, with a legally enforceable right to obtain better terms and conditions if information is denied.
- Time off with pay for union representatives carrying out duties or training connected with collective bargaining, or without pay for union members attending internal union activities.
- Time and facilities for carrying out workplace ballots.

The right to time off can be enforced by a claim to a tribunal (see p. 292). It is available to shop stewards, staff representatives and other labour representatives. It enables them to prepare for negotiations, draw up plans, consult other members and officers, and negotiate. The amount of time off is that which is 'reasonable' for carrying out duties and training in connection with their industrial relations functions.

Quite separately, union members have the right to take off time for union activities, such as voting, attending union conferences and other matters of internal organisation. This right does not attract pay.

Union membership agreements, or closed shops, can be negotiated with management but since the Employment Acts 1988 and 1990, refusal of employment on the ground of unwillingness to join the union is unlawful.

All companies with 250 employees must include in their annual report a statement of the measures taken to provide information to, and to consult with, employees on matters of concern to them (Companies Act 1985).

Rights within the union

There is no general right to join a trade union. Such a right does exist if it is the practice within, say, an industry or section of industry for employees to belong to a particular union in accordance with a union membership agreement. In that case, if you are employed or are seeking to be employed (even if you do not have a job or a job offer), you have the right not to be unreasonably excluded or expelled from membership. You can complain to a tribunal if you are refused.

The relationship between you and your union is governed both by the union rule book and by statute. The rule book, together with custom and practice, sets up contractual rights entitling you to the benefits and the procedures contained in it. In addition, the rules of natural justice will generally apply to any disciplinary hearing within the union. These are the right to be given notice of the allegation made against you, the opportunity to state your case and to be heard by an impartial body within the union.

You have the right under the Trade Union and Labour Relations (Consolidation) Act 1992 to resign and not to have unjustifiable disciplinary action taken against you. You can complain to a tribunal (see p. 292) which can set aside the decisions of the union and award compensation.

Discipline is unjustifiable if it is on the grounds of failing to participate in or support industrial action, even if a majority of the members involved voted in favour. Similarly, disciplinary action for refusing to break your contract of employment, or for following calls for action in breach of the union's rules, is unjustifiable. Disciplinary action means expulsion, fines, deprivation of benefits or any other detriment. It also includes advising another union not to take the person into membership because of, for example, refusing to support industrial action by the first union.

The Independent Review Committee of the TUC operates to protect you if you have been expelled from your union and lost your job as a result. Such situations will be very rare, but the Committee works by putting pressure upon unions and the using internal power of the TUC to enforce compliance.

Political activities

A union may resolve to have a political fund and to require its members to pay contributions, part of which go into the fund. Activities of a party political nature must be paid for out of the political fund and not out of the general fund of the union. You have an absolute right to refuse to contribute to the political fund and must not be disadvantaged for so doing (Trade Union Act 1913). Ballots were held in all unions which had political funds, pursuant to the Trade Union Act 1984 (now the Trade Union and Labour Relations Consolidation Act 1992), and all passed resolutions favouring the continuance of such funds.

In Northern Ireland the system is reversed, in that all members are contracted out of the political fund and it requires a positive statement by an individual to join in the fund.

Election of officers

Since the Trade Union Act 1984 and the Employment Act 1988, all officials who have voting rights, or who attend and speak at the governing bodies of trade unions, must be elected by secret postal ballot every five years.

13.2 Contracts of employment

Not everyone who works has a contract of employment. Employment law generally protects only employees. In discrimination cases, people applying to become employees and people under a personal contract to do work are also covered. A distinction is most frequently drawn between employees and the self-employed. It is easier to see than to define. The label used is not decisive as to what the parties to the contract intended. All the relevant circumstances have to be examined to see if the person is in business on his or her own account.

Employed or self-employed?

You will generally be an employee, and not self-employed, if the economic reality of the relationship is that you are not in business on your own account. You and your employer owe each other obligations which include, on your part, the requirement to obey instructions and to do the work yourself; and on your employer's part to provide work and to accept the work done. Once a self-employed person completes the work, the contract ends, even if a subsequent identical contract is given and there is in fact no break in the relationship. Since there are tax advantages to the worker and tax and other advantages to the employer in establishing self-employed status, these are superficial temptations. Self-employed workers are denied access to employment protection legislation and are unprotected by the employer's compulsory insurance against industrial injuries. Unless you genuinely want to go into business on your own account, taking the risks inherent in such a practice, you should resist offers to become self-employed, and in any event the courts are more likely to find that you have a contract of employment.

Certain categories of worker are given employment protection rights although strictly they are not employees. For example, apprentices enter into fixed-term contracts which impose particular obligations upon the apprentice and the employer. There is a strict obligation to give and accept instruction in the trade and termination generally requires the apprentice's parents' consent.

Civil servants work under terms of service with the Crown and do not have contracts of employment. This includes some National Health Service workers. Nevertheless, they have access to most of the employment legislation, and where they are excluded they have their own arrangements, for example, in relation to redundancy pay.

People who hold office may or may not be employees, depending on the nature of the relationship with their 'employer'. Directors of companies, for example, may be office holders under company law and also be employees of their companies. Trade union officers hold office by virtue of their election in some cases, and are also employees of their union. Police officers hold office and are not employees.

Homeworkers may or may not be employees, depending on the nature of the relationship and upon whether they are engaged in business on their own account, applying the 'economic reality' and 'mutual obligation' tests.

Casual workers may be self-employed or employees only for the time when they are engaged, even though they continue to work day after day for the same employer and take on all the appearances of a regular employee. If you can establish that all your contracts as a casual worker are linked under an 'umbrella' contract, spanning a period long enough (i.e. two years) to entitle you to bring a claim under the employment legislation, you will be able to take advantage of your rights.

Trainees on Training Agency schemes may or may not be employees, depending on the type of scheme and the arrangements for pay, but are covered by health and safety and discrimination legislation.

What's in a contract?
Every employee has a contract of employment. For most people, this means a written statement of the main terms given to you shortly after you started work. Nevertheless, you are still an employee working under a contract of employment even if nothing is written down. The fact that you have agreed to work and your employer has agreed to pay you constitutes a contract of employment. True, if a dispute arises as to the rate of pay or entitlement to bonus it will be more difficult for you to prove your version is correct, but that does not detract from the fact that you have contractual rights. A contract will generally consist of terms and conditions which may be identified in any of the following forms.

Written statement
Within thirteen weeks of your starting work, your employer must provide you with a statement, in writing, of the particulars of your terms of employment (EPCA 1978). These must include: the date your employment started and whether any previous employment is regarded as continuous with it; the rate of pay or the method of calculating it and how often it is paid; hours of work; entitlement to holidays, holiday pay, sick pay, and whether or not a pension scheme exists; the length of notice required to be given by each side; job title; any disci-

plinary rules which apply to you and the name of any person to whom you can apply if you have a grievance or are dissatisfied with any disciplinary action, and the procedure which you must follow. Details of disciplinary rules need only be given if your employer employs at least twenty people. For all of these, cross references can be made to more detailed documents, such as those described below. If you are not given a written statement you can make a claim to a tribunal and if successful you would get compensation (see p. 292).

The written statement provides strong evidence of what the agreed terms are, but does not in itself constitute the contract of employment. That is much broader than the written statement, so you can challenge the terms in it if they are not those to which you agreed. Do not sign that the terms in a statement are correct. By all means give a written receipt, but only agree that you have received the document and not that you accept its contents being true.

The Trade Union Reform and the Employment Rights Act 1993 will amend these rights to include in the statement information on whether employment is temporary or permanent, the place of work and whether you are required to work outside the UK. The statement will have to be given after two months.

Collective agreements

Frequently many of these terms and conditions will be determined by agreements negotiated by trade unions on your behalf. The fruits of the negotiations between unions and employers are incorporated automatically into your contract of employment, since either your written statement or the custom and practice at your workplace will generally say so. Collective agreements generally set substantive terms and conditions such as wages and hours, and will also provide the machinery for the resolution of disputes, discipline and grievances.

Itemised pay statement

Every time you are paid you are entitled (EPCA 1978) to a written statement setting out the gross pay, any variable or fixed deductions, net pay and, if not all the pay is paid in the same way, the method of payment for each part, for example, where a bonus is paid less frequently than basic pay. If you have fixed deductions for each pay period, it is sufficient for management to give you a statement in advance of what the fixed deductions are, and they must reissue it at least annually. If you are not given an itemised pay slip then you can make a claim to a tribunal (see p. 292).

Works rules

Management may publish on notice boards or in employee handbooks a set of works rules. These do not necessarily form part of your contract, so that if you break any of them you may not automatically be breaking your contract of employment. At most, they are management's instructions about how the job is to be done and are not to be treated as rules cast in stone – they can be challenged if you make a claim to a tribunal arising out of, for example, your dismissal for breaking one.

Wages council orders and Agricultural Wages Boards

Since 1909, protection was given to workers in industries where there is low trade union organisation and where workers are notoriously prone to exploitation. The Wages Act 1986 cut down the rights of workers engaged in a range of industries including catering, garment manufacture and retailing. On 30 August 1993, all wages councils were abolished.

If agricultural workers are not paid the minimum rate wages inspectors employed by the Department of Employment can prosecute the employer. A court can order the employer to pay a fine and to make payments of arrears of wages or repayment of deductions unlawfully made (for example, for accommodation). In addition, proceedings can be brought either by you or the wages inspector in the county courts. Workers engaged in agriculture have minimum basic wages set by the Agricultural Wages Boards though the government is considering abolishing them.

Breach of contract

Since it takes two to make a contract, changes to it must be agreed by both. Otherwise there is a breach of contract which, it is sufficiently serious, entitles you to say the contract is at an end and to walk out. Alternatively, you can refuse to accept that the serious action or omission by your employers has brought the contract to an end and you can continue to work, while reserving your rights to make a claim in the courts for breach of contract. A breach occurs when either party fails to carry out the agreed terms, or terms which have been implied by the courts or by custom and practice, or when you are dismissed with no or insufficient notice, unless you have committed 'gross misconduct' (see p. 288). A sufficiently serious breach of contract will also entitle you to bring a claim of unfair dismissal (see p. 292).

Contractual obligations

This paragraph contains the main contractual obligations between you and your employer. The method and frequency of wages or salary are as set out in your written particulars. If you were employed before 1987 (when the Wages Act 1986 took effect) and were entitled to be paid in cash, management must obtain your agreement before changing to other forms of pay.

If deductions are made unlawfully from your pay you can make a claim to a tribunal (see p. 292). Deductions are lawful only if you have given your consent in writing or if this is provided for in your contract. However, there are exceptions allowing management to make deductions in respect of: overpayment of wages and expenses; payments by law to public authorities; payments to third parties, for example to trade unions; or deductions following a strike or other industrial action. The 1986 Act applies not just to employees but to all workers.

Hours of work are determined by agreement either with you or with trade unions. There are no restrictions on the maximum or minimum number of hours to be worked by men or women, or the times of the day and days of the week when work may take place. There are some restrictions on the hours of young people below the age of eighteen. There is no definition of a 'part-time worker' but in order to claim rights under the employment legislation you need to have worked for at least sixteen hours a week, or alternatively for eight hours a week for more than five years. There is no statutory obligation to offer holidays, or to pay for them, or even to offer or pay for bank holidays.

As long as management pay you they have no obligation to provide work. The right to work may be enforced only by:

- Employees who are offered the opportunity to earn commission or a bonus (and therefore cannot achieve this if they are denied the right).
- Artists, actors, singers and performers whose careers are advanced by exposure.
- Highly skilled craft workers who need to keep their hand in.

Although management is under an obligation to provide adequate storage accommodation for your clothing if you work in a factory, they are not generally liable to recompense you for losses unless they are aware of a history of thefts and have done nothing, or they know you are required to bring tools or clothing to work in order to carry out your job. In that case, it is more likely that you can claim.

There is no right to search you, for example, on leaving the work premises, unless you have agreed this in your contract or accepted it by long-standing custom and practice. Security officers have no general powers to search or detain you. If you damage your employer's property you may be liable to compensate them if the damage is caused by your lack of care. In practice, damage to property or injury to fellow workers does not result in claims against workers.

If you are injured at work you can claim compensation on the basis that your employer has not provided a safe system of work.

Management have no right to impose a suspension or lay-off without pay and without your agreement. Suspension with pay pending the investigation of an allegation of misconduct against you is often provided for in agreements, but unilateral suspension without pay for economic or disciplinary reasons is unlawful. If you accept that management's needs for your work have diminished, you can claim redundancy pay (see p. 289) if you are suspended or reduced to less than half pay for more than four weeks. If there is no work at all, you can also claim a guarantee payment of £14.10 per day (1993) for up to five days a quarter (EPCA 1978).

You are entitled to see personal data held by your employer on computer or in a form other than manual records (Data Protection Act 1984). If the data is inaccurate, you can apply to a County Court or the High Court for its rectification or removal, and you can claim damages for loss you have suffered and for distress caused to you. Your employer must comply with a request for the data within forty days (see also p. 75).

You owe a duty of fidelity to your employer while you work and some aspects of that survive your leaving. While you are employed, you must not disclose confidential information, but you can use information which you remember (you must not remove and use your ex-employer's documents after you leave) unless there are clear written restrictions in your contract – known as restrictive covenants – forbidding this. Then, such restrictions will be upheld provided they do not stop you earning a living and they are reasonable for the protection of your ex-employer's interests. A covenant is unreasonable if it restricts you for too long or to too narrow a geographical area, or if it excludes you from your main types of work. Information relating to your employer's specific trade secrets must be kept confidential even after you leave.

While employed, you must work only for the one employer during your working hours, but in the absence of some implied restriction on your working for others, you can work in your own time as you wish. Any money you make arising out of your employment belongs to your employer and you must account for it. If you produce written material for publication, your employer has the copyright over it (Copyright Act 1956). If you make inventions or create patents management gets the benefit provided your normal duties include the likelihood of your making inventions. If you invent something of outstanding benefit to management, you can claim a fair share of the profits (Patents Act 1977).

You are under a duty to obey instructions, provided these are lawful, reasonable and within the scope of the contract you have agreed. Other instructions will constitute breaches (or even the tearing up by your employer) of the contract, for example, if you are instructed to do something which is against the criminal law, or which is unsafe, unreasonable or outside the scope of the duties you have agreed to perform. If your contract is in any way illegal (for example, because of your intention to avoid tax by being paid cash in hand), you can claim no rights under it or the employment legislation.

You are under no obligation to disclose previous convictions, unless you are applying for a job in certain professions or occupations where disclosure is obligatory. You are entitled to answer 'no' to questions aimed at probing convictions which have become 'spent' after periods of time, for example, five years for a fine (Rehabilitation of Offenders Act 1974 see p. 173). Answering negatively is neither a lie nor grounds for dismissal.

Discrimination is unlawful on the grounds of race, gender and being married. In Northern Ireland, race is not protected, but discrimination on the grounds of religious belief and political opinion is.

On leaving, management is not obliged to give you a reference. Neither is your employer under a duty to make sure that any reference is fair and accurate.

You have a right to time off without pay to be a member of a local council, health authority, school or college governing body, water authority or magistrates' bench, or for jury service. If this right is denied you can claim to a tribunal (see p. 292)(RPCA 1978). The amount of time off is that which is 'reasonable' taking into account the effect of your absence on your employer's business.

Whistleblowers

Workers who bring attention publicly to unsafe or unsound industrial or working practices may well find themselves in danger of victimisation by their employers. There are very few specific provisions in the law aimed at protecting such workers and their freedom of speech. A worker can rely on the unfair dismissal legislation although it may often be possible for an employer to show that as a result of the whistleblowing activities there has been misconduct. The claim by the employer will be that the worker has broken the obligation to be faithful to his employer (a duty that has been much developed by the courts in recent years). It is often the case, however, that employers alive to the political embarrassment of declaring that the whistleblowing activity was the real reason for the dismissal will be caught out by presenting a patently sham reason for their action. The worker may be able to show, for instance, that there has been no real damage to the employer or that the employer had not warned the worker it would lead to dismissal.

In addition, an employer may sue workers who have disclosed confidential information. In no circumstances can a worker reveal the trade secrets of the employer (which are widely defined sometimes to include simple processes). Ex-employees may also be prevented by their contract of employment from revealing other information confidential to the employer – to stick, the clause must not prevent the worker from being able to work in the future and the information must be defined.

Injunctions may be obtained where such contracts are broken leading to lengthy 'gagging' of ex-employees in some cases.

Whistleblowing cases have often concerned Health Service employees, for example, Graham Pink and Wendy Savage. As cuts are made in funding and conditions in hospitals deteriorate there is more and more pressure on those inside the system to prevent them from speaking out. Indeed guidance notes for staff on relations with the media have been published by the NHS which stress patient confidentiality and internal grievance procedures. A further problem in this area is the tension between often highly restrictive contractual clauses against speaking out and the rules of professional conduct which allow and indeed require nurses to act whenever they see falling standards of care. Where professional codes are incorporated into the contract of employment it is arguable that the final decision remains with the worker according to his or her professional rules. Professional codes often require individual responsibility for decisions which can remove much managerial prerogative in the assessment of whether the 'whistleblowing' is in breach of contract.

The Trade Union Reform and Employment Rights Act 1993 introduces a right not to be unfairly dismissed or victimised if a worker (who is a health and safety representative) takes action when he or she believes workers to be in serious and imminent danger. Whether this extends to whistleblowing activities has yet to be tested – the wording is clearly open to restrictive interpretation by the courts.

13.3 Drug taking, drinking and workers' rights

Drug addiction like alcoholism should be treated like an illness. ACAS in its advice booklet 'Discipline at Work' urges employers to have a policy covering both problems. However, employers usually treat drug taking as misconduct. Reasons given are that drug taking, unlike alcohol, can be a criminal offence and employers themselves can commit an offence under the Misuse of Drugs Act 1971 if they know that illegal drugs are being used or distributed on their premises. Tribunals usually find that dismissal is a reasonable response to drug taking or being under the influence of drink or drugs at work. Factors that a tribunal are likely to take into account include: whether the conduct was on or off duty; safety at work; contact with children or young people; the effect on the employer's reputation and business; the illegality of the employee's actions. So off-duty conduct will not usually merit dismissal in itself, though it may if it affects the employee's ability to do the job or the employer's reputation. Even if the employee has been convicted of a drug offence, the employer must conduct a proper investigation before dismissing, otherwise it will be unfair as there may be mitigating circumstances. In one case, for instance, the employee did not smoke the cannabis found in his garden.

Personal problems causing temporary drug taking or drinking have sometimes been seen as a factor that employers should take into account and restrict themselves to a warning rather than dismissal. Tribunals often accept that an employer is entitled to assume that there is a safety risk in drug taking or drinking without there being any evidence. So a worker up on disciplinary charges connected with drugs or alcohol would do well to provide evidence that there was no safety risk.

The Transport and Works Act 1992 has introduced new measures which include a new criminal offence relating to people controlling vehicles (trains, trams, etc.) whilst being unfit through drink or drugs.

13.4 Women

The Equal Pay Act 1970 and the Sex Discrimination Acts 1975 and 1986 give women (and men) the right to equal treatment and opportunities. Most of the progressive developments have come, however, from European legislation – Article 119 of the Treaty of Rome and the directives on equal pay and equal treatment. The UK government changed the law in 1983 and 1986 to comply with rulings of the European Court of Justice which also extended women's rights through the case law. Pay and matters governed by your contract are dealt with in the Equal Pay Act; non-contractual benefits and opportunities are dealt with by the Sex Discrimination Act (for other aspects of sex discrimination see p. 208).

Equal pay
You are guaranteed equal pay if you are doing work which is the same as, or broadly similar to, that of a man, or if you are covered by a job evaluation scheme which gives you similar scores to a man doing different work, or if you are doing work which you consider to be of equal value to a man's. Pay is widely defined and includes all aspects of remuneration including pension contributions. In addition, Article 119 of the Treaty of Rome enables you to claim in an industrial tribunal for discrimination in pay matters which is overt and direct even if you cannot point to a male worker. For example, entitlement to redundancy payment or pension benefit which differs between men and women is unlawful even though there may be no man with whom you can compare yourself. The Equal Pay Act excludes claims for pensions and retirement benefits, so you must claim under Article 119.

In a job evaluation scheme, if your job scores less than that of the man under you, you will have to prove that the scheme discriminates, for example, giving undue weight to characteristics and abilities commonly possessed by men, or undervalues those of women. You can also compare yourself with a man who is doing work which is of 'equal value' to yours whether or not his job has been evaluated under a job evaluation scheme. You make your claim to a tribunal (see p. 292) which will decide whether to refer your claim for analysis to an independent expert appointed under the Equal Pay Act. Unless your employer can convince the tribunal that there are no 'reasonable' grounds for making the comparison, your claim is then assessed in a lengthy and cumbersome process which involves examining the work you do and that done by your comparator(s). The tribunal may accept or reject the expert's report.

Management may defend the inequality in a claim under any part of the Equal Pay Act by saying that the difference is genuinely due not to sex but to a 'material factor'. The material factor has to be objectively justified by the employer. The measures chosen by the employer must correspond to a real need on the part of the employer and be appropriate to achieving the objects pursued and be necessary to that end. This may include additional responsibility, the pressure of market forces, seniority or the 'red circling' of a particular comparator on the grounds of prior employment history.

If you win, the tribunal can award arrears of pay for up to two years prior to the making of the claim and can change the terms of your contract to give you equality.

Sex discrimination at work

The Sex Discrimination Acts 1975 and 1986 outlaw discrimination at work on the grounds of sex or the fact of being married. It is direct when management treat you less favourably than they treat a man, or would treat a man if there were one in your place. It is indirect when a requirement applies equally to men and women but is such that the proportion of women who can comply with it is considerably smaller than the proportion of men who can, and which management cannot justify and which is to your detriment because you cannot comply. For example, an age barrier to recruitment or promotion might unfairly prejudice women who have been out of the economy for the purpose of child care. Or reserving certain benefits and opportunities to full-time workers could prejudice women if they form the majority of part-time workers.

Discrimination can occur at the recruitment stage, in advertisements and in the terms and conditions which are offered. If you are denied transfer, promotion, training, benefits, facilities and services, or if you are dismissed or subjected to any other detriment, you can make a claim to a tribunal (see p. 292).

The Sex Discrimination Acts exclude discrimination relating to retirement benefits including a pension. A requirement that women retire at a different age from men is unlawful. Other claims relating to retirement must be made under European law, Article 119 or the Equal Treatment Directive.

Certain jobs may lawfully be reserved for men, if management proves that being a man is a 'genuine occupational qualification' for the job. These are narrowly defined and include jobs requiring authenticity, for example, acting; physical contact with men or working in a country whose laws and customs mean a woman could not effectively do the necessary work.

Special procedures exist for seeking information before you make a claim (see chapter 9).

Maternity

A pregnant worker who has two years' service with the same employer has three rights: to maternity leave, to statutory maternity pay and not to be dismissed on account of her pregnancy. If you have less than two years' service you can complain under the Sex Discrimination Continuity of Employment.

You must notify management in writing twenty-one days before the start of your leave and at the same time confirm that you intend to return. You can also be asked in writing after your confinement to confirm your intention to return. In any event, you must give twenty-one days' written notice of the date on which you intend to return. Your employer can seek medical confirmation, and you yourself can postpone the date of return by up to four weeks on medical grounds. You must notify management in writing twenty-one days before the start of your leave, and at the same time confirm that you intend to return. You can also be asked in writing after your confinement to confirm your intention to return. In any event, you must give twenty-one days' written notice of the date on which you intend to return. Your employer can seek medical confirmation, and you yourself can postpone the date of return by up to four weeks on medical grounds.

Maternity pay

You may be entitled by your contract or collective agreement to be paid while you are on leave, and to be paid above the minimum statutory maternity pay (SMP) levels. You can take advantage of whichever is better. SMP is available if you have been employed for twenty-six weeks including the fifteenth week before the expected week of confinement, and you have average weekly earnings' above the lower earnings limit for the purposes of social security contributions (EPCA

1978 and Social Security Act 1986). You need not be working at the fifteenth week, providing your contract continues into it (for example, you could take some holiday entitlement). SMP is available from the eleventh week before confinement and lasts for eighteen weeks.

You do not get SMP if your pay is below the lower earnings' level. You are entitled to SMP at a higher rate for the first six weeks of absence provided you have been employed for two years at sixteen hours per week (or for five years at eight hours per week) by the fifteenth week before confinement. You then receive twelve weeks' pay at the lower rate (£47.95 in 1993).

No dismissal

It is automatically unfair to dismiss you on account of pregnancy or to fail to offer you a suitable available vacancy. If a redundancy has occurred during your maternity leave and it is not reasonably practicable to give you your old job back, you must be offered suitable alternative employment on no less favourable terms. However, if the number of employees at the time of your taking leave is five or fewer, including you, management can refuse to take you back on the grounds that it is not reasonably practicable to offer you a suitable alternative vacancy.

Claims

If you are denied any of the above rights you may make a claim to a tribunal. As from October 1994, these rights will be improved by the Trade Union Reform and Employment Rights Act which makes dismissal on pregnancy grounds unlawful irrespective of length of service, and provides for fourteen weeks' maternity leave for all women and better health and safety protection.

13.5 Health, safety, sickness and disability

Health and Safety at Work Act 1974

This Act imposes duties on all employers to ensure so far as is reasonably practicable the health, safety and welfare of their employees. This means providing safe plant and systems of work, and making arrangements for the safe handling, storage and transport of all articles used at work. Information, instruction, training and supervision should be provided so as to ensure employees' health and safety.

If management break these obligations, the Health and Safety Executive inspectors can issue prohibition or improvement notices requiring the work to be stopped or the machinery to be improved and they also have power to prosecute.

If your trade union is recognised for collective bargaining (see p. 270) you have the right to appoint union safety representatives who are given rights under the Act to time off with pay and to carry out inspection of the workplace and of relevant documents. Employers must consult safety representatives on health and safety arrangements. Claims for time off can be made to a tribunal or complaints about safety can be made to the Health and Safety Executive.

Regulations and a Code of Practice set out employers' obligations to provide first-aid facilities, including first-aid boxes and trained first-aiders, the number depending on the nature of the risk and the number of employees. In hazardous work-places there should be one qualified first-aider where more than fifty persons are employed and two where more than 150 are employed.

Accidents and industrial diseases causing the loss of more than three days' working time must be notified to the Health and Safety Executive.

The Fire Precautions Act 1971 requires a fire authority to give a certificate to the occupiers of any workplace other than low-risk premises where an exemption has been granted or when there are fewer than twenty employees. This imposes duties on employers to ensure that fire precautions and means of escape are provided and maintained.

Employers must keep workplaces clean, at a reasonable temperature (a minimum of 16°C or 13°C when the work requires severe physical effort), free from humidity, well ventilated, well lit, well provided with toilets and clean floors. Dangerous machinery must be guarded or, when this is not practicable, other suitable steps taken. Cranes must be kept in good mechanical order and be regularly inspected. If you are working on processes involving danger to your eyes you must be provided with and wear eye protection. Adequate drinking water and washing facilities must be provided. The atmosphere must be kept free of harmful dust and fumes.

Some of these obligations apply in all circumstances – they are 'absolute' duties and any breach of them will be a breach of the law. On the other hand, some depend on what is practicable, in which case a lesser standard will suffice. Many of these obligations arise from regulations implementing European Community directives which came into force on 1 January 1993. They replace many of the previous Factory Act provisions.

Mines and quarries

Extensive protection is given to workers in these industries. Inspectors may be appointed by a union under the Mines and Quarries Act 1954; they are given specific powers and duties to enforce the legislation.

Construction sites

These must be kept safe, excavations and demolitions must be fenced or secured and machinery must also be fenced.

Agriculture

Agriculture, forestry and nurseries are covered by the Agriculture Act (Safety, Health and Welfare Provisions) 1956 and regulations made under it.

Other industries

Specific regulations cover, for example, working with asbestos, wood, civil engineering, lead, nuclear radiation and in foundries.

Sanctions

For breach of any of the above, the Health and Safety Executive may bring proceedings in the criminal courts and may issue prohibition and improvement notices.

Compensation

In addition to possible prosecution, many breaches of the above laws give rise to claims by injured workers for breach of statutory duty or negligence. Every employer is under an obligation to provide:

- A safe system of work.
- Competent staff, i.e. if another worker is careless you can sue the employer for failing to supervise him or her.
- A safe place of work.
- Safe and adequate plant, machinery and materials, and adequate supervision.

A civil claim is made in either the County Court or the High Court depending on the seriousness of the injury or the disease you have contracted. Legal aid is available. You must claim within three years of the injury or disease, although you can sometimes claim later if you did not know that you were suffering from an injury or disease which is attributable to your employer's negligence. If successful, you will be awarded damages to compensate you for your injury and for financial losses such as loss of wages and expenses.

Sick pay

Many contracts and collective agreements contain arrangements for payment during times of sickness. If these are better than the minimum statutory sick pay (SSP) you are entitled to them by your contract. If you have made sufficient social security contributions you will be entitled to SSP, payable by your employer and fully reimbursable from the state. Provided you earn more than the lower earnings' level you qualify for SSP for the first twenty-eight weeks of absence, excluding the first three days. You get SSP at the higher or lower rate according to your average weekly earnings, but you are entitled to no more than twenty-eight weeks' SSP in any three-year period.

The Disabled Persons (Employment) Acts 1944 and 1958 and Regulations prescribe a quota of 3 per cent of the workforce to be registered disabled persons. This applies to an employer of twenty or more employees. For some jobs, priority is given to persons holding 'green cards' and you need a special permit before a non-disabled person can be employed. In fact, there is little regard for and even less enforcement of these laws. Long before the law on unfair dismissal was enacted, it was a criminal offence to dismiss a registered disabled person unless the employer could show a reasonable cause.

The Companies Act 1985 requires companies with 250 employees to make a statement in their annual report concerning the employment of disabled people.

13.6 Dismissal

The termination of a contract of employment by the unilateral act of your employer is a dismissal. It can take many practical forms. You may be dismissed with or without or with less than your contractual notice. You may be made redundant or offered early retirement. You may resign in protest at your employer's words or behaviour – this is called constructive dismissal if your employer's action is serious enough. You may be given an ultimatum in which you can either resign or be dismissed. You may be the victim of a process of 'squeezing out' over a period of time. If you are on a fixed-term contract, management may refuse to renew it on its expiry. Or they may refuse to take you back after a strike, or to re-engage you after your dismissal during a strike. Or they may refuse to offer you a job after you have been on maternity leave.

In reality, there are only two kinds of dismissal in law upon which you can take action. You can either claim wrongful dismissal, which is when you are given less than your contractual period of notice or denied access to agreed procedures prior to dismissal (that is all it means); or you may claim unfair dismissal because the reason given by your employer, or found by a tribunal on your claim, is insufficient, and management acted unreasonably in dismissing you for that reason in all the circumstances (EPCA 1978).

Notice
You are entitled to periods of notice depending on your length of service and the written statement (see p. 274) must include a note of your contractual entitlement. After one month's service you are entitled to one week's notice and thereafter at the rate of one week for each year of service up to a maximum of twelve weeks. Of course, your contract

may provide for longer periods than this, but if nothing is said, you are entitled to a 'reasonable' amount of notice which may exceed the statutory minimum.

If you do not get your contractual or statutory notice, you can sue for breach of contract in the County Court. If you have been denied access to a contractual procedure for challenging dismissal, your notice period is extended by the notional period during which you would have pursued your rights internally.

You lose your right to notice if you are dismissed for gross misconduct, a term not defined in any statute but taken to mean conduct by you which shows that you no longer intend to be bound by the contract and which, if proved, deprives you of your rights.

Reasons for dismissal

Provided you have been employed for two years at the date of dismissal, you are entitled to particulars, in writing, of the reasons for your dismissal. Following a written request, management must provide them within fourteen days. If this is not forthcoming, you can claim to a tribunal (see p. 292) which has the power to declare the reason for dismissal and to award two weeks' pay. If you are claiming unfair dismissal, you should seek written particulars in any event and add this to your claim if management does not comply.

Unfair dismissal

In order to claim unfair dismissal, you must have worked for two years' at sixteen hours per week, or for five years at eight hours per week (minima), unless you are claiming on the basis of race, sex or trade union discrimination. You can claim at any stage up to the age of sixty-five, unless there is a lower normal retirement age at your workplace.

If you bring a claim to a tribunal (see p. 292) management must show what the reason was for your dismissal. It must fit into one of the following categories: conduct, capacity, redundancy, a legal restriction (for example, not having proper working papers) or some 'other substantial reason' which could justify the dismissal. Few employers have difficulty putting forward a reason, so the main dispute focuses on the reasonableness of the employer in deciding to dismiss for that reason. Since the circumstances in which dismissal arises are numerous and varied, there is not space here to deal with this complex area of the law. Clear rules have emerged for dealing with sickness, reorganisations, criminal acts committed within the employment context, poor performance and refusal to obey instructions. Nevertheless, each case is to be treated on its own merits and tribunals on the same facts could reach quite different conclusions.

Remedies for unfair dismissal

If you win your case, the tribunal must first consider whether you wish to be reinstated and, if so, must decide whether it is just and equitable to order that. If not, compensation should be awarded to take account of the losses you have suffered up to the date of the hearing and the amount of time you are likely to be unemployed, or if you have a job, to compensate you for any loss in pay in the new job. If you have claimed unemployment benefit, your losses are calculated after taking account of what you have received. In addition, you should also get a payment equivalent to a redundancy payment (see below) which is called a basic award.

After dismissal, you must take steps to try and find alternative work and if you do not your compensation may be reduced by a percentage. Also, it may be reduced and the tribunal may refuse to order reinstatement if you have contributed to your dismissal by your own actions.

In 1990–91 only 45 per cent of applicants who reached a tribunal hearing succeeded. The median award of compensation was £1773. Reinstatement was awarded in fewer than 3 per cent of cases.

Breach of procedure

The existence of a disciplinary procedure in your contract of employment or collective agreement is important for both unfair and wrongful dismissal. If you are denied your rights, you may claim an injunction in the High Court to prevent management acting upon your dismissal or taking other disciplinary action until the procedure has been exhausted. This means you are to be treated as still employed, although perhaps not being required to work, until the full trial of your case for wrongful dismissal. You can get legal aid for this. Also, in unfair dismissal proceedings a failure to go through either the agreed procedure or to adopt the rules of natural justice (giving notice of an allegation, an opportunity for you to say what you think, and an open-minded management) may result in the dismissal being unfair. In other words, a potentially fair dismissal can be made unfair if proper and reasonable procedures are not followed.

13.7 Redundancy

Redundancy occurs when management's requirements for work of the particular kind you are employed to do has ceased or diminished, either temporarily or permanently. If you are dismissed for this reason, or put on short-term working (receiving less than half pay) or are laid off for four weeks or more, you can claim a redundancy payment (EPCA 1978).

The payment is based on your age, length of continuous service and weekly pay. You are entitled to one and a half weeks' pay for each year of continuous employment when you are aged between forty-one and sixty-three inclusive, one week's pay between the ages of twenty-one and forty inclusive, and half a week's pay for each other year.

Weekly pay does not include all your earnings and so, for example, voluntary overtime is excluded but regular commission and bonuses are included. The maximum weekly pay allowable for redundancy purposes is £205 (1993).

You lose your right to a redundancy payment if you turn down an offer made by your employer to re-engage you on a new contract if the offer is of suitable alternative employment – the kind of work which would be regarded as suitable for you – and you have unreasonably refused to take it. The unreasonableness is judged by what your own circumstances are.

Before you are made redundant, you have a right to claim a reasonable amount of time off with pay in order to look for work or to retrain. And, if you accept an offer of new employment with the same employer or one of its associates, you have the right to a four-week trial period during which time you can quit the job and be regarded as redundant. In other words, you do not prejudice your rights by taking the job for a trial period.

As with unfair dismissal, you need two years' continuous employment to qualify for these redundancy terms. Your entitlement to redundancy pay is reduced if you have reached the age of sixty-four.

If management dispute that there is a redundancy situation, for example, by claiming that there has simply been a reorganisation of the business without any lessening of the requirements for employees, or if you dispute the amount of money paid to you, you can make a claim to a tribunal, though you will lose your right to redundancy pay in the circumstances described above (see p. 292). If your employer has gone bust you can make a claim for redundancy pay and other outstanding debts including notice and holiday pay to be made by the Secretary of State for Employment (EPCA 1978 and Insolvency Act 1986).

Consultation

If your union is recognised for collective bargaining, management are under an obligation to consult it at the earliest opportunity about a proposal to make any dismissal (Employment Protection Act 1975). There is a minimum consultation period: thirty days if ten or more employees are to be dismissed, ninety days for a 100 or more. If the union claims that there has been no or inadequate consultation, it can make a claim to a tribunal which can then make a 'protective award' of compensation in favour of the employees who have been dismissed without the necessary consultation having taken place.

Takeovers, mergers and transfers

If the business in which you work is transferred as a going concern to another employer, the Transfer of Undertakings Regulations 1981 protect your terms and conditions with the new employer. Recognition of your union and all your contractual terms go over to the new employer. If you are dismissed as a result of the transfer, you can claim unfair dismissal which will be automatically unfair unless management proves that the dismissal was on account of an organisational or technical reason associated with the transfer.

Payment

The total amount of any redundancy payment is to be paid by your employer, without reimbursement from the state. You are entitled to a written statement of the calculation.

13.8 Industrial action

There is no right to strike in the UK. What is regarded as a fundamental or constitutional right in other countries becomes an immunity from some forms of civil action in the courts in the UK. Persuading people not to work and to break their contracts has always been unlawful in common law. If it is done in contemplation or furtherance of a trade dispute, as narrowly defined by the Trade Union and Labour Relations Act 1974, and if a ballot in favour of the action has been held, union leaders are 'immune' from normal civil liability.

Restrictions on the freedom to strike are placed on police and prison officers, apprentices (who must make up the time) and merchant seafarers; limited action by postal workers is also restricted by law.

A trade dispute is a dispute between workers and their own employer about terms, conditions, suspension, duties, engagement of workers, allocation of work, discipline, union membership, negotiating procedures and union facilities. In the course of such a dispute you can persuade people not to work. But if you do it on behalf of the union because you are a lay or full-time officer, or if the union adopts your actions, the union must conduct a ballot, and such calls for action will only be lawful if taken within four weeks of the result of a successful ballot. The ballot must ask all those likely to be asked to breach their contracts whether they are in favour.

It does not matter what form the industrial action takes – it can be a strike, work to rule, ban on overtime (whether it is voluntary or compulsory), withdrawal of cooperation, boycotts – they are all forms of industrial action and involve breaches of contract. As such, all those engaged in action are liable to their employers for breach of contract. In practice, employers do not sue their workers for the losses suffered by them as a result of each worker's breach of contract. What is more likely is an action against the union. Unions can be sued in their own name for damages if industrial action is taken which is unlawful. Much 'secondary action', that is action taken against an employer who is not a party to the main trade dispute, is unlawful. If the union has organised this, an injunction can be granted to prevent it, and claims for damages of up to £250,000, depending on the size of the union, can be awarded.

Equally likely is that employers may dismiss all of those engaged in industrial action. If all of you who take industrial action at the same workplace are dismissed and none is re-engaged within three months none of you has any claim. After the three-month period, selective re-engagement is permissible. This means that you are always at risk whatever form of action you take. You have no claim if at the time of dismissal you are taking part in unofficial industrial action.

Employers sometimes withhold pay for all or part of the time that you have been engaged in limited industrial action. They are entitled only to deduct a proportion of pay representing the proportion of your time lost by your action.

Since the Employment Act 1988, ballots in favour of industrial action must be taken at each workplace where workers are to be called upon. Action in pursuit of union membership agreements (see p. 271) is always unlawful.

Picketing of your own workplace (but nowhere else) during the course of a dispute is lawful provided that your purpose is peacefully to persuade people not to work or to communicate information. A Code of Practice (and one court decision) recommends that there be a limit of six pickets on each entrance, but different numbers may be appropriate in different circumstances. Offences under public order legislation (see p. 23) are the most likely criminal charges to arise out of picketing.

13.9 Claims

Most claims in this chapter are brought before industrial tribunals. Legal aid is not available, but an extension to the green form for preparation and/or counsel's advice can be granted. Legal aid is available if you are taking a case such as an injunction to the High Court. Help can be obtained from the Equal Opportunities Commission, the Commission for Racial Equality or, in certain cases, from the Commissioner for the Rights of Trade Union Members.

Claims in time

The first point to check is whether you are in time to bring a claim. Deadlines are strict, usually three months from the action complained of. Make sure you fill in, or have filled in on your behalf, the 'Originating Application to an Industrial Tribunal' form (IT1) and that it reaches the Central Office of Industrial Tribunals for England and Wales, or for Scotland or for Northern Ireland, within the appropriate time.

Documents

The organisation against which you are claiming – usually an employer but sometimes a trade union – will reply in a set form. You may ask for further particulars of any matter they raise, and you can also be asked to give particulars. Before commencing proceedings in a race relations or sex discrimination claim you may issue a questionnaire seeking to obtain information from your employer about the actions and policies you are challenging. If you have been dismissed, write a letter seeking particulars, in writing and within fourteen days, of the reasons for your dismissal.

An important step in the proceedings is the 'discovery of documents'. You are entitled to see all documents relevant to your claim, including internal notes and minutes, which are particularly important in respect of claims for discrimination. If the employers do not provide documents, you can seek an order from the tribunal to this effect.

Representation

You can be represented at a tribunal by anyone you like. If you are claiming unfair dismissal, the employers start the case and bring their witnesses. Otherwise you start.

If you think the hearing is likely to last more than one day you should tell the tribunal so that they can fix a block of time for it. Otherwise the case will be adjourned with an interval in between.

The case is generally conducted by the Chairman (the statutory term) who is a lawyer, but the tribunal also consists of a person nominated by employers' organisations and one by employees' organisations. They have an equal say in the decision.

Awards

Tribunals can award compensation, make recommendations of reinstatement or re-engagement, and order employers to rectify discriminatory acts and policies.

Appeals

Appeals on points of law go to the Employment Appeal Tribunal (EAT) in London or Edinburgh or to the Northern Ireland Court of Appeal. The EAT consists of a High Court Judge and a person nominated by employers and one by employees. Legal aid is available. You may be represented by anyone you like at the EAT, and appeal from its decisions lies to the Court of Appeal, the Court of Session in Scotland or the House of Lords. This can only be on a point of law, and you must have the permission either of the EAT or the Court of Appeal or Court of Session in order to take the case further.

13.10 Further information

Useful organisations

The best source of advice is your trade union. The TUC will direct you to an appropriate union. Their address is:

Congress House
Great Russell Street
London WC1B 3LS
Tel: 071 636 4030

Advisory Conciliation and Arbitration Service (ACAS)
Regional offices in Newcastle, Leeds, London, Bristol, Birmingham, Nottingham, Manchester, Liverpool, Glasgow, Cardiff and the Labour Relations Agency in Belfast.

Commission for Racial Equality
Elliott House 10–12 Allington Street
London SW1E 5EH
Tel: 071 828 7022.

Commissioner for the Rights of Trade Union Members
Sunley Building
Piccadilly Plaza
Manchester M60 7JS
Tel: 061 832 9111.

Equal Opportunities Commission
Overseas House
Quay Street
Manchester M3 3HN
Tel: 061 833 9244

Equal Opportunities Commission for Northern Ireland
Chamber of Commerce House
22 Great Victoria Street
Belfast BT2 2BA
Tel: 0232 242752

Fair Employment Agency
Andras House
60 Great Victoria Street
Belfast BT2 7BB
Tel: 0232 240020

Health and Safety Commission
1 Baynards House
1 Chepstow Place
London W2 4TF
Tel: 071 221 0870

Labour Relations Agency
Windsor House
9–15 Bedford Street
Belfast BT2 7NU
Tel: 0232 321442

Bibliography

J. McIlroy, *Industrial Tribunals*, Pluto Press, 1982.
R. W. Painter and K. Puttick, *Employment Rights*, Pluto Press, 1993.
C. Palmer, *Discrimination at Work*, Legal Action Group, 1992.
D. Pannick, *Sex Discrimination Law*, Oxford University Press, 1986.
M. Rowland, C. Kennedy and I. McMullen (eds), *The Rights Guide to Non-means-tested Benefits*, Child Poverty Action Group (annually).
Tolley's Employment Handbook, 1991.
Lord Wedderburn, *The Worker and the Law*, Penguin, 1986.

14

The rights of travellers

This chapter deals with:

*   The right to travel.
*   The right to stop.
*   The right to a site.
*   The right to housing.
*   The right to education.
*   The right to healthcare.
*   The right to welfare benefits.
*   The right not to be discriminated against.
*   Government proposals for law changes.
*   Further information.

14.1 The right to travel

As with most other rights under English law, you can do what you like ... unless it breaches criminal law or someone else's rights under civil law. As a traveller, you are subject to broadly the same laws as anyone else. So you have the right to pass and repass on the highway, but no special right to stop and park your caravan or other vehicles. As will be explained later, however, special extra laws may currently apply to you if you are defined as being a 'gypsy'.

14.2 The right to stop

Where can you stop, legally, and park and live in a caravan? The answer to this is: a legal site. A legal site is:

*   A piece of land you own, which has any necessary planning permission. You are the owner and occupier.
*   A piece of land owned by someone else, including a local council, which is laid out as a site with any necessary planning permission, with a site licence and where the site operator and yourself have agreed you can stay. You are a licensee, with very limited rights if it is a local authority gypsy caravan site.

- A piece of land, not necessarily laid out as a site, where no planning permission or site licence for the parking of an inhabited caravan is required because you are doing seasonal agricultural or forestry work for the landowner (usually a farmer), or in a limited number of other cases where you are staying for short periods on open fields.
- A piece of land where one or more caravans have remained continuously for over ten years and where no valid planning enforcement notice has been served nor planning application turned down during that time. In these cases, if you own the land or the landowner allows you to stay, you can apply for a certificate of Lawful Established Use and Development and that Certificate is the same as a full planning permission. If you can prove that caravans have been on the land since at least 1963 or even 1948, then planning powers will not be able to be used against you automatically.

Other than the four cases above, you may be liable to have planning (enforcement) action taken against you or be moved on, except in certain cases where the owner of the land you are on is unknown.

What follows is a checklist to help you identify not only how much the right to stop has been reduced, but also which powers may be used against caravans or other vehicles on any particular type of land.

Designation

Your rights, if you are a gypsy, to be provided with a legal site will be dealt with later. We shall see how certain local councils have a duty to provide adequate numbers of caravan site places for gypsies who live in, or regularly come to, their area.

Once the Secretary of State for the Environment is satisfied that adequate accommodation for gypsies has been made or does not need to be, he or she may 'designate' the area of the county, district, group of districts or London borough. This order gives extra powers to authorities and the police against you if you are a 'person of nomadic habit of life' who is not on a legal site. It affects you if you are on highway land, occupied land (if the occupier does not want you there) or unoccupied land. It is unlikely, though possible, that these powers would be used against you on your own land. They can be used against those who stop without permission on a legal council or private site and against those without licence to occupy such a site.

On land included within the three categories above, the local council or the police could prosecute you, and the local council could get a magistrates' court order which would allow them to tow off the caravans that belong to you and others on the land. The police have powers to arrest anyone obstructing the legal eviction and anyone doing so can be prosecuted separately.

Powers of councils in 'designated' areas are additional to powers of landowners to evict. See 'If the landowner wants you moved off' below.

Own land

Whether or not the area is designated, if you live on land where you have freehold or leasehold title, you may still fall foul of the law. If it is not a legal site, you must get planning permission and a site licence. If you do not seek planning permission from your local district or borough council, it may decide to take out a planning enforcement notice against you. If you do not appeal against this, or you do not win your appeal, you can subsequently be fined, face High Court injunctions to prevent the occupation of your land, and even, finally, be imprisoned for contempt of court and have your land sold to pay unpaid fines.

If your planning application is turned down due to your race or ethnic group (and this could be difficult to prove), there would be a breach of the Race Relations Act 1976. If this has happened to you (or you suspect it has), contact the Commission for Racial Equality at the address at the end of this chapter. Note also that in any planning appeal over a gypsy caravan site, the shortage of sites for travellers in an area is a 'material consideration' for the planning inspector to weigh up. The Department of the Environment is proposing to change this policy and others relating to gypsy sites, but has not yet made the change. See the end of this chapter for a summary of the proposed changes.

Type of land

If you have no title to the land, the type of land may decide if and how anyone can be moved from it. Outside London, highway verges are both wider and more plentiful in rural areas, as is common land. There are many powers to prosecute and/or move on travellers (or anyone else) under the Highways Acts, but some councils and some police do not wish to make matters worse by using these powers, unless it is really necessary. In the case of common land, there may be legal complications about moving you on, unless that bit of common is already covered by an express ban on caravan parking. If it is, there should be a sign up saying so.

Some of the remedies enable prosecution, some enable eviction and some do both. It is always important to check paperwork to see what the effect of the legal action will be, if it is successful.

Who owns the land?

If the land is neither highway verge nor common land and has a definite owner, the length of time you can stop on it will depend on a number of factors, including the number of caravans and the way that you and other travellers operate, as well as the level of complaint from others round about. Councils with too few sites may feel that it is unwise to evict you too quickly. Others may not feel limited by this. Action depends on the decision of the particular landowner.

If the landowner wants you moved off

There are now two methods that a landowner can use. The more important one has only been in use since 1 April 1987. It has been used much less since a 1991 Home Office Circular advised restrictions on its use. It is section 39 of the Public Order Act 1986. Under it, if certain conditions are satisfied, the police may direct any or all of the people on the land to leave it. You may be prosecuted if you fail to do so, or if you return to the same place within three months, unless (in either case) you have a legal defence that you did not go onto the land as a trespasser, or a reasonable excuse for failing to leave the land quickly when directed.

Before a senior police officer can use section 39, he or she must reasonably believe that two or more people entered the land as trespassers with the intention of living there for a time, and that the occupier has taken reasonable steps, themselves or through an agent, to ask you to leave. That officer must also consider the arguments for using the section and balance them against the arguments against.

If you and others have more than twelve vehicles (including caravans) between you there are no further conditions and the most senior police officer present may direct you to leave. If there are fewer than twelve vehicles, that officer must also reasonably believe that there has been damage to property on the land by one or more of you, or that threatening, abusive, or insulting words or behaviour by any of the trespassers have been used against the occupier of land, a member of their family, agent or employee. In addition, the landowner may use the civil courts to get a possession order against those of you who are on the land. The court need only give have two days' notice of such a County or High Court hearing, at minimum.

Other powers exist under Public Order legislation, covered elsewhere in this book (see p. 23).

If the landowner wants to let you stay

In this case, unless you are a seasonal worker or staying only days on open land, the landowner may be pressed by planning officers to move you and, if you have gathered for a festival or other event in numbers, you could be prosecuted for unlawful assembly.

14.3 The right to a site

Local authorities have had powers to establish caravan sites since 1960. Each county council, London and metropolitan borough council now has a *duty* to provide all 'gypsies' with sites. The duty extends towards those who are gypsies as defined by the Caravan Sites Act 1968: 'Persons of nomadic habit of life, whatever their race or origin.'

That duty is to provide 'adequate accommodation' for gypsies 'residing in or resorting to' their area, 'so far as may be necessary'. In London and metropolitan boroughs, the legal duty is limited to provision for fifteen caravans 'at a time'. Elsewhere, there is no legal limit, just the number of caravans (regularly, in practice) residing in or resorting to the area. But this general duty gives no particular right to any traveller to claim a site place from a particular local council. What dissatisfied travellers have had to do is to take individual councils (and sometimes the Secretary of State for the Environment as well) to the High Court for their failure to provide adequate sites, or the Secretary of State's failure to direct the council to provide them, as he or she has power to do.

This has resulted in a number of councils being found to be in breach of their duty and, in one case, being told that their decision to evict a group of travellers from their land was 'unreasonable ... and a void decision'.

If you are seeking a site place, you should keep in touch (preferably in writing) with the local council you have most connection with, hold on to evidence of your continuing stay in the area, and keep pressing for the building of a necessary site.

14.4 The right to housing

It can obviously be very difficult for any nomadic person to secure rights to housing. It is hard enough if you are not nomadic and settle in an area with some legal accommodation. Some areas have large numbers of families in hotels or bed and breakfast accommodation. If you are single or childless and neither elderly nor disabled, it will be difficult for you to get council housing, whether or not you are a traveller. All housing authorities have their own distinct rules for acceptance onto their housing lists and for deciding who gets priority once they are on the list.

If you are a traveller, you face daily difficulties if you have no legal accommodation to stop on or in, and these are dealt with elsewhere in this section. But it is important for you to remember that you have the right to seek council housing and to be considered for it, just as much as anyone else. You may also have rights to be provided with (or helped to get) accommodation by a local council housing department if you are judged to be 'homeless' (for example, you are being evicted from a piece of land or a highway verge, and you have nowhere legal to go and live in your caravan), and have a 'priority need' for accommodation (if you have children living with you, or elderly or disabled people). If it is decided that you are homeless and have such a priority need, then the council can avoid its duty to provide you with accommodation only by showing either that you have a 'local connection' with another council's area that is stronger than your connection with theirs, or that you made yourself intentionally homeless (for example, you were in housing or on a legal site, perhaps even some time ago, but left this legal accommodation for no good reason).

It is important to note that there is no duty on any council housing authority to provide you with a site for your caravan. In London and metropolitan boroughs, the duty, if it exists, to provide gypsy sites and for the homeless is upon the same council; in shire counties, the duty to provide accommodation for homeless people rests on the district council, while the duty to provide caravan sites for travellers is on the county council.

If you are looking for settled accommodation, or even if you want to put your name on a waiting list for a possible caravan site, you should visit the local council housing offices, preferably in the area that you have most connection with, unless there is a good reason for selecting another area (risk of violence from another member of the family, or someone else, for example). When you visit the housing offices, ask them what sort of provision is available. Do they have a site for travelling people? Does it have spare places on it? Where is it and how do they decide who goes on to it? If you have no interest in such a site, instead give the housing officer all the details about your living arrangements in your caravan. Remember that there are two separate ways of getting council accommodation and that you can apply to be put on a council house waiting list without being homeless. Before you leave the council office, make sure that you have got a decision from them both about your application to go onto the council house waiting list, as well as any decision about whether you are 'homeless'. Ask them to give you a written note of those decisions, or of when they will be made. Keep that record safe.

If you apply to be dealt with as homeless, the council housing department should give you a quick answer. If necessary, visit them regularly. Find out the name of the housing officer or other person that you need to speak to and try to speak to the same person each time.

If you are applying for a council house, make sure you keep in contact with the housing department by telephone or letter as the council house waiting lists are revised every six months or year in many areas and you have to make sure that you stay on the list each time until they make you an offer. It is possible to be on more than one council house waiting list at once.

Finally, you have the right to see all information on the housing department files. You may have to pay a charge if you want copies. If you do not read, or feel more confident with someone assisting you, then ask a sympathetic councillor, council travellers' officer, teacher, health visitor or some other person that you trust to go with on those visits, who could not only give you assistance, but also act as an independent witness.

14.5 The right to education

Traveller children aged between five and sixteen have the same legal right to education as anyone else. Other travellers who are not of compulsory school age have the same right to seek state education as anyone else of comparable age.

It is obviously difficult to claim or seek these rights if you do not have a legal place to stop. If your child is of school age, then simply take the child to the state school nearest to where you are and ask them to provide education. It will be very helpful, both for the child and the local education authority, if you present children at school at age five or even shortly before. But if there have been difficulties in getting your children to school at an earlier age, do not hesitate to take them at *any* age. You have a legal duty to present them at school, and the local education authority has a legal duty to provide them with appropriate full-time education.

Once you have met the school secretary, headteacher or another teacher, they may say that there will or could be difficulties which stop them admitting your child. It is important for you to stand your ground. Those practical difficulties are for the school or the local education authority to work out. If they ask you to go away for a few days, ask them exactly why you are being asked to do so. It is a good plan to be firm but polite! If one or more of your children is refused education at a school, or there are many obstacles put in front of her or him, then you should approach the Chief Education Officer for that council by going to the local town or county hall.

Many traveller children start school later than five and attend only from time to time. If you keep moving because of work or other reasons, then you only have to make sure that your children are in school for 200 half days (100 full days) during the September to July school year. If your children have started late or attended irregularly, they may be judged to have special needs, which may include remedial help with reading or even the necessity for them to go to a special school. There are rules about the way in which this decision on special needs is made, and you will almost certainly need the assistance of a literate friend to help you through this process.

In conclusion, remember that your school age children have a right to be educated and a right to have their needs considered in the same way as any other child. If the school or education department is planning to make (or making) decisions that you do not understand or disagree with, keep asking them questions at every stage, so that they tell you exactly what they are doing, why they are doing it, and what the likely result will be. What is most important is that you do not give up and withdraw your child or children from school if you do not understand what is happening. Taking a child away from school is likely to damage the child's education more than it challenges the local authority over the decisions they have made about that child's education.

The Children Act 1989 puts responsibilities on courts and local authorities to make decisions about children in the best interests of those children. There are beginning to be some court decisions about its effect on travellers and homeless families which demonstrate that these people have rights too.

14.6 The right to healthcare

Everyone has a right to healthcare from the National Health Service. What this means in practice is that no hospital should ever turn away someone who is the victim of accident or illness, whoever that person is and whether or not they have paid any national insurance contributions. When you go to a dentist or take a prescription to the chemist, however, you will only get certain benefits free or at a reduced price if you are a child, someone who suffers from a long-term illness or disability (for example, diabetes) or if you receive income support, a pension or family credit.

Although many travellers go to casualty departments when they have an accident or illness, it is much more sensible to register with a local doctor if you are in an area, or expect to be, for more than a few weeks. Lists of doctors should be available at main Post Offices, and the best way is to visit the doctor you pick from the list and give her or him the exact details of those members of your family who wish to register with them (dates of birth and so on). Some doctors are prevented from taking extra people onto their list if it is already too long, and so you may have to go to several doctors before you find one that will allow you to register with her or him. If you are turned down by all the doctors, whether or not it is because you are a traveller, find the address and phone number of the Family Practitioner Committee in the local phone book. Contact them (if possible in writing, after a telephone call) telling them that you have been turned down by the doctors concerned, the reasons you have been given by the doctors, and any other reasons you believe may have affected the decision.

If there is an accident or illness within your family and you believe it may be unsafe to move the person concerned you can telephone any local doctor and ask them for emergency help. Try to make sure that there is somebody else with you when you make that call, if that is possible, so there is no doubt that you made it and when you made it.

In practice, health visitors may have more contact with your family and friends, especially around the time that any children are born. Ask a health visitor for advice about registering with a doctor and for help with getting your rights to healthcare, even if you are regularly being moved from place to place.

The major changes to the National Health Service within the last few years are deterring some doctors from accepting traveller and other mobile families onto their lists. It is becoming increasingly important for all Health Service consumers to assert their rights to healthcare.

14.7 The right to welfare benefits

It is commonly believed that if you do not have a settled address then you are not entitled to welfare benefits. This is untrue. You are as entitled to welfare benefits if you move around as if you stay in the same place. But it is obviously more difficult to claim them; you may get long delays while the papers relating to you go from office to office of the Social Benefits Agency. Agency officers may also presume fraud, or the intention to defraud, more easily in those who are more mobile.

If you and any members of your family that you live with do not have any income, or only a very small one, then you can apply for income support on form IS1 which you can get from a Post Office or social security office. If you are on a site or in a house, you may be able to claim housing benefit and for this you approach the local council housing department. If you have children under sixteen living with you, you are entitled to child benefit, whatever income you have. If you do not have a settled house or site to stop on, your child benefits may be paid at the end of each three months, unless you can make an arrangement for it to be paid through a close friend, relative or council officer, or it can be added to any income support that you are receiving each week.

You may also be entitled to other benefits, such as extra heating allowances, as caravans are probably more difficult to keep warm than houses. In addition, there are other benefits for the disabled and those who look after them and you can get leaflets about all these from main Post Offices or discuss them with the local social security office. At the end of this chapter, there are details of a guide to many of these benefits and how to claim them.

Particular difficulties often arise with lost birth certificates or with people proving their identity. These two issues may well be linked. If you are having difficulty with either of them, approach your local advice centre, Citizens' Advice Bureau or local social services department to help you get your money, especially if it is an emergency.

Unless you are not required to be 'available for work', due to your age, pregnancy, lone parent status, etc., you are required to be not only 'available for work' but also 'actively seeking work' in order to receive income support payments.

14.8 The right not to be discriminated against

This subject is dealt with elsewhere within this book in general terms (see chapter 9), but the following relates particularly to discrimination against 'gypsies' (falling within one or more racial or ethnic groups of such).

The National Union of Teachers has described the prejudice against travellers as being similar to that suffered by many other ethnic minorities, and sometimes as fierce.

For many years, it was said that the Race Relations Acts covered gypsies as much as any one else, but no one was ever prosecuted for incitement to racial hatred against gypsies (and in very few other cases, either, it must be said) and there are only two notable cases that the Commission for Racial Equality dealt with concerning travelling people (see below).

Recent changes in the law and practice now mean that a gypsy applicant (and far from all travellers will come within the racial or ethnic definition 'gypsy') for a planning permission or a council house is covered by the Race Relations Act 1976. If someone produces material, including a leaflet, book, play, film, television or radio programme which is likely to stir up racial hatred against gypsies, then they can be criminally prosecuted, providing the Attorney General consents to the prosecution. The Court of Appeal decided in the summer of 1988 that gypsies were one or more ethnic groups and were protected by the Race Relations Act. A 'No Travellers' sign on a public house could indirectly discriminate against gypsies, as they would be a large proportion of the group 'travelling' (that is, caravan-dwelling) who would be refused service. Unless, therefore, there is justification for the sign, it is in breach of the law.

If you have been refused service in a shop or a pub, or been prevented from entering premises normally open to any member of the public by an objectionable sign, or you know of planning policies which ban all gypsy caravan sites being approved in an area, or in some other way you suffer discrimination in treatment by virtue of your origins as a traveller, then it is extremely important that you complain rather than expecting that it is something that you have to put up with. Complain to the local Community Relations Council for your area, if you know where it is, or complain direct to the Commission for Racial Equality in London, whose address is below.

14.9 Stop press

The Criminal Justice and Public Order Bill being discussed by Parliament in January 1994 will, if passed, include provisions to: end the duty on local authorities to provide sites for gypsies; end grant aid for such sites; reduce the numbers of vehicles present to six before the police can use the special eviction procedures (see p. 299); give the police extra powers to seize vehicles (and to charge for the removal, retention and destruction); create new criminal offences of trespassing with the intent of intimidating others or obstructing or disrupting their activities; give local authorities the power to ban assemblies of over 20 people; and give local authorities the power to direct unauthorised campers to leave the land making it a criminal offence not to obey the direction.

14.10 Further information

Useful organisations

The Advisory Committee for the Education of Romany and Other Travellers (ACERT)
Moot House
The Stow
Harlow
Essex CM20 3AG
Tel: 0279 418666

Commission for Racial Equality
Elliott House
10–12 Allington Street
London SW1E 5EH
Tel: 071 828 7022

National Gypsy Council
Greenhills Caravan Site
Greengate Street
Oldham
Greater Manchester OL14 1DQ
Tel: 061 665 1924

The Romany Guild
50–56 Temple Mills Lane
Stratford
London E15
Tel: 081 555 7214

The Romany Rights Association
c/o Eli Frankham
The Bungalow
Romon Bank
Walpole Street
St Andrews
Wisbech
Cambridgeshire PE14 7HP
Tel: 0945 780326

Save the Children Fund
Head Office
Mary Datchelor House
Grove Lane
London SE5 8RD
Tel: 071 703 5400

Bibliography

C. Brand, *Mobile Homes and the Law*, Sweet and Maxwell, 1986.
B. Forrester, *The Travellers' Handbook*, Interchange Books, 1985.
B. Lakhani and J. Read (eds), *National Welfare Benefits Handbook*, Child Poverty Action Group (annual).
Travellers on the Road, NCCL Factsheet, June 1987.

Index

acquittal 166, 168
actual bodily harm 24
adoption 172, 176, 266–7
advertisements: complaints 106–7,
   205, 213–14; race discrimination
   204–5; sex discrimination
   213–14, 282
affray 24
agents provocateurs 219
Agricultural Wages Boards 276
agricultural workers 276, 286
AIDS/HIV 64, 190
Anton Piller orders 65–6
appeal(s) 44; against bail 170;
   Court of 167, 168, 294; from
   Crown Court 167–8; to House of
   Lords 168, 294; immigrants 239,
   240–1, 242; from industrial
   tribunals 293–4; on points of law
   167, 293; right of 167–8; *see also*
   mental health review tribunals
apprentices 273, 291
arrest 119–20, 161; breach of the
   peace 138; children 264; citizen's
   139; by customs officers 69–70;
   for fingerprinting 141–2; information on 142; police powers
   25, 27, 138–42, 154–6;
   prevention of terrorism 154–6;
   searches on 136, 142; specific
   powers 141; subject to
   conditions 140–1; summary
   138–40; without warrant
   138–42
arrestable offences 136, 138–9;
   serious 70, 133, 139–40, 145,
   148–9
assault 25–6; indecent 139; by
   police 99, 166; on police 25–6;
   on prisoners 180, 190

assemblies 3, 6–13; offences 26–7;
   see also protest actions
assembly: freedom of 2, 112;
   unlawful 299
asylum seekers 223, 231, 241–3
authorship, false attribution of
   35

bail 161, 167, 168–70
bailiffs 66
banned organisations 52, 155, 157,
   159–60
banning orders 5–6, 15, 19, 26
barristers: complaints 104
bind-overs 11, 28–9
blasphemy 41–2
breach of the peace 25, 28, 138
British Board of Film Classification
   53
British citizenship 243–4, 261–2
British Rail: complaints 109
broadcasting: complaints 52–3, 71,
   105–7; controls on 40, 51–3, 54,
   208
Broadcasting Complaints
   Commission 52–3, 71, 106
Broadcasting Standards Council 52,
   106
buggery 139, 216, 218, 219
bugging, electronic 58
buses: complaints 109
by-laws 2, 13, 14

cable programming 53–4, 208
care orders 258, 264, 266
care proceedings 172, 265–6
casual workers 274
cautions 150, 264
censorship 51–4, 184–5
charge 161, 168

charities: collections 13; discrimination by 204, 213
children and young people 222, 257–67; abduction 262; access to records 76, 81, 84–5; citizenship/nationality 261–2; courts and 45, 264–7; decision making 259–61; fines 30; immigration 234–5; intimate searches 69; leaving home 260–1; medical treatment 260; money/financial support 261; naming 259; obscenity and 40; parental responsibility 258–9; police detention 144, 146, 150, 151, 152, 264; religion 259–60; sexual orientation 220; spent convictions and access to 176–7, 178; travel/passports 262; *see also* education
Child Support Agency (CSA) 261
citizen's arrest 139
Citizen's Charter 126–7
civil servants 273–4
clubs: discrimination 204, 212
Commission for Racial Equality (CRE) 196, 198, 200, 205–7, 226, 298, 306
committal proceedings 165–7
community care: complaints 94
compensation: employees 270, 275, 277, 286, 289, 293; victims of crime 110–11
complaints 89–127, 154; access to health records 82, 83; credit reference agencies 79; customs searches 70; prisoners 181–2, 185; sex discrimination 210, 213–14; *see also under* advertisements; broadcasting; press
computerised records 73–7, 173, 278
confessions 146, 150, 165
confidence, breach of 47–9, 56–7, 190; employees and 279–80
consent: age of 216; children 76, 81, 260; mental patients 254–5; search of premises 133
conspiracy to corrupt public morals 219–20

construction sites 285–6
contracts of employment 273–80, 289; breaches 276, 291–2; collective agreements 275; employed or self-employed? 273–4; itemised pay statements 275; low wages and 276; obligations 276–9; whistleblowers 279–80; works rules 275–6; written statement 274–5, 287
copyright 71, 278; cut-price copies 50–1, 65; defences 50; meaning 49–50; 'moral rights' 51; passing off 51
councils *see* local authorities
court(s) 101–2; access for prisoners 180, 182; Appeal 167, 168, 294; children and 45, 264–7; complaints 102–3; contempt of 33, 42–7, 66, 135; County 102, 196; Crown 163, 164–5, 166–8, 169–70; High 102, 170; House of Lords 168, 294; magistrates' 102, 164–6, 169; of Protection 255; small claims 102; youth 264–5; *see also* European Court of Human Rights; European Court of Justice
credit reference agency records 78–9
criminal damage 26
criminal injuries 110–11
Crown Prosecution Service 162
cruising 217–18
custody officers 143, 144, 147, 150
custody records 70, 143, 147, 148
Customs and Excise, H.M. 41, 67–70, 156, 161

data protection 73–7, 173
Data Protection Registrar 74, 75, 77, 173
death penalty 125
defamation 34–9, 107; defences 37–9, 46, 174; publication and 35–6; spent convictions and 174, 179; who can sue? 36–7
defence, conducting own 163–4, 165–6

defendants: after protest actions 16, 17–18, 20–3; children as 264–5; rights of 120–1, 161–79

demonstrations 1–2, 3, 6–9

deportation 157–8, 240–1

detention 119–20; after charge 146; children 144, 146, 150, 151, 152, 264; clock 144–5; conditions in 148, 156; conduct of interviews 150; customs and excise 67–70; denial of bail 168–9; fingerprints 151, 152; identification by witnesses 152–3; immigrants 239–41; legal advice 148–9; limits and extensions 143, 145–6; medical treatment 148, 156; notification of 139, 140, 149–50, 156; photographs 151, 152; by police 142–54; prevention of terrorism 113, 149, 154–7; review of 144; rights of suspects 146–54; samples 151–2; searches 67–70, 147–8; stopping and 131; without charge 139, 143–4, 145; *see also* under mental patients

disability: discrimination 225–6; employment 225–6, 287

dismissal: breach of procedure 289; constructive 287; notice 287–8; reasons 288; reinstatement 270, 289; remedies 289; unfair 221–2, 270, 276, 279–80, 281, 284, 287, 288–9, 292; wrongful 173, 287

disorderly conduct 11, 25

DNA samples 152

doctors: general practitioners, complaints against 91–2; misconduct 93; negligence 93; searches by 147–8

drugs 148–9; employees and 280–1; obscenity and 40; search powers 67, 129, 136, 147

education: admissions 262–3; behaviour/discipline 263–4; compulsory 262; curriculum 263; immigrants 237–8, 239, 243; overseas students 202, 237–8, 239; prisoners 191; race discrimination 201–2; records 80, 85;

right to 124, 262–4, 302–3; sex discrimination 211–12; special needs 263, 302; travellers 302–3; trusts 211

either way offences 164

elections: meetings 12–13; right to free 124; right of reply 54; trade union officers 273

electricity: complaints 108; officials' right of entry 61–2

employment: access to medical reports 82–3; drug taking/drinking 280–1; health and safety 284–6; hours 277; immigrants 236–7, 243; injuries 190–1, 277, 286; misconduct 276, 277–8, 288; part-time 277, 282; prisoners 190–1; race discrimination 198–201, 205, 279, 293; records 85–6, 278; redundancy 278, 289–91; references 279; self- 273–4; sex discrimination 213, 214, 269, 279, 282–3, 293; sexual orientation and 220–2; sickness and disability 225–6, 286–7; spent convictions and 170–1, 173, 175–8, 279; time off 271, 279; women 281–4; workers' rights 268–95; *see also* contracts; dismissal; industrial action; industrial tribunals; trade unions

Employment Appeal Tribunals (EATs) 221–2, 293–4

entry, right of: mental patients and 64, 249; officials 60–6; racial material and 208; *see also* searches

Equal Opportunities Commission (EOC) 212, 214–15, 221, 227

European Commission of Human Rights 112, 113, 114–17

European Convention for the Protection of Human Rights (ECHR) 112–13, 225, 232; Articles 32–3, 56, 118–24, 185; complaints under 111–17, 181–2; Protocols 124–6; value of 118

European Court of Human Rights 33, 112, 113, 116–17, 223

European Court of Justice 112, 281
evidence 162, 165; destruction of 65–6; detention and 143–4, 145, 146; inadmissible 150; searches and 134, 136, 138, 157; spent convictions and 172–3
excluded material 134–5, 138
exclusion orders 155, 156, 157–9
expression, freedom of 32–55, 112, 121–2

fair comment defence: defamation 37–8, 174
false imprisonment 99, 166
family cases 265–7
films 53
financial professions: complaints 104–5
fine levels 29–30
fingerprints 138, 151, 152, 155, 156, 242; arrest for 141–2
firearms 136, 140
fire brigade: right of entry 61
force, use of 147, 151; entry and search 137; excessive 99, 154; mental patients 248, 249; prevention of terrorism 155; prisoners and 189
forced labour 118–19
fostering 65, 176, 203, 223–4

gas board: complaints 108–9; right of entry 61–2
general practitioners: complaints 91–2
Gillick principle 259
goods, facilities and services: race discrimination 203–4; sex discrimination 212–13
government, central: complaints about departments 89–90
graffiti 208
grievous bodily harm 24
gross indecency 139, 216, 217, 218–19
guardians *ad litem* 265, 266, 267
guardianship: mental patients 251–2
gypsies *see* travellers

harassment 59; racial 199–200; sexual 210–11
health services *see* medical treatment
highways: obstruction 3, 9, 10, 13, 14, 27–8; right to use 3, 13, 296; roadchecks 9, 132, 139
homeworkers 274
homosexuality 215, 216–25; ban on promoting 224–5
hospital orders 252
hospitals: complaints 92–3; special 255; *see also* mental patients
housing: access to records 80, 83–4; officials' right of entry 62; race discrimination 202–3; sex discrimination 212; sexual orientation and 222; travellers' right to 300–2
Human Rights *see* European Commission of Human Rights; European Convention for the Protection of Human Rights; European Court of Human Rights

identification: defamation victims 36–7; DNA 152; suspects 140–1, 152–3, 155; by witnesses 21, 152–3
immigrants 231–46; children 234–5; controls 136, 231–3, 238–41; employment 236–7, 243; fiancés and fiancées 234; husbands and wives 234; parents and grandparents 235; refugees 223, 231, 241–3; rights to British nationality 243–4; settlers 233–6, 237, 242; sexual orientation and 222–3; temporary visits 237–8; visa nationals 233, 238–9
importuning 216–19
indecency offences 40–1
indecent assault 139
Independent Television Commission (ITC) 51–2, 53, 54, 106
indictable offences 164
industrial action 268, 269, 272, 291–2; secondary 292

industrial tribunals 46, 270, 275, 277, 279, 281, 282, 288–9, 292–4; appeals 293–4; awards 293; documents 293; race discrimination 196, 198–9, 200, 293; representation 293; sex discrimination 210–11, 214, 221–2, 281, 282, 293

infectious diseases 64–5

information: freedom of *see* personal records; and ideas, right to receive 55; withholding 155–6

injunctions: confidentiality and 49, 56–7; libel 34; race discrimination 207; secondary industrial action 292; unfair dismissal 289; whistleblowers 279–80

injury, personal: crime victims 110–11; employees 190–1, 277, 286; police as cause 154

innocence, presumption of 120, 161

insulting behaviour 216, 217, 219

insurance: complaints 104–5; medical reports 82–3; sex discrimination 213; spent convictions and 170–1, 174

interviews 184, 264; conduct of 150; *see also* questioning

intimidation 5, 7, 27, 43

inventions 278

Irish National Liberation Army (INLA) 155, 159

Irish Republican Army (IRA) 155, 159

job evaluation schemes 281, 282

judges 167

juries: disclosures 43; free speech cases 34; official secrets trials 34, 48; trial by 164–5; verdicts 167

jury service 256, 278

juveniles *see* children and young people

knives 26, 129

landlords 59, 133, 202

law centres 163

leaflets 13

legal advice 101–2; right to 148–9, 156, 162–3, 188, 254; *see also* solicitors

legal aid 35, 71, 102, 286, 289; applications 163

legally privileged material 135, 138

legal observers: protest actions 15–16

legal representation 162–4; right to 145, 193, 254

lesbianism 215, 216, 217, 219, 220, 222, 223–4

libel 34–9, 46

liberty, right to 119

licence applications 46, 176, 178, 199

life, right to 113, 118

List 99: 177

local authorities: access to meetings 86; ban on promoting homosexuality 224–5; complaints 90–1; sex discrimination 215; race equality and 207; rights of entry 64–5; travellers and 296, 297–8, 299–300, 306

McKenzie advisers 163–4, 188

magistrates: extensions to detention 145–6; warrants 64, 133–4, 249

magistrates' courts *see under* courts

mail: interception 57–8; mental patients 255; prisoners 184–5; unwanted 60

malicious falsehood 35, 70–1

malicious prosecution 99, 166

marches *see* processions

marriage: discrimination and 209, 279, 282; immigrants 234; right to 122, 185, 223

maternity 283–4

media: complaints 71, 105–7; privacy and 70–2; *see also* broadcasting; press

medical records, access to 80–3, 190

medical treatment: children 260; complaints 82, 91–4; right to 148, 156, 180, 190, 303–4; travellers 303–4 meetings 11–13; offences 26–7, 159–60; stewards 11–12

mental health review tribunals 248, 250, 251, 253–4

mental patients 69, 247–56; access to health records 81–2; appeals 251; applications for compulsory detention 248–52, 253; categories 247–8; detention of offenders 252–3; discharge 250; guardianship 251–2; immigrants 241; nearest relative 250–1; right of entry and 64, 249; rights in mental hospitals 254–6; voluntary 247, 249, 255

mines and quarries 285

mortgages: sex discrimination 212

motor vehicles: stop and search 129–33

names: children 259; suspects 140–1

national security 57, 58–9, 74; spent convictions and 175, 177, 178; *see also* terrorism

naturalisation 243–4

neighbours 59

newspapers: sale 14; *see also* press

non-discrimination notices 206–7, 214, 221

notes, right to make 153–4

Notices of Rights and Powers 137

notifiable diseases 64–5

nuisance 59–60

nurses and midwives: complaints 93

obscenity 39–40; mailed 60; phone calls 59

obstruction: highways 3, 9, 10, 13, 14, 27–8; officials 62; police 9, 10, 27

offensive weapons 26, 130

officials: disclosure of convictions by 178; power of entry 60–6

ombudsmen: financial professions 104–5; health services 92–3; local government 84, 86–7, 90–1; parliamentary 89–90, 181

open government 86–7

parents 151, 178, 259–61; access to children's records 76, 81, 84–5; divorce/separation 258–9, 261; immigration 235; responsibility 258–9; sexual orientation 223–4

Parliament: demonstrations near 7; petitions to 13

Parliamentary Commissioner for Administration (PCA) 89–90, 181

part-time workers 277, 282

peddling 14

personal records 73–88, 134

pests and vermin 65

petitions 13

photographs: indecent 40; by police 151, 152, 155; right of privacy 51, 71

picketing 2, 6, 7, 9–11, 292; secondary 10

planning officers: right of entry 62–3

plays 208, 224

police: *agents provocateurs* 219; arrest powers 25, 27, 138–42, 154–6; assault by 99, 166; assault on 25–6; civil actions against 99–100; complaints against 94–101, 154; criminal actions against 100; detention 142–54; immigrants' registration with 238; industrial action 291; obstruction 9, 10, 27; picketing and 10–11; protest actions and 18–20; public meetings and 12–13; reporting of spent convictions 176, 177–8, 179; search of premises 99, 133–8, 142, 157; stop and search of persons and vehicles 129–33, 157; use of force 99, 137, 147, 151, 154, 155

Police Complaints Authority (PCA) 96, 97, 99, 101

Police Consultative Committees 101

police stations 142; bail at 168–9; *see also* detention

posters 14, 40

Post Office: complaints 109

postponement orders 45

pregnancy 283–4

press: complaints 35, 71–2, 105; contempt of court and 42–7; protest actions and 16–17, 23; racial hatred and 208; right of reply and 54–5; *see also* libel

Press Complaints Commission (PCC) 35, 71, 105

prisoners 180–95; access to courts 180, 182; access to lawyers 182–3, 185, 188, 193; allocation 186–7; categorisation 186; cellular confinement 188, 189–90; complaints/ requests 181–2, 185; discharge 184, 194; discipline/adjudication/ punishment 187–9; education 191; exercise 189, 191; letters 184–5; life sentence 193–4; marriage/founding a family 185; medical treatment 190; parole 192–4; race discrimination and 182, 204; reading/writing materials 191–2; reception 181; segregation and transfer 187, 188–90, 252–3; telephones 185; unconvicted 183, 184, 187, 190, 191; visits 183–4; women 185–6; work 190–1

Prison Rules 180, 181

privacy, right of 56–72, 112, 121

privilege, defence of: defamation 38–9, 174

processions 3–6; offences 26–7

professions: complaints 91–4, 102–5; disclosure of spent convictions and 175–8; race discrimination 199, 201

prohibited articles 129–30, 131

prohibited steps orders 258, 259, 265

protest actions: historic right of peaceful 1–3; organisation of 14–23; regulation of 3–14; stewards 11–12, 15–16; *see also* public order offences

public interest 49, 134, 177; as defence 49, 50, 71–2, 87

public order offences 2, 4–5, 7, 10–11, 12–13, 23–30, 42, 207–8, 219, 299

public utilities: complaints 107–9

questioning 144, 145, 146, 155–6

race discrimination 122, 196–208, 226–7: advertisements 204–5; clubs 204; defined 196–8; direct 196–7; education 201–2; employment/training 198–201, 205, 279, 293; goods/facilities/ services 203–4; housing 202–3; indirect 197; local authorities and 207; overseas students 202; positive 201; prisons 182, 204; responsibility for 198; travellers 208, 305–6; victimisation 197–8

racial hatred 13, 42, 207–8

racially inflammatory material 208

radio: censorship 52; complaints 52–3, 105–6

rallies 3, 6–9

rating officers: right of entry 63

recordable offences 142, 151

records, personal 73–88, 134

redundancy 275, 289–91

refugees 223, 231, 241–3

rehabilitation of offenders *see* spent convictions

religion 208; blasphemy 41–2; children 259–60, 263; freedom of 121; in schools 263; sex discrimination 213

reply, right of 38, 54–5

residence orders 258, 259, 260, 262, 265

restriction orders 252, 253

restrictive covenants 278

riot 23–4

roadchecks 9, 132, 139

road traffic offences 111

samples 70, 151–2

searches: Anton Piller orders 65–6; on arrest 136, 142; by customs officers 67–70; employees 277; intimate 68, 69, 70, 147–8; personal 67–70, 129–33, 142, 147–8, 156, 157; pocket 68; in police stations 147–8; premises 99, 133–8, 142, 157; prevention

of terrorism 157; prisoners 181; prison visitors 184; racial offences 42, 208; records 132; 'rub-down' 68, 69; safeguarded material 134–5; strip 68, 69, 131, 147, 184; use of force 137, 147; vehicles 129–33; warrants 42, 133–4, 137, 208; without warrant 99, 136, 157
secrecy, official 34, 47–9, 87
Section 8 proceedings 265
secure accommodation orders 264–5, 266
security services 58–9
seizure of property 66, 131, 137–8, 147, 157, 208
'serious harm' exemption: access to health records 80, 81–2
sex discrimination 122, 208–15, 227–8; advertisements 213–14, 282; areas covered by law 209; complaints 210, 213–14; contractual terms 213; defined 209–10; direct 209, 282; education 211–12; employment 213, 214, 269, 279, 282–3, 293; goods/facilities/services 212–13; housing 212; indirect 209–10, 282; local authorities 215; mortgages 212; sexual harassment 210–11; social security 215; victimisation 210
sex shops/cinemas 41
sexual offences 45, 176, 190, 217–20, 265
sexual orientation 215–25, 228–9; armed forces 216, 217; ban on promoting homosexuality 224–5; civil law 220; conspiracy to corrupt public morals 219–20; employment 220–2; housing 222; immigration 222–3; men and criminal law 216–17; offences 217–20; parental rights 223–4; policing and *agents provocateurs* 219; public displays of affection 217, 219; sexual activity 218–19; transsexuals 223; transvestites 223; women and criminal law 216; young people 220

silence, right of 128, 150–1, 155–6, 162
slander 34–9
social security: officials' right of entry 63; sex discrimination 215
social work records, access to 80, 84–5
soliciting 216–19
solicitors: for children 265, 266; complaints 103–4; duty 148, 149, 163; prisoners' access to 182–3, 185, 188, 193; protest actions and 16, 17, 18, 21–2; *see also* legal advice; legal representation
special procedure material 135, 138
specific issues orders 258, 265
spent convictions 37, 170–9, 279; access to children and 176–7, 178; defamation and 174; effect of 172; evidence in legal proceedings 172–3; exceptions 174–6; further offences 172; going abroad 174; police reporting of 177–8; unauthorised disclosure 178–9
sport: race discrimination 204; sex discrimination 212, 213
statutory undertakers 132–3
stolen goods 129–30, 131
stop: police powers to *see under* police; right to 296–9
street collections 13
street trading 14
strict liability contempt 44–5, 46–7
strikes *see* industrial action
summary offences 164
summonses 140, 161
supervision orders 266
sureties 29, 168
surveillance 58–9
suspects, rights of 128–60; *see also* arrest; detention; questioning
suspicion, grounds for 128, 130–1

tax officials: right of entry 63–4
telephones: complaints 107–8; use by prisoners 185; tapping 57–8; unwanted calls 59–60
television *see* broadcasting

tenants 59, 83, 171, 222
terrorism: defined 154; international 154, 155, 157–8
terrorism, prevention of 113, 137,
  140, 149; arrest and questioning
  155–6; banned organisations 52,
  155, 157, 159–60;
  examination/detention at
  ports/airports 156–7; exclusion
  orders 157–9; roadchecks 9;
  searches 157
threatening, abusive or insulting
  words or behaviour 10, 24–5,
  208, 299
trade disputes 9–10, 291
trade unions 268; ballots 271, 272,
  273, 291, 292; closed shops 271;
  collective bargaining 269, 271,
  275, 284, 290; consultation 271,
  290; election of officers 273;
  political activities 272–3; race
  discrimination 199, 201; recognition 270–1; rights against
  employers 269–70; rights within
  271–2; safety representatives
  284–5; sexual orientation and
  222; time off for 271; why join?
  269; *see also* picketing
trainees 200–1, 274
transport complaints 109
transsexuals 223
transvestites 223
travel agents: complaints 109–10
travellers 296–307; designation and
  297–8; discrimination and 208,
  305–6; education 302–3; health
  care 303–4; housing 300–2;
  proposed changes in law 306;
  right to stop 296–9; right to
  travel 296; sites 296–7, 299–300,
  301, 306; welfare benefits 304–5
trespass 58, 59, 99, 299
tribunals 58, 102; access to 46;
  Employment Appeal 221–2,

293–4; mental health review
  248, 250, 251, 253–4; Special
  Educational Needs 263; *see also*
  industrial tribunals
truth, defence of: defamation 37,
  174

Ulster Defence Association (UDA)
  52, 159
uniforms, political 26, 160

VAT officials: right of entry 63–4
victimisation: employment 270,
  279, 280; race discrimination
  197–8; sex discrimination 210
video cassettes 40, 65, 50–1
violence: obscenity and 40; public
  order offences 23–6
violent disorder 24
voting rights: mental patients 255

wages 275, 276–7, 278; equal pay
  269, 281–2; industrial action and
  292; maternity pay 283–4;
  redundancy payments 289–91;
  sick pay 286–7
wages council orders 276
wards of court 260, 261
watching and besetting 27
water companies: complaints 108;
  officials' right of entry 62
whistleblowers 279–80
witnesses 29, 120, 166; children as
  265; identification by 21, 152–3;
  interference with 43, 169
women: employment rights 281–4;
  prisoners 185–6; *see also*
  lesbianism; sex discrimination
word processed documents 75
workers' rights 268–95; *see also*
  employment
work permits 236–7

young offender institutions 264